WEiRD
LAS VEGAS
AND NEVADA

Weird

Las Vegas
and Nevada

Your Alternative Travel Guide to Sin City
and the Silver State

by JOE OESTERLE and TIM CRIDLAND

Mark Moran and Mark Sceurman,
Executive Editors

WeiRD LAs VeGAS AND NEVADA

Published by Sterling Publishing Co., Inc.
387 Park Avenue South, New York, NY 10016

© 2007 Mark Moran and Mark Sceurman
Distributed in Canada by Sterling Publishing
c/o Canadian Manda Group, 165 Dufferin Street
Toronto, Ontario, Canada M6K 3H6
Distributed in the United Kingdom by GMC Distribution Services,
Castle Place, 166 High Street, Lewes, East Sussex, England BN7 1XU
Distributed in Australia by Capricorn Link (Australia) Pty. Ltd.
P. O. Box 704, Windsor, NSW 2756, Australia

10 9 8 7 6 5 4 3 2 1

Manufactured in China.

Photography and illustration credits are found on page 255
and constitute an extension of this copyright page.

Sterling ISBN 13: 978-1-4027-3940-8
Sterling ISBN 10: 1-4027-3940-0

For information about custom editions, special sales, premium
and corporate purchases, please contact Sterling Special Sales
Department at 800-805-5489 or specialsales@sterlingpub.com.

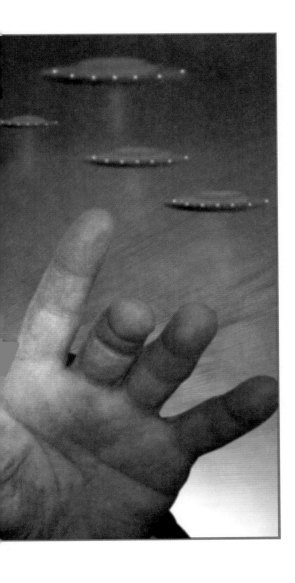

CONTENTS

Foreword: A Note from the Marks

Our weird journey began a long, long time ago in a far-off land called New Jersey. Once a year or so, we'd compile a homespun newsletter called *Weird N.J.*, then pass it on to our friends. The pamphlet was a collection of odd news clippings, bizarre facts, little-known historical anecdotes, and anomalous encounters from our home state. The newsletter also included the kinds of localized legends that were often whispered around a particular town but seldom heard outside the boundaries of the community where they originated.

We had started *Weird N.J.* on the simple theory that every town in the state had at least one good tale to tell. The publication soon became a full-fledged magazine, and we made the decision to actually do our own investigating to see if we could track down where all of these seemingly unbelievable stories were coming from. Was there, we wondered, any factual basis for the fantastic local legends people were telling us about? Armed with not much more than a camera and a notepad, we set off on a mystical journey of discovery. Much to our surprise and amazement, a lot of what we had initially presumed to be nothing more than urban legends turned out to be real—or at least to contain a grain of truth, which had sparked the lore to begin with.

After a dozen years of documenting the bizarre, we were asked to write a book about our adventures, and so *Weird N.J.: Your Travel Guide to New Jersey's Local Legends and Best Kept Secrets* was published in 2003.

Soon people from all over the country began writing to us, telling us strange tales from their home state. As it turned out, what we had perceived to be something of very local interest was actually just a small part of a larger and more universal phenomenon.

When our publisher asked us what we wanted to do next, the answer was simple: "We'd like to do a book called *Weird U.S.*, in which we could document the local legends and strangest stories from all over the country," we replied. So for the next twelve months, we set out in

fifty states. And indeed, we found plenty of it!

After *Weird U.S.* was published, we came to the conclusion that this country had more great tales than could be contained in just one book. Everywhere we looked, we found unwritten folklore, creepy cemeteries, cursed locations, and outlandish roadside oddities. With this in mind, we told our publisher that we wanted to document it *all* and to do it in a series of books, each focusing on the peculiarities of a particular state.

One place that we'd traveled to many times and knew we could count on for weird stories was the state of Nevada, and the city of Las Vegas in particular. Think about it: a vast wide-open terrain dotted here and there with Old West ghost towns and extraterrestrial landing sites. And in the middle of all this, the world's most visited tourist attraction—a surreal fantasyland where time as we know it ceases to exist, where day and night and desert and oasis meld together as one, and the lines between what is real and what is illusion begin to blur.

Once we'd made the decision to forge ahead into this uncharted weird territory, we set out to find authors on whom we could count to be our eyes and ears in Nevada. The first person we asked was our old friend from *Weird N.J.*, Joe Oesterle. A native of New Jersey not being from Las Vegas himself, we knew that he'd be the perfect man to report on the city's strangeness, because he could observe it in the same way that the vast majority of people do—as outsiders looking in—sojourners, strangers in a very strange land.

Of course, we'd also need an inside man on the job, someone who was immersed in the day-to-day weirdness that is life in Las Vegas and Nevada. For this we chose Tim Cridland. The first time we met Tim, he was in a carnival tent on the boardwalk in Seaside Heights on the Jersey Shore. Dressed in a silk-and-lamé genie outfit, Tim was impaling long metal skewers through the flesh of various parts of his anatomy. As if that wasn't enough to convince us that he was sufficiently weird for the job, we'd later learn that Tim lived in Las Vegas when he wasn't on tour with his traveling band of sideshow carnies. He had also spent years wandering around the infinite deserts, isolated canyons, and mysterious mountains of Nevada collecting stories of the ghosts, graveyards, and unexplained phenomena there.

We knew that if there was a weird tale to be uncovered anywhere in Las Vegas or Nevada, Joe and Tim would be the ones to find it. Along the way we met a few other fellow travelers—Skylaire Alfvengren, Janice Oberding, and Troy Paiva—who also made invaluable contributions to this book.

Each of these great writers possesses a quality that we refer to as the "Weird Eye." The Weird Eye is what is needed to search out the sort of stories we're looking for. It requires one to see the world in a different way, with a renewed sense of wonder. And once you have it, there is no going back—you'll never see things the same way again. All of a sudden you begin to reexamine your own environs, noticing your everyday surroundings as if for the first time. And you begin to ask yourself questions like, "What the heck is *that* thing all about, anyway?" and "Doesn't anybody else think that's kind of *weird?*"

So come with us now and let Joe and Tim take you on a tour of Sin City and the Silver State, with all of their strange sites, quirky characters, spirited specters, and unexplained mysteries. It's all part of a state of mind we like to call *Weird Las Vegas and Nevada.*

—Mark Moran and Mark Sceurman

Introduction

WWW.JOEARTISTWRITER.COM

When the Marks first called me to contribute to this book, I thought, "I live in southern California, what could I possibly know about Las Vegas?" But after chatting with them for a few minutes, for some reason still unknown to me, they felt passionately that I was the man for the job. So, ever the professional, I slammed down my double martini, made a call to Bobby Chocolate Pudding (my bookie) asking for yet another week's extension, and started work on this project "toot sweet."

Spending the better part of four months in Las Vegas, I researched and wrote by day, and enjoyed the vices the city had to offer by night. I met more hitmen, hookers, magicians, and midgets in that one third of a year than most people could hope to meet in a lifetime.

The way I figure it, taking all my hours at the blackjack table into consideration, Mark and Mark will have to hire me to write and illustrate a half a dozen or so more books for them before I can break even on this one. Of course, if Bobby Chocolate Pudding finds out

where I've been hiding, it's going to be that much harder for me do write or draw anything . . . what with my fingers being broken and all.
–Joe Oesterle

I grew up in Washington State and while living in Seattle published a photo-copied magazine, what was know as a 'zine, devoted to the weird. My 'zine was called *Off The Deep End*. My intent was to publish information so strange even "normal" anomalist researchers could not accept it. It was an experiment in rotating belief systems, and part of the experiment was not taking beliefs too seriously, especially your own.

I had always had an attraction to weird information, from *Ripley's Believe It or Not!* to the writings of Charles Fort. It was another one of my strange interests that would bring me toward Las Vegas, where I live today.

I always had a fascination with sideshow acts and feats of the fakirs of the Far East. I put together an act and joined up with some like-minded people. Together we created a show that toured America and Europe. I left that show to start my own and began to live the life of a nomad. And all the while, Nevada beckoned me. I knew that Las Vegas was a vortex of weirdness. In my *Off The Deep End* days, people had been sending me videotapes of the Las Vegas local news. George Knapp, a reporter for KLAS-TV, had been doing a series of reports on Area 51 and the rumors that it was a government-run base for flying saucers.

I had spent some time in Reno, staying with my good friend Jim Keith, a conspiracy researcher, the week before his mysterious death, on my way to the Burning Man Festival, but I moved to Nevada permanently when I was asked to be in a Vegas show called "Shock", which played at one of the diviest casinos on the Strip. After the show, and the casino it was in, turned into a pile of rubble (as things tend to do in Vegas), I got together with Robert Allen, the show's producer. We put together a new project, "*Haunted Vegas Tours*", which now operates out of the Greek Isles Casino, just off the Strip. Next we put together the "*Haunted Laughlin Tour*", devoted to the ghosts and legends of the Colorado River region. My experiences as a researcher were put to good use putting together these tours and also in writing this book. Many who know me only for my stage persona, Zamora the Torture King, will be confused as to my involvement in this book, while those who know me well will understand completely.

People who live outside Nevada think all that there is in Nevada is in Las Vegas. People who live anywhere else in Nevada think that the only part of the state that is not part of Nevada is Las Vegas; they see it as a suburb of Los Angeles. I hope that I have pleased both groups in the selections I have chosen for this book. Nevada is one of the weirdest states in the Union, at least per capita. It has some of the strangest prehistoric history, it has more abandoned towns than any other state, and since one of its main revenues is tourism, there is always a new and weird roadside attraction to compete for attention. There is always something weird to do in Nevada, so whether you are a paranormal-obsessed multimillionaire who wants to put a hotel in space or just a tourist looking for something to do, take a journey through *Weird Las Vegas and Nevada*. *–Tim Cridland*

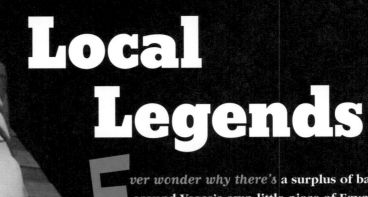

Local Legends

Ever wonder why there's a surplus of bats flying around Vegas's own little piece of Egypt? Or fear waking in your hotel room, atop a dead body? Or doubt that we ever really went to the moon? Every town has legends, but those in Las Vegas are as distinctive as the town itself. Go anywhere— restaurants, Laundromats, pawnshops—and you can be entertained for hours with tall city tales. Most can't be confirmed, but pretty much any local can recite them to you. Take a few moments away from the tables to contemplate the legends of Sin City and you'll find a veritable jackpot of weirdness.

Las Vegas is not the only place in Nevada where one can take a legendary gamble on life. Many have tested fate's odds over time, hoping to strike it rich in Nevada's mining industry, or by trying the marriage/divorce thing (sometimes more than once). Larger-than-life stories abound from both. Fact is, the legends here are as big and loud and 24/7 as Vegas itself. Care to play?

The Dead Body Under the Mattress

Visit any schoolyard in America, and odds are you will find one wise-beyond-his-years eighth grader who will tell you, with all the certainty that only someone who has lived thirteen years on this planet can muster, that his uncle knows a guy who knows a guy who worked at a hotel in Vegas, and that guy told his uncle's friend about the honeymooning couple who slept on a dead body.

The story has a number of variations, but the basic premise is always the same. A newly married couple, usually from the Midwest, either gets married in Vegas or flies to Nevada's most famous city to celebrate their nuptials. Often the bride and groom have "saved themselves" for their wedding night, so their initial night of ardor is a blessed one in the eyes of God. The eager husband gallantly carries his blushing bride over the threshold of the specialty suite. They drink champagne from each other's glasses, kiss passionately, and tumble in a heated frenzy onto the bed.

The next morning the lovebirds awake and notice an odor. The pair put in a call to housekeeping and leave for an exciting day. Upon their return, the duo notice that the smell has graduated into a stench. Since the maid failed to remove the offending aroma, the newlyweds take it upon themselves to locate the origin of the pungent scent. As they move couches and dressers, it becomes apparent the foul fragrance is coming from the bed itself. They each grab one end of the mattress, tug it off,

and are horrified to find a decaying corpse lying in a precut compartment of the box spring.

As it turns out, this urban myth is partly true. The gruesome story has been confirmed in a number of hotels from Atlantic City to Pasadena, but ironically there has never been a documented case in Sin City itself. So why in almost every retelling of this tale does this grisly incident take place in Vegas?

Go ask that smart little eighth grader. He has all the answers.

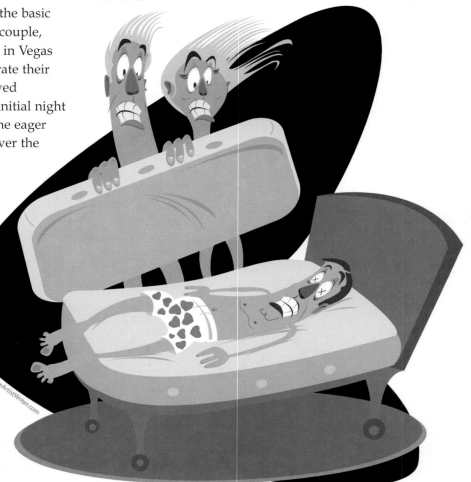

www.JoeArtistWriter.com

Cave Legends

Legends of spirits and portals to other worlds have long been associated with some of Nevada's caves, often times preceding the appearance of the white man in the region.

One such place is Cave Valley Cave, located near the Utah border at, appropriately enough, Cave Valley. A Mormon explorer named George Washington Bean found this cavern in 1858 and discovered "thousands" of footprints and other signs of human occupation inside. Local Indians told him the cave had been forbidden place for many generations and they would not enter it.

They also said that, years before, two women had entered the cave and remained inside for six months. When they returned, they wore new clothing. The women said that deep inside the cave they had entered a valley, which was filled with vegetation, animals, and water. There was also a tribe of people, who had given the women the clothing. According to the Indians, these subterranean inhabitants were responsible for the footprints that Bean found.

Nearby is Cave Creek Cave. Also feared by the Indians, Cave Creek Cave is most infamous for the appearance of the spirit of a Civil War soldier. In 1865, the cave attracted the attention of six soldiers stationed nearby at Fort Ruby, who set out to explore it. They constructed a boat inside the cave, to navigate its water system. After paddling five hundred yards, they were stopped by a wall of rock that seemed to have water flowing underneath it. One of the soldiers plunged in, presumably to find out what was on the other side. A few minutes later the soldier's corpse floated to the surface.

In a letter to the *Eureka Daily Sentinel* dated June 22, 1887, John T. Baker said that after hearing the story of the soldier's death he was compelled to explore the cave. He entered and found the soldiers' boat. "I arrived at the wall and was intently gazing on the spot the infortmate [sic] made the fatal plunge," Baker wrote, "and wondering what could induce a sane man to be so inconsiderate, when to my terror a soldier stood before me." Baker wrote that he returned to the cave the next week and the apparition returned too, this time speaking to him. In a follow-up letter to the *White Pine News* dated July 16, 1887, Baker says the soldier told him that he came to the cave with the intention of ending his own life and making it appear an accident to his fellow soldiers. The cause of his discontentment was a thwarted love affair with a lady from the valley. "I am doomed to stay in this solitary and lonely cavern for ages yet to come, as punishment for the self-destruction of my body and human life," the spirit told Baker.

The women said that deep inside the cave they had entered a valley, which was filled with vegetation, animals, and water.

The cave has been explored several times since Baker's experience, most notably in 1939, when searchers found a small figure of a Chinese idol, its arms folded across its chest, at the location where the soldier took his life. A 1981 exploration also noted the idol and nicknamed the chamber the Chinese Jinx Room after one of their rubber rafts deflated next to it. It is unclear as to whether the Chinese idol is an artificial or a natural formation. Cave Creek Cave is now blocked by bars and no longer accessible to the public.

Bottomless Pit

If there is a cavern world beneath Nevada, miners may have broken into it from time to time. The June 26, 1915, issue of the *Goldfield Weekly Tribune* describes the finding of a "bottomless pit" at the Volcano mining camp. The mining drill broke through into a huge cavern, and rocks thrown in could not be heard to hit the bottom. There was never a follow-up to this report, and not much gold was found either. Daniel Cronkhite, in his book *Recollections of a Young Desert Rat*, tells of how he visited the abandoned camp, now called Hannapah, in 1967. He and some friends entered one of the mines, where they all heard sounds of activity from below.

Gabbs Valley Underground River

The September 8, 1893, *Los Angeles Times* reported that a prospector named John L. Obendorff found a subterranean river after breaking into a natural cave while working at the Monarch Mine in Gabbs Valley, Nye County. He explored the river for two miles. He found that it had fish and was able to catch an eight-inch-long trout.

Tommyknockers

Mining is peppered with superstitious stories the world over, from dragons and giant humanoids to vast subterranean cities. Herbert Hoover, our thirty-ninth President, who worked briefly as a Nevada hard-rock miner, commented on the universal belief in mine spirits, a supernatural extension of miners' anxieties. They were not only guardians of "the treasures of the earth," but an unearthly scapegoat for malfunctions and disasters.

"Think, for instance," Hoover wrote, "of the dead darkness in which the miners' lamps serve to distort

every shape, the uncanny noises of restless rocks whose support has been undermined, the approach of danger and death without warning, and the sudden vanishing or discovery of good fortune."

Nineteenth-century mining was not only a dank, dismal, claustrophobic pursuit , but was also extremely dangerous. Cave-ins and fires were the most obvious hazards, but there were many other ways a miner could die. There were times on the Comstock when someone met his maker every week. According to *Territorial Enterprise* reporter Dan DeQuille, "So many men have been killed in all the principal mines that there is hardly a mine on the lead that does not contain ghosts, if we are to believe the miners."

A glance through the headstones of the Virginia City cemeteries reveals that miners traveled from Germany, Ireland, and England, primarily Cornwall, home of some of the world's oldest mines. Along with their skills, the Cornishmen brought their belief in Tommyknockers, mine spirits known as bucca in their homeland.

Descriptions of Tommyknockers were frequently found in Nevada papers. When visible, they "take the form of little old men. Small bodies with ugly heads and big ears and noses . . . [wearing] peaked hats, leather jackets and leather boots." Another report described them as "little, withered, dried up creatures . . . about the size of a two-year-old." One Nevada City miner quit when he spied "a little old man with whiskers comin' out of the mine pile."

In 1884, the *Virginia City Evening Chronicle* reported two men who, climbing into an abandoned mine, "heard the click of hammers. . . . Following up the sound, they were astonished to see two striking hammers hard at work on the head of a rusty drill which was being deftly turned by unseen hands. Although not a soul was in sight, they heard a lively conversation." The men snagged a

couple of skeptics, who corroborated their story.

Other tales tell of pixie axes tapping away alongside miners, revealing rich ore veins to men the 'knockers favored. They knocked on walls and caused timbers to creak to warn of impending cave-ins. It was believed the first man to hear the knock was jinxed, likely not long for this earth. Helpful yet mischievous, Tommyknockers were also blamed for throwing pebbles, stealing tools, and derailing ore cars. Miners would leave room at the end of the bar for their wee guardians and often fashioned tiny bucca effigies at the mouths of mines for luck.

Not one single 'knocker has ever been captured, although their footprints were found in winter snows. Old-timers have an explanation as to why the knockers have kept a low profile in this century: electricity! They still exist, but hide in the deepest, darkest recesses of abandoned workings.

Again in *Recollections of a Young Desert Rat*, Daniel Cronkhite relates his 1967 encounter with mine spirits while exploring the abandoned timber shafts of Hannapah in Nye County: "I had descended some 50 or 60 feet when I stopped and hung on a time-worn rung of the ladder, listening intently. Deep in the blackness beneath me I heard 'tick, click, tap, rap' and other various sounds which sent the flesh on my back crawling."

His friends asked what was going on, to which he responded, "The Tommyknockers are here," before scampering back up. "Reaching the surface, we all peered down into the questionable pit and listened again—and they, too, heard the warning of the little people."

Gremlins of all stripes change with the times, and some folks believe 'knockers have simply moved into other mechanized industries. By the same token, it's been said that there is hardly a miner working underground in Nevada today who does not believe in these little people.

Reno's Happy Divorce Traditions

For better or worse, Reno is known for quickie divorces. It only follows that some traditions would evolve from the ashes of the many marriages that have dissolved at the Washoe County Courthouse, traditions designed to bring luck to those who contemplate taking the plunge again.

One tradition starts as close as the pillars of the courthouse itself. It is said that by kissing a pillar after obtaining a divorce, a newly single person ensures a more successful marriage the next time around. This particular legend was featured in the June 21, 1937, issue of *LIFE* magazine, which focused on Reno's naughty nightlife and quickie divorces. The issue's cover portrays a young woman kissing a courthouse pillar.

But then, once the pillar is kissed, what to do with the wedding ring? Reno has the answer. One merely has to walk a block from the courthouse to the Virginia Street Bridge, a.k.a. Wedding Ring Bridge or the Bridge of Sighs. Here the newly divorced can ask for better luck in selecting a mate, then toss their rings into the Truckee River below.

No one is sure where this custom originated, but it was probably encouraged and helped along by those who scavenge the Truckee River in search of gold and platinum in the form of wedding bands; a diamond sparkling in the water makes the quest especially lucrative.

Hollywood has done its part to keep the customs alive. In *The Misfits,* Marilyn Monroe's character is a newly divorced young woman eager to get on with her life. Two of the movie's early scenes were filmed outside the Washoe County Courthouse. Hundreds of people stood across North Virginia Street one day in July 1960 and watched the filming. Some say Monroe kissed a pillar; others say she did not. And if Marilyn actually kissed a pillar, which one did she kiss? No scene showing the kiss made the movie.

Wedding Ring Bridge is also featured in *The Misfits* and in the 1939 film *Reno,* which shows a divorcee tossing her ring into the Truckee.

Was It Only a Paper Moon?

Bill Kaysing's book, *We Never Went to the Moon* was published in 1974 and put into words what a surprisingly high percentage of Americans had already suspected, that the moon landing was just another TV production. Kaysing was the former head of technical publications for the Rocketdyne Research Department of the Propulsion Field Laboratory in Simi Hills, CA.

But even before Kaysing's book was published, the belief that the moon landing was faked and that part of the hoax originated in Nevada was already deep in the public psyche. There's a scene in the James Bond film *Diamonds Are Forever*, released in 1971, where Bond infiltrates a secret space research facility outside Las Vegas. His cover blown, he flees his pursuers and inadvertently finds himself in a soundstage with a simulated moonscape and astronauts (or astro-nots, as Kaysing calls them) in action. Bond steals their moon buggy, breaking through a wall and onto the Nevada desert.

Nevada has a few qualities that make it a likely location for a hoaxed moon landing. It has isolated territories and restricted military bases, such as Area 51, where top-secret programs play out on a regular basis. And parts of the state actually look like the lunar landscape.

Astronauts did some of their training at the Nevada Test Site; at least, that's the public story. The first training mission there was in February 1965. Over time, the astronauts would visit Sedan and Schooner craters and the volcanic formations of the Timber Mountain caldera. Training there continued well into the televised moon landings. Photos released by Test Site officials show the astronauts in training, wearing incomplete space suits and sometimes just civilian clothing. It's as though showing them in a complete suit would have aroused too much suspicion; but training without the full suit would seem to negate the whole point of the exercise.

Recently, author B. Brandon Barker wrote a satirical science fiction novel about a fake moon-landing project at the Nevada Test Site, entitled *Project EMU*. To drum up publicity for the novel, he created a Web site that promotes its contents to be "true," and was surprised when someone posting to the site's discussion board actually backed up some content as fact. John Nesbit, a former air force mechanic who was stationed at Nellis Air Base in the '70s, wrote, "I do not know about Operation EMU, but it was a NASA training thing. That's what we were told. Only later did it come out that it was much broader than that. . . ."

You don't have to be an astro-not with top-secret clearance to enjoy Nevada's moonlike features. Lunar Crater is a 430-foot-deep volcanic crater near Tonopah, just a few miles down a bumpy dirt road off Highway 6. Make sure to pack some Tang in case you blow a tire and have to wait for mission control to send a tow truck.

Luxor Light Goes Batty

The giant black glass pyramid of the Luxor Hotel & Casino is known for its brilliant beam of light, which shoots skyward into the night. It's the world's most powerful searchlight, shining so many miles up into the sky that astronauts are able to pick out Las Vegas and airline pilots can see it from hundreds of miles away. There are some Las Vegans who insist that the light be capped because it brings bad luck to the city. Until this is done, they say, the city will remain cursed.

But this is Las Vegas, and the light has become a landmark, one to which not just humans are drawn. Each night, when darkness finally falls and wind sweeps across the city, the light also attracts thousands of flying insects: bugs, beetles, moths, and whatnot. And this creates the ideal all-you-can-eat buffet for bug-eating creatures, such as the bats that swarm in from as far as twenty miles away, looking for a bite to eat.

While Las Vegas made a huge effort to rid the city of palm tree–dwelling rats a few years back, no such campaign is planned for the Luxor's bats. The Luxor doesn't seem to mind the bats that drop into its light for dinner from time to time. No sense in fighting nature. The bugs probably have a different viewpoint, but in this town gambling is king, queen, AND the oo-la-la. Some of the insects that fly into the Luxor's light will live to fly another night; some will end up in the belly of a hungry bat. It's nature's way. Roll the dice!

And Your Little Sphinx, Too!

The searchlight at the Luxor is not the only thing that locals think is cursed. The same can be said for the casino's sphinx, which was built facing east toward the rising sun and incoming airplanes. However, the sphinx should have been built facing west, as the Egyptians did with the real one. Some think Las Vegas is cursed because of the inadvertent positioning gaffe.

Ancient Mysteries

This will jolt some of those smart Easterners, the fellows who say Nevada is so raw and new. They think we have no past, no background of antiquity.

—Nevada governor James Graves Scrugham.

There's no telling exactly when the hairy man-beasts believed to be our distant relatives first started dragging their knuckles around, but when they did, they might have done it right here in the land that would become Nevada. Or at least some people think so. Nevada is home to some of the oldest human remains ever found in North America, left over from those times in prehistory when the topography was covered with lush greenery.

In the 1920s and '30s, the search for "early man" was all the rage, and Nevada had plenty of contenders for the role. These early men, if that's what they were, left behind tantalizing traces of themselves and the civilizations they created. Mummies of red-haired giants, "ancient writings" in hidden caves, tales of a mysterious pale-skinned tribe that predated the Europeans' arrival, all fuel the belief that there were people here long before the textbooks tell us there were.

Is it possible? Were there human inhabitants living, loving, and working in Nevada before the dawn of history? Read on and decide for yourself.

Lost City Beneath Lake Mead

In the fall of 1924, one of the most important archaeological finds in North America's history was discovered near Overton in the southern Nevada desert. Brothers Fay and John Perkins were prospecting for gold in a remote area when they happened upon the remnants of a lost civilization. The men dutifully notified Nevada governor James Scrugham of their find. Scrugham had a special interest in Nevada's ancient history and was quick to realize the importance of the discovery. Wasting no time, he summoned eastern archaeologist and Indian expert Mark Raymond Harrington to the find. Soon worldwide attention would be focused on Nevada and its Lost City, a series of Indian ruins that extended the thirty-mile length of the Muddy River.

The city was believed to date from 1500 to 2000 B.C. In their first dig into the ruins, Harrington's party uncovered a complex of forty-six prehistoric structures, the largest of which had over one hundred rooms. The archaeologist determined they had been built by Puebloan Indians, who had apparently come from northeastern Arizona or southern Utah around A.D. 700. The Lost City complex, which ultimately included one hundred sites along the Muddy River and over fifty along the Virgin River, was one of the longest continually occupied areas in ancient North America.

Nearly six miles square, the site, which became known as El Pueblo Grande de Nevada, stirred the imagination and intrigued scientists and scholars who came to the desert to see the ancient ruins for themselves. They went about their work, methodically salvaging, tagging, and categorizing their finds. But time was not on their side. Plans for a project that would dam part of the Colorado River and redirect its flow were already in the works.

The fascinating history of the Lost City of El Pueblo Grande de Nevada is preserved at the Lost City Museum in Overton, which owns one of the most complete collections of early Pueblo Indian artifacts in the Southwest. Starting with the Desert Culture that lived here ten thousand years ago, the display features many treasures recovered from the Pueblo Grande before it was forever submerged beneath the waters of Lake Mead, formed with the completion of the Hoover Dam (Boulder Dam). As the waters of the lake began to swell, most of the ancient Pueblo Grande was lost forever. Even so, there are still miles of ruins along the Moapa Valley yet to be excavated and studied.

Alan LeBaron and the Cascadian Race

According to the theory of Captain Alan LeBaron, who explored the area from 1912 to the 1930s, the human race originated in the American Southwest. All the races and cultures of earth started in what is now called Nevada and its vicinity, and migrated to other lands when the climate changed to its current arid condition.

A report published by the University of California, Oakland, summarized LeBaron's hypothesis: "Capt. LeBaron's investigations are based on the theory that the high plateau forming most of Nevada and parts of Utah and Arizona is the oldest land on earth. There are geological maps that show that this area has not been submerged under the sea for more than 40 million years. It is therefore argued that it is the logical place to find the origin of man."

In paleogeography, the study of ancient land masses, this area is known as Cascadia. LeBaron, therefore, called the first humans the Cascadian Race. LeBaron's theories were fomented when, in 1912, he found what he recognized as Egyptian hieroglyphics on a rock in Nevada. LeBaron knew what he was seeing: He was born in Egypt. Eventually, he convinced the Hearst newspaper's Examiner Foundation to fund his explorations. It is no surprise that his discoveries were reported with great fanfare on the front pages of the *San Francisco Examiner*.

The first of these reports concerned findings near Yerington. Here, in 1924, LeBaron discovered what he called the Hill of a Thousand Tombs. The "tombs" were about two feet square, concealed by stones fitted together without mortar. Inside each enclosure was a layer of gray sand and a circle of yellowish red sand. Some of the sand was sent to San Francisco for analysis and was shown to be bone lime and the remains of teeth.

LeBaron believed that these were the burial places of human heads, so ancient that they had disintegrated into dust. Additionally, he discovered ancient writing at this location that he identified as Egyptian, Babylonian, and Mesoamerican.

But his most remembered findings were yet to come.

LeBaron was asked by Nevada governor Scrugham to explore Lehman Cave and others in the vicinity of Ely. LeBaron found nothing to interest him at Lehman, so he turned his attention to caves on the northeastern slope of Mt. Wheeler, near the narrows of Baker Creek.

Upon entering cave number 3, LeBaron states, "I stopped in amazement. Here there were no Egyptian, Babylonian or Mayan characters like those at Yerington and which I had hoped to find in the Baker Caves. But here was something equally stunning: the smooth wall of the cave was covered with painted hieroglyphs distinctly Chinese in character."

Strangest of all was the discovery of what the Examiner described as "a skull . . . of a man who was nearly seven feet tall and whose cheekbones proclaimed him to be Chinese

University of Nevada student William Fong, who had formerly attended the University of Canton in China, confirmed that the writing was Chinese, recognizing, among others, the words "chief", "wolf", "grotto", "trees", "water", "temple". Fong stated that these were ancient Chinese characters, dating them to the Chang dynasty. The antiquity of the writing was further confirmed by John Endicott Gardner, an expert in Oriental languages from Berkeley.

Strangest of all was the discovery of what the *Examiner* described as "a skull . . . of a man who was nearly seven feet tall and whose cheekbones proclaimed him to be Chinese, but whose gray-brown hair proved a Caucasian mixture."

Sacrifice of the Fairest

LeBaron's next exploration, again financed by the Examiner Foundation, would plant him firmly in the history of Nevada. While he was exploring near the Colorado River, a member of the Paiute told him of an area with rocks covered with strange images. LeBaron traveled to a place that would be called Grapevine Canyon. Accompanying him on the trip was Las Vegas resident B. M. Bower, a writer of western novels, who chronicled the events for the *Examiner*. When she reported her story, Bower gave her readers their money's worth:

PLACE OF ANCIENT HUMAN
SACRIFICE FOUND IN NEVADA:
HUGE ROCK WHERE "FAIREST OF THE TRIBE"
WAS OFFERED TO THE GOD OF RAIN

read the February 1, 1924, headline.

LeBaron believed that markings in the area indicated that there was a tomb nearby. Bower wrote, "The rocks are so eroded that many of the more exposed carvings are obliterated or seen as vague indentations in the sloping face of the natural tomb. But enough of the carvings remain intact . . . to show the strange blending of Maya, Aztec, Manchurian and Egyptian characters; as if here in the groping minds of this vanished people were born the rudimentary beginnings of the written language of the whole human race."

On one of the rocks were found symbols: the death mask, a small triangle, the lotus flower, and the sign for rain. LeBaron's translation, as reported by Bower, was explained as such: "Here as in Egypt, the lotus flower undoubtedly was the symbol meaning the fairest, or the flower of the tribe. Following that is the sign of the rain-god. Could anything be more briefly eloquent of the last desperate, though futile, attempts of a perishing people to appease the wrath of an implacable god? Translated into

words, the ideographs would read 'Here we sacrificed one of our fairest to the god of rain.'"

An extreme change of climate was a fundamental part of LeBaron's theory. He would later summarize this in an interview: "This land of Cascadia was destroyed when the growth of Sierra Nevada range shut off forever the warm winds from the Pacific. It was the progressive drying up of a land, a process which endured for ages, and in the end forced all living things to migrate or perish."

According to LeBaron, this migration caused the dispersion of the symbols found at Grapevine Canyon to other parts of the word. The Cascadians became the Chinese, the Egyptians, the Aztecs, and eventually all the

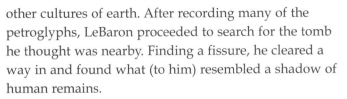

other cultures of earth. After recording many of the petroglyphs, LeBaron proceeded to search for the tomb he thought was nearby. Finding a fissure, he cleared a way in and found what (to him) resembled a shadow of human remains.

LeBaron's theories caught the eye of the Theosophy Society, which stated in its journal, "The discovery of 'Cascadia' . . . illuminates as by a lightning flash [Blavatsky's] enigmatic reference to 'ruins strewn along and beyond the Rocky Mountains.'" Not everyone else was so believing. Nevada's more remembered amateur archaeologist, John Reid, wrote to a colleague, "This Captain LeBaron is identified with no institution, he is out on his own accord." This was true, but he was

accompanied by J. C. James, a geologist of the University of Nevada, to the caves near Ely, and Dr. Eliot Blackwelder, professor of geology at Stanford University, would join LeBaron at the Grapevine Canyon site. Although scientists may not have agreed with LeBaron's theories, they did verify some of his finds.

LeBaron continued his search for the Cascadian Race, finding artifacts in the Imperial Valley of California and heading into the northeastern edge of Death Valley.

Sticking fast to his theory, in March 1927 he said of the Southwest to the *Los Angeles Times*, " the human race originated here . . . this was the garden of Eden." Three years later he would tell a San Francisco paper that Cascadia was a "land literally flowing with milk and honey, with giant sequoia, hardwoods and fruit-bearing trees."

Unfortunately, LeBaron never produced the book he intended to write about his finds, and today his theories are as dimly remembered as the somewhat implausible theory of the Cascadian Race.

Tremendous Triassic Shoe Sole

Amateur geologist Albert E. Knapp was strolling through Fisher Canyon in the Humboldt Mountains on the morning of January 25, 1927, when he happened upon a strange fossil. It lay right-side up, atop a pile of rocks. He bagged the relic, which to him seemed to be the imprint "from the heel of a shoe which had been pulled up from the balance of the heel by suction."

What appeared to be the shoe's leather remnants were thoroughly petrified. The rear two thirds of the print were intact and remarkably well preserved. The right side of the print appeared worn down, and an indentation, apparently made by the wearer's heel bone compressing the shoe's sole, was evident.

Knapp believed the rock in which the shoe print was found to be Triassic limestone, which ran in a belt through the canyon hills he'd been exploring and which is conventionally dated at between 180 and 225 million years of age. A writer for the *San Francisco Examiner* suggested that," it may be that the wearer, in flight from pursuing dinosaurs, trod in a bed of clinging clay. In drawing out the foot, the shoe—if it was actually a shoe—may have been wrenched loose from its thongs, leaving the sole behind."

Lovelock mining engineer (and collector of anomalous data) John T. Reid acquired the print and brought it to New York, where he had it examined by paleontologists, geologists, and the American Museum of Natural History. "The analyses proved up any doubt of the shoe sole having been subjected to Triassic fossilization," Reid proclaimed.

He also had microphotographs made by the Rockefeller Institute, which showed the distinct imprint of a quality piece of leather (dinosaur hide?), apparently hand-stitched in double rows. The stitching was done with a thread finer, smaller, and more delicate than that used by shoemakers of the day. "The microphoto magnifications are twenty times larger than the specimen itself, showing the minutest detail of thread twist and warp, proving conclusively that the shoe sole is not a resemblance," Reid told the press, "but strictly the handiwork of man."

> **The fossil caused much feather-ruffling among scientists and the press. . . . If the print was genuine, it would place the emergence of modern man a whopping four million years further back in time.**

The fossil caused much feather-ruffling among scientists and the press, as the very age of the human race was called into question. If the print was genuine, it would place the emergence of modern man a whopping four million years further back in time. One newspaper proclaimed the print "proof that human beings not only existed during that remote period but that they were sufficiently advanced in culture to manufacture and wear shoes of modern design."

Samuel Hubbard, curator of California's Oakland Museum, commented, "There are whole races of primitive men on earth today, utterly incapable of sewing that moccasin. What becomes of the Darwinian theory in the face of this evidence that there were intelligent men on earth millions of years before apes were supposed to have evolved?" The print's greatest proponents—professors Soddy, Joly, and Strut of the University of Oxford—argued for the existence of mankind for millions of years. Soddy believed that a long-ago "radium-conquering" superrace had departed from Earth "to some sphere in space where conditions were more favorable for human life." If they could harness space flight, one must assume they could make a decent pair of shoes.

Sadly, the files collected on the Triassic shoe sole are said to have vanished from the American Museum of Natural History.

Mystery of the Ophir Skull

Bones of questionable antiquity have a habit of popping up in the western states. An intriguing skull was uprooted in Virginia City and written about by Dan DeQuille of the *Territorial Enterprise*. He gives no date for the find, but it must have been before 1869, as that was the year the discoverer was killed in a railroad accident. As DeQuille recounts, the find of "a human skull of a very ancient and curious type" was made three hundred feet below the mouth of the Ophir Mine. It was unceremoniously dumped on the ground with a load of ore, but was snatched up by a U.S. District Court judge by the name of A. W. "Sandy" Baldwin. Baldwin brought the skull to a friend named William Shepard, who promptly put it on display at his Palace Saloon. Was the skull the oldest known record of human existence in North America? Or a hoax perpetrated by bored miners playing "dupe the scientist"?

DeQuille came to the conclusion that the skull "was that of a man belonging to a prehistoric race" who met his demise by stumbling into a chasm or standing on a patch of earth that gave way beneath his weight.

In 1874, Professor J. D. Whitney brought the skull to the California Academy of Sciences in San Francisco. He had had plaster casts made, one of which was examined by Dr. James Blake, who noted the resemblance to certain South American skulls of great antiquity.

Professor Whitney was eager to have the skull sent to Harvard and examined in Europe, but Shepard wouldn't have it. One cast was said to have been acquired by a French scientist in 1878, while the other was sent to famed craniologist Dr. J. Wyman at Cambridge University. Professors there concluded the skull belonged to a member of a prehistoric North American race.

And what of the Ophir skull itself? It's said to have perished in the great Virginia City fire of October 26, 1875, which destroyed most of the city's downtown, taking this mysterious hint of an unknown past with it.

Spirit Cave Man

Thousands of years ago, much of Nevada lay deep beneath the waters of Lake Lahontan, a massive inland sea that covered over eight thousand square miles of western and central Nevada, northeastern California, and parts of Utah, Oregon, and Idaho. As the waters slowly receded, waves swept against the shoreline of volcanic bedrock, digging out caves and rock shelters.

Prehistoric man living in this region used these caves as places of shelter and burial. In an attempt to learn more about how these ancient people lived, archaeologists have studied many of Nevada's caves. One of the most famous is Spirit Cave in the northern Nevada desert somewhere near the Stillwater Range, east of Fallon.

Because the exact locations of archaeological sites are protected under the Archaeological Resources Protection Act of 1979, only certain state employees and archaeologists who hold valid state and federal antiquities permits are privy to facts about the location. Don't even bother citing the Freedom of Information Act; this information is exempt from FOIA. However, like many such burial caves, Spirit Cave is located on public land and people occasionally stumble onto the site by accident.

One of the most intriguing discoveries of Spirit Cave was made in August 1940 by archaeologists Sydney and Georgia Wheeler, who were studying the caves and rock shelters near Grimes Point. After unearthing textiles and other artifacts, the Wheelers found the partially mummified remains of an ancient man who would later be known as Spirit Cave Man.

The remains were carefully unearthed and taken to the Nevada Museum, where they were kept under lock and key until they could be studied. More than fifty years would pass before science, through a new radiocarbon dating, carbon-14 analysis, could accurately determine that Spirit Cave Man lived and died over 10,600 years ago.

This makes Spirit Cave Man the oldest Nevadan in known history and indeed the oldest North American. An examination determined that life was not easy for the five-foot two-inch man; he suffered chronic back pain, gum disease, and infections.

In the past several years, Spirit Cave Man has become the center of a bitter controversy between anthropologists and scientists who want to study his remains and Native Americans who claim him as their ancestor; thus, they say he should be reburied so that he can continue his journey on to the next world. The battle has moved into the federal courts; under the 1990 law called Native Americans Grave Protection and Repatriation Act, the tribes claim the right to rebury Spirit Cave Man without further scientific testing.

The place we call Nevada has changed dramatically in the centuries since Spirit Cave Man lived and walked upon this land. When he died, his grieving family and friends prepared him for burial. They could not have imagined our world ten thousand years distant, as they lovingly wrapped him in a rabbit skin blanket and buried him there within the dark and silent stillness. *—Janice O.*

Chinese Explorers in Fu-Sang

In August 1925, the director of the Chinese Information Service in Paris, announced to the world that America had been discovered by the Chinese in A.D. 458.

This allegation would be made again and again over the years. It is based, for the most part, on an account from *Chu I Chuan: The History of the Liang Dynasty*, an account by the Buddhist missionary Hui-Shen.

Hui-Shen traveled across the "Eastern Sea" to a place that he called Fu-Sang, where he remained for forty years. When he returned, he recounted the strange people, customs, flora, and fauna of what maverick scholars believe is now called America, with Fu-Sang being the name given the California coast.

Henriette Mertz, a Chicago-based patent attorney and amateur historian, was the first person to connect places from the two accounts to American geographical features. She published her theories in the 1953 book *Pale Ink*. In it she maps out what she believed was the Classic journey, mountain by mountain and river by river. The fourth section of the Classic, she claims, is an account of a journey from what is now Washington State to Nevada. Among the places Mertz believes can be recognized in the book are Mahogany Peak and Capitol Peak at the head of Paradise Valley.

Hendon Mason Harris was a Baptist missionary living in China who was also convinced that the Chinese had discovered America. In 1972, in an antiques store in Seoul, he found what would become known as the Harris Map. This map, which probably dates from the Ming dynasty, and is very likely a copy of earlier maps, has three references to Fu-Sang.

Near Fu-Sang is an area called Double Rainbow Land, of which Harris says, "We could suppose that it was northeast of Southern California, and toward the Grand Canyon. Rainbows in the desert are very lovely, and often appear in double form." Harris also believes that the Paiute and Shoshone Indians are of Chinese descent.

If the Chinese did explore Nevada in ancient times, this would explain the findings of ancient Chinese writing in the state. Chinese writing has been found near Virginia City and, as we said earlier, Alan LeBaron found other examples near Ely and Searchlight. Chinese coins of the Han and Sung dynasties, accompanied by Chinese inscriptions of their value, have been found all over Nevada and California. Were they brought by early explorers? Stay tuned.

Keyhole Canyon Artifacts

Time has a way of burying things, often under dirt and sand. When someone uncovers something that doesn't fit with the orthodox viewpoint, the tendency is to ignore it until time buries it again. This seems to be the case with the strange artifacts found at Keyhole Canyon.

Keyhole Canyon, located near the towns of Nelson and Searchlight in the southern end of the state, is renowned for its petroglyphs. That's what brought Paul Mercer and members the Clark County Mineral Society, of which Mercer was the president, to the location on a February day in 1948.

Mercer split off from the rest of the group and entered a small cave, looking for more Indian rock writing. Inside he saw an object jutting out of the sand-covered floor of the cave. He began to expose it, and more strange objects came into view. Soon he uncovered what Nell Murbarger called "several hundred pounds of the most amazing and mystifying Stone Age art ever found in Nevada!"

Murbarger was a prolific writer on Nevada history, whose work appeared regularly in the *Los Angeles Examiner*, the *Salt Lake Tribune*, and *Desert Magazine*. She wrote about Mercer's discoveries in the May 1956 issue of *Nature* magazine and an issue of the *Salt Lake City Tribune*'s Sunday magazine.

Mercer, she said, had unearthed fifteen handmade artifacts, all appearing to be pre-Columbian and Mayan in origin. Most impressive to Murbarger was a "thirty-inches high clay water jug, modeled in the form of a man's head and torso" and "a Mayan-type human-form idol, twenty-two inches [in] height, and carved from a solid chunk of basalt."

The artifacts are strangely out of place, thousands of miles north of their seeming place of origin, and remain unexplained. Mercer could find no reason that they should be there, and no other similar artifacts were found in the region.

The present location of the artifacts is unknown. Aside from Murbarger's articles, little attention has been given to them. Thankfully, Murbarger took photos of the puzzling pottery, or we might have no record of it at all.

Perhaps because of the ancient mysteries it holds, Keyhole Canyon is the site of an annual Masonic ritual. Every third Sunday in September, the lodges of southern Nevada have an "open-air" initiation ceremony. The keyhole-shaped entrance opens into a naturally formed lodge, with a large boulder serving as an altar. If you are planning on sneaking a peek at this secret ritual, be warned. On the night of the ceremony, the surrounding mountains are patrolled by "Tylers," Masonic guards with very modern walkie-talkies.

At left, a Mayan-type human-form; below, a clay water jug.

Red-Headed Giants of Lovelock Cave

John Reid was a mining engineer and self-taught archaeologist who lived in Lovelock in its early days. Although Reid was an amateur archaeologist, he was well respected and considered to be an important

intellectual in what was still pioneer territory.

In 1866, when he was eleven years old, the young Reid was on a cattle run with some other boys, including Natchez, son of Chief Winnemucca. They camped outside of Lovelock Cave, but the Indians would not enter the cave, because they feared "evil spirits." That night they told Reid the legend of the cave. It was a story he never forgot.

The tale was essentially the same that Sarah Winnemucca tells in her book *Life Among the Paiutes, Their Wrongs and Claims*. "Among the traditions of our people is one of a small tribe of barbarians who used to live along the Humboldt River," Winnemucca writes. "It was many hundred years ago. They used to waylay my people and kill and eat them." She goes on to say that the tribe would attack their tribe and that this led to a war that went on for three years. The conflict came to a grisly end when the people-eating tribe was trapped in Lovelock Cave. "My people asked them if they would be like us, and not eat people like coyotes or beasts . . . but they would not give up."

"They filled the mouth of the cave with brush and wood, and set it on fire, telling the barbarian tribe that if they surrendered they would put out the fire. No word came from the cave and after the fire went out, they were never seen again. "My people say that the tribe that we exterminated had reddish hair."

Disregarding the Indians' fears, Reid entered the cave, but all that was visible was bat guano. This, however, was not necessarily a bad thing.

In 1911, Reid, along with David Pugh, formed the Sunset Guano Mining Company. They began to haul out carloads of guano, and it was at this time that artifacts were found, including human bones and mummified bodies.

Reid, in letters to the University of California, stated

that they had found feather boas and other artifacts as well as, at the south end of the cave, some human skeletons. In the north end of the cave they found some dried-up, mummified bodies, all of them having red hair. One of them was "six feet six inches tall." Reid considered this one a "giant." Over the next few decades, there were several archaeological excavations of the cave. It was evident that there had been a massive fire in the cave. It was filled with soot, and, in places where the cave floor was intact, grass had been burned "to the depth of a foot or so." There was also evidence of a battle at the cave.

Because of the finds at Lovelock Cave, and finds in the area of other giant-size skeletons and mummies and of stones with strange markings, Reid theorized that the Southwest was once inhabited by a race of red-haired giants who had an advanced knowledge of mathematics and astronomy. He found astronomical markers, one a sixty-ton rock that he believed had been moved to its location and then sculpted. He also found what he called "calendar stones," which he spent hours deciphering. Reid eventually came to believe that the red-haired giants were related to the Mayans.

But what became of the artifacts? There are many stories. It is said one skeleton was taken by a local Masonic lodge for use in its ceremonies. The Nevada Historical Society in Reno was supposed to have some of the skeletons and one of the calendar stones. Some skeletons collected by Reid had indeed been purchased by the Historical Society in 1948. Strangely, they were misplaced, until they were found in 1977.

In the 1980s, authors Sheilagh Brooks, Carolyn Stark, and Richard H. Brooks published an article about these skeletons in the Nevada Historical Society's magazine. It was essentially a debunking article, saying that Reid had mismeasured to get the heights he reported. The red

hair, they said, was the result of dye in the hair, exposure to elements, or both.

The Lovelock Review Miner reported that two skeletons, one measuring eight feet tall and the other almost ten feet tall, were recovered from a weathered-out dry lakebed. At least one was covered with some kind of shroud. The *Review Miner* of September 29, 1939, reported another giant skeleton, seven feet seven inches in height, found at the Friedman Ranch near Lovelock.

Clarence "Pike" Stoker was involved in the original mining and evacuation of Lovelock Cave. For years he had a small museum, with exhibits of early life in Lovelock and artifacts of Lovelock Cave, operating out of his house. The museum closed in the early '70s, and in 1978 its exhibits were acquired by the Humboldt Museum in nearby Winnemucca.

If you go to the Humboldt Museum and ask nicely, they will show you their Lovelock Cave skulls. The skulls are not on public display, but locked away in a cabinet in a back office. There seems to be nothing abnormal about them. The quarter resting against the jaw of one of them gives some idea of their size.

Until someone finds a giant mummy tucked away in an attic somewhere or in the hidden recesses of some forgotten collection, the tribe of red-haired giants remains one of the legends of Nevada's ancient history.

So had Reid's giants been slain? Maybe not. Even in the article, the authors admit that they had little information about the skeletons. Some were just fragments; few were marked with information. "It is assumed that Reid must have collected these specimens from the Pyramid Lake area and the Humboldt Sink. The time period to which these remains date is undetermined," they wrote. If these skeletons were missing for almost thirty years, more could still be found.

Celtics Sing and Sheer Sheep in the Silver State

Add the Irish to the list of possible early explorers of Nevada. Mabo the Melodious, the Celtic god of music, is immortalized in a petroglyph at Cane Springs in Clark County. His face is in the form of a lyre, with letters in the ancient Ogam script incorporated into the design, spelling, "I sing stanzas to music." Mabo, whose face can be a lyre or a harp, is found at many locations in Nevada.

Depiction of Celtic games, with names like "hurling the caber" and Camanachd are also found. The Cane Springs site depicts some kind of game resembling baseball, with commentary written in Gaelic.

Scholars who advocate the pre-Columbian exploration of America by Irish and Nordic explorers say that they landed on the East Coast, so how did these inscriptions end up in Nevada?

They walked, says maverick scholar Barry Fell. The markings were not left by the original Celtic colonists, but by their ancestors. Fell writes in his book *Bronze Age America* that this westward migration may have taken "centuries." The Celts blended, both culturally and physically, with Norse colonists on their journey, and both groups influenced Native Americans.

Life was not all music and games for the ancient Celt-Americans. On the journey west, they encountered Rocky Mountain bighorn sheep and created an industry around them. "In Nevada, I was told of persistent legends that the region was formerly in the possession of a now-vanished people called 'sheep-eaters,'" states Fell.

Petroglyphs depicting looms, needles and thread, weaving sticks, and other wool-working tools, accompanied by old Gaelic script, are found all over the Valley of Fire and the Lost City area. The Celtic goddess Sulis, patron of spinning and weaving, is found near these depictions.

Other Celtic deities are represented in Nevada petroglyphs. The Irish god Ogma the sun-faced, who is associated with occult sciences, makes many appearances. Good news, maybe, for Las Vegas gamblers hoping to latch on to a little of the legendary luck of the Irish.

Fabled People and Places

it's no surprise that the vast desert lands that surround Las Vegas, where a stretch of road can seem endless and a drop of water elusive, have inspired fantastic tales of people and places. Anyone who has ever sat under the scorching Nevada sun, watching heat waves ripple the scenery, can understand that this place would be fertile ground for the stuff of imagination. We know for a fact that some storied places do exist, like the atomic test sites and Area 51. But how about the nymph creatures who entice swimmers to their deaths within our lakes? Or the buried treasure from failed mining expeditions?

Just as the painted panorama of the desert is twisted by the rising heat, so are the tales of fabled people and places in our minds. One blink and you see something that wasn't there a minute earlier. When it comes down to it, only one thing is certain: Nevada has its share of things that couldn't be real, shouldn't be real, and probably aren't real . . . but might be.

Encountering a Water Baby is very bad news. They like to drag people into their watery lair and drown them.

Singing Mountain

Sand Mountain, also known as Singing Mountain, is located off Highway 50, approximately twenty-five miles east of Fallon. Each year the popular site, which is under the management of the U.S. Department of the Interior and the Bureau of Land Management, is visited by thirty-five thousand outdoor enthusiasts who come to the 4,795-acre recreational area to sand board, hike, drive their dune buggies and dirt bikes, camp, and have fun.

Of those who come to the six-hundred-foot-high dune, many want to hear the eerie booming sounds emitted when the wind shifts across the sands. While there are several acoustical, or so-called booming or singing, dunes in the world, in the United States there are only a few; two in California, two in Hawaii, and Nevada's Sand Mountain, which many consider to be one of the best places in the country to witness the phenomenon of booming.

Scientists explain that Sand Mountain sings or booms as a result of the vibrations and movement of the smooth, rounded grains of sand and the warm, dry climate. But the local Paiute Shoshone peoples have an entirely different explanation. According to their beliefs, the singing is the hissing of Kwasee, an ancient serpent that lived with their people where they were created at the sacred mountain, Fox Peak in the Stillwater Range.

Kwasee and his wife lived beneath the Stillwater

Mountains; together they journeyed across what is present-day western Nevada (Pyramid Lake, Lake Tahoe, and Walker Lake) dispensing wisdom and spreading joy everywhere they went.

When his wife died, Kwasee was so saddened that he buried himself in the sand at the foot of the Stillwater Range, and there he remains to this day. According to the elders, Kwasee is still alive beneath Sand Mountain and continues to bestow his guidance and protection upon them. Tribal leaders have requested that the Bureau of Land Management close Sand Mountain to motorized vehicles two months each year so that they can conduct their ceremonies.

Hidden Waters

In sharp contrast to its parched surface, the underworld of Nevada is teeming with water. The area was once a great inland sea, as evident from fossilized remains of prehistoric sea creatures. Apparently, the water seeped below the surface, feeding a network of subterranean rivers, lakes, and an ocean. Since earliest times, there has been speculation of a subsurface connection between Lake Tahoe and Pyramid Lake.

The July 1883 issue of the *Carson City Morning Appeal* contained a story by Sam P. Davis entitled "The Mystery of the Savage Sump." The fanciful tale concerned two men who had discovered a hole at the bottom of Tahoe that they plugged and opened up at will, thereby controlling flooding of the Virginia City mines. Although the story was fiction, it was inspired by speculation that water in the mines originated from the lake. Reports in a Tahoe newspaper doubtless fueled this

speculation and Davis's imagination. One account, in September 1866, concerned the sighting of a cone-shaped column of water rising from the lake opposite Saxon's Mill; it left a whirlpool when it subsided. The other, from July 1883, concerned two men who were fishing near Carnelian Bay when their boat began to revolve in circles and they sighted a hole in the lake floor at the axis.

Wally's River

Lest you think that stories of underground water systems are all culled from the yellowed pages of antiquated newspapers, be assured that the hunt for Nevada's underground rivers continues today.

Robert Wallace "Wally" Spencer was no wide-eyed kook; he was literally a rocket scientist. In the late 1980s, Spencer found what he believed was a 500-million-year-old river that flows from Canada to beneath Nevada and out to the Pacific Ocean. Spencer, who was originally looking for oil, used satellite photos, imaging radar, and a radiation detector mounted on the back of a four-wheel-drive pickup truck in his explorations. He had traced the river for six miles, in which it rose from 40,000 feet underground to a mere 385 feet beneath the surface at a location in Nevada. If harnessed, "It could turn Nevada into the garden of Eden," Wally told the attendees of the first Nevada Water Summit. Unfortunately, Spencer was unable to convince the state to help fund his search, so he continued on his own, keeping the underground river's location a secret. He died in 2003 at age seventy-three without tapping into his waterway, but his friends and business partners continue the quest.

Nevada's (Other) Underworld

In the 1940s, a man named Richard Shaver published a series of tales about a race of people who lived in underground caverns, some beneath the inhospitable surfaces of Nevada. He said that they were the remnants of an advanced race, most of whom had fled earth when radiation levels became too high. The ones left behind, most of them, were called Deros. They had gone into the caverns to escape the radiation, but it had already damaged their bodies and minds. Shaver alleged that the subterranean dwellers had access to abandoned technological devices that they barely knew how to operate and would occasionally aim these machines' rays at the surface world, causing all kinds of havoc.

Shaver's stories were published in the science fiction magazine *Amazing Stories.* The editor, Ray Palmer, published them as fact, causing a great deal of controversy and a significant increase in magazine sales.

Although Shaver's popularity waned in the early '50s and the man himself died in 1977, there has been a small but dedicated group of people who are convinced of the reality of the cavern world he described.

River of Black Gold

Larry Hahn is looking for the legendary underground River of Black Gold, found by Earl Dorr in 1927.

Larry first heard of the River of Black Gold from a customer of his surplus store in the 1970s. These days Hahn's Surplus is the headquarters of Exploration Inc. of Nevada, soon to be Kokoweef Inc., after the mountain Dorr descended into some eighty years ago. His company is actively searching for an entrance to the underground realm.

In a report, Earl Dorr describes exploring an underground cavern system for four days, accompanied by a civil engineer. The two men descended five thousand feet into a cave, where they found many chambers, an immense one with "a flowing river on the floor of the canyon, which rises and falls with the tides regularly."

Dorr had heard of these caverns from three brothers named Peysert, whom Dorr said he'd known since childhood. They had mined in the caverns for six weeks and extracted a large amount of gold. Dorr says of their find: "When the tide is out, there is exposed on both sides of the river from 100 to 150 feet of black sand, which the Peysert brothers report is very rich in placer gold." Dorr and Morton removed some of the sand, and Dorr's sample was assayed at $2,144.47 per yard.

Dorr is said to have blasted shut the entrance to this cavern, not long after he had found it, after becoming convinced that other miners were coming to jump his claim. He then persuaded some Los Angeles–based investors to back a mining operation, but the Crystal Cave Mining Company stopped looking for the cave when they found zinc. Disenchanted with the project, Dorr deserted it. He died in 1957 after being injured in a mining accident.

Larry Hahn took over the quest for the lost river in the 1980s, convincing many investors to chip in for drilling equipment and the likes. Every June there is an investors' meeting at the mining camp, located in the Ivanpah Mountains just a few miles from Whiskey Pete's Casino and a surprisingly short distance off I-15. Hahn is convinced that they will soon find the proof that will take the River of Black Gold out of the realm of legend and bring real wealth to himself and his investors.

Water Babies

People who camp near Pyramid Lake sometimes hear unusual whimpering sounds coming from the shoreline late at night. To some it sounds like the meowing of a cat; others say it is exactly like the crying of a baby. Legend tells us that these noises emanate from powerful tiny creatures known as the Water Babies, whose crying is said to coax curious people to swim out to their doom.

Water Babies are hideous, humanlike creatures that, according to Native American legend, can be found in all the lakes of Nevada. They are also found in springs and other bodies of water. All the tribes of the Great Basin have tales of the Water Babies. And although they're called babies, these evil little creatures are really dwarf people who have "the bodies of old men and the long hair of girls."

Encountering a Water Baby is very bad news. They like to drag people into their watery lair and drown them. If you escape that fate, just hearing a Water Baby can kill you. They are considered an omen of doom, bringing illness and death. Even to speak of the Water Babies is taboo. Certain shamans, though, can communicate with them without harm—it was the shaman's job to explain to the Water Babies why the tribe was using their water.

As with the Tommyknockers of miners' lore, it is best to try to make friends with these guys if you run into them. At Lake Tahoe, if Indians wanted to go onto the lake, they would fill a basket with corn and pine nuts, seal it in pitch, and sink it into the lake. If that didn't appease the Water Babies, they might not make it back from fishing.

The Tahoe Washoe have many legends about Cave Rock, a singular stark boulder on the eastern shore of the lake, which an early newspaper described as the "water prison of the demons." One legend concerns a warring tribe that had held the Washoe prisoners. The Great Spirit set the Indians free by putting their captors in a cave below Cave Rock, trapping them underwater. Their wailing and moans can still be heard on certain nights. Some people also say that Water Babies congregate at the cave, although it is unclear if the babies and the spirits of the Washoes' former captors are the same phenomenon.

Water Babies seem to have one foot in the spirit world and the other in the physical. Sometimes when they are heard, small footprints are found on the beach the next day. A rock in Owens Valley, on the Nevada–California border, is covered in tiny footprints that are attributed to a Water Baby by the local Numu-Paiute tribe.

But the ultimate Water Baby physical evidence was related to Nevada historian Philip Earl. "I was told that somebody had a corpse of a Water Baby in a big vat of alcohol," says Earl. It was allegedly hit by a car and is said to be at the Stillwater colony near Fallon. "I have not seen it. I've been told by two people. In this job, you get told all kinds of crazy things."

Death in the Devil's Hole

Perhaps Death Valley's name is what gives the land its sinister, otherworldly reputation. Certainly, the subzero elevation, the searing heat, and the moonscape panoramas also lend themselves to the aura of mystery that surrounds the region straddling the Nevada–California border.

The most infamous of the entrances into Nevada's underground water system is Devil's Hole, located in the Nevada section of Death Valley. A small hole in some rocks that holds a perpetually ninety-three-degree pool of water, Devil's Hole leads deep into the Southwest's underground water system.

Divers explored Devil's Hole in the 1950s, reaching a depth of one hundred and fifty feet. They suspected that the waterway connected to nearby Devil's Hole Cave, a long, vertical tunnel with water of similar temperature at the bottom. Another diving exploration, which took place in June 1965, ended in tragedy. Paul Giancontieri, eighteen, and David Rose, twenty, both from Las Vegas, vanished in Devil's Hole. They were part of a group of four young men who had gone to the hole for recreational diving. When Giancontieri did not return, Rose went in after him and also failed to surface. Despite a four-day-long recovery attempt, the young men's bodies were never found.

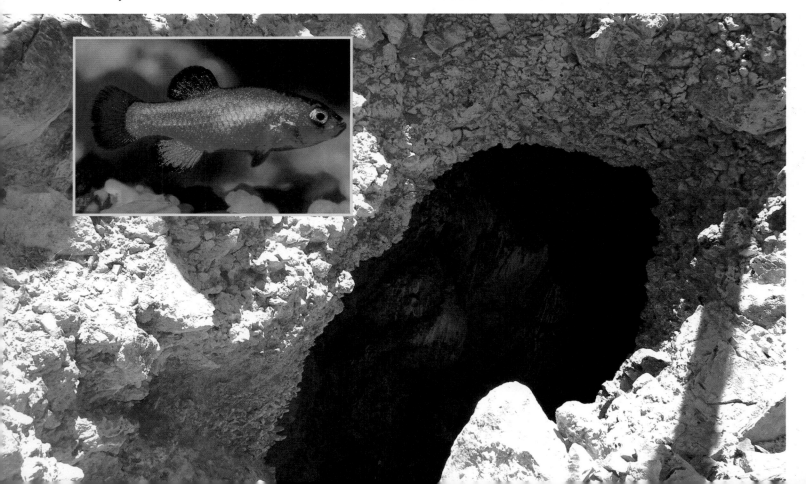

Devil's Hole continued its journey into infamy in the late 1960s. Cult leader Charles Manson was obsessed with finding a hole in the desert where he and his followers could hide from the coming race war he was trying to provoke. After the war was over, Manson and his followers planned to emerge from their hideout in the desert and take power. Manson based his quest for the hole both on lines in the Book of Revelation referring to the "bottomless pit" and on Hopi Indian legends. Former Manson family member Tex Watson wrote about the hole in his book *Will You Die For Me?*, saying Manson told him that it was an "underground paradise beneath Death Valley where water from a lake would give everlasting life and you could eat fruit from twelve magical trees."

After a three-day meditation in the desert, Manson became convinced that Devil's Hole was the entrance to the bottomless pit and that the water acted as a door. All he and his followers had to do was drain it or swim through it to reach the underground paradise. They never got around to testing this theory, though.

Currently a chain-link fence and motion detector devices that link to satellites surround Devil's Hole. They are there to protect an endangered species of pupfish, a prehistoric, minuscule population whose only home is this portal into Nevada's underworld.

Atomic Testing Museum

There are a multitude of reasons to visit Vegas, the spectacular shows, fine dining, and of course legalized gambling, but ten will get you twenty the average person on the Strip did not come to Las Vegas to visit a museum.

It would also seem like a safe bet to assume that lounging poolside, working on your tan, and sipping fruity tropical drinks would be vastly more appealing than the prospect of going to some stuffy institution for a detailed history of nuclear testing in Nevada. That bet, however, especially for lovers of the weird, is not a sure thing.

From the outside, the eight-thousand-square-foot Atomic Testing Museum doesn't seem very tempting. It's a fairly sterile-looking building, like something you'd see at a typical community college. But the fun is all inside. Upon entering the museum, you are bombarded with a compelling one-and-one-half–minute movie depicting the history and need for (depending on your politics) atomic weaponry.

Images of Hitler invading Austria turn quickly to Einstein, FDR, and the Manhattan Project. Suddenly Japan declares war on America, and the United States answers back by leveling Nagasaki and Hiroshima. The visions of jubilant Americans on the streets celebrating the end of World War II are in stark contrast to the devastation in the Land of the Rising Sun. Russia enters the picture by exploding an A bomb of its own, and before you can say "fallout shelter" the Cold War has begun. Nevada, with miles and miles of uninhabited space, becomes the perfect place to conduct the dangerous but necessary (again, depending on your politics) testing of weapons of mass destruction.

Next stop, the Atomic Age Gallery. If there is one thing America is better at than making bombs, it's jumping on a trend and making a quick buck. Among the memorabilia of the atomic age's prime years, 1950–1960, are toys (Atomic Ray Guns), candy (Atomic Fire Balls), and literature (Superboy comics; Superboy is asked to drink atomic chemicals, and government scientists are saddled with the unenviable burden of explaining to the Lad of Steel that a fissionable explosion is currently going off inside his rib cage, and with every breath our Kryptonian hero takes, he will emit a nuclear fire).

Around the corner is a facsimile of the concrete bunkers used at the original test sites. Audiences have to enter the utilitarian room before the timer runs down to zero. As the giant doors slam shut, the patrons take seats on long wooden benches. A blast of hot air precedes a thunderous boom, followed by a detailed movie chronicling how the atomic bomb changed history, politics, the economy, and popular culture.

While many parts of the museum look like they were grabbed from B-movie sci-fi sets, they are actual representations of the era. It's hard not to snicker smugly at the mannequins representing the typical American family as they futilely take cover under their tables and chairs during a routine bomb drill.

The experience becomes more educational and interactive as you pass the exhibits of Geiger counters and enter the hands-on area of the institution. Here guests can use robotic arms that once handled radioactive materials, or sit in front of a modern-day computer screen and solve the problem of where to store hazardous waste.

To get the most out of your tour, speak to one of the volunteers on-site. Many of them worked at test sites between 1951 and 1992, when the worldwide moratorium on nuclear testing was declared. They're full of fascinating first-hand facts that are not included in the actual tour.

One guard told a story of how a test went off accidentally in the middle of the desert when he and some of his colleagues were far from the safety zone. "It was a little frightening," the man explained matter-of-factly. "At first there was this blast of heat, and a wall of sand was flying right at us; then we heard the explosion." He also offered, "We were always told not to look directly at the explosion, but it was hard not to take a peek. They were some of the most beautiful colors I ever saw when these explosions went off. The sky was just so beautiful."

Visit the Atomic Testing Museum on 755 East Flamingo Road. If you miss a little gambling or a little swimming pool time, it won't be the end of the world. And even if it is, you couldn't ask for a more appropriate place to be.

Ancient Atomic Warfare in Nevada?

On the Nevada side of Death Valley, U.S. Route 95 borders the eastern portion of Death Valley National Park, about 140 miles north of Las Vegas. You'll encounter vast deserted stretches of giant salt deposits (left over from when the valley, like California, was an inland sea).

Somewhere around here a 19th-century American explorer named Captain Ives William Walker claimed to have stumbled upon the vitrified ruins of a mile-long city.

Among these ruins, there was, according to Walker, liquefied rock surface that looked to have "been attacked by a giant's fire-plough."

Walker's mysterious observation first crops up in a 1977 book by Rene Noorbergen called *Secrets of the Lost Races*. The Walker discovery has taken on the aura of fact and spread through the literature of what speculative researchers characterize as "ancient atomic warfare." Basically, ancient atomic warfare is a term that helps explain geological anomalies like patches of fused green glass found in deserts around the world. After all, nuclear detonations at the Atomic Testing Site just outside of Las Vegas, Nevada, turned desert sand into glass, right?

Well, lightning strikes and meteor impacts cause the same reaction. Except that many of these questionable patches lack the characteristic patterns created by lightning and meteors. So what caused these anomalies, then?

Speculative researchers like David Hatcher Childress *(Technology of the Gods: The Incredible Sciences of the Ancients)*

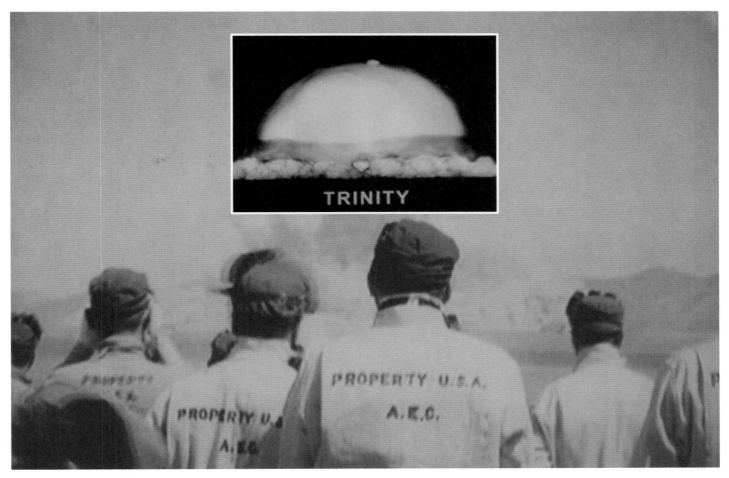

TRINITY

and Charles Berlitz *(World of Strange Phenomena)* look no further than ancient East Indian adventure narratives like the *Bhagavad-Gita* to posit their theories. These stories include descriptions of super-weapons like the Iron Thunderbolt, a death-dealing mega-bomb that eerily formed giant umbrella-shaped clouds in its wake. The Bhagavad-Gita was written around 500 B.C.

Squelching further the notion of Ye Olde Armageddon is the added fact that it's impossible to find a single archeologist, geologist, or any "-ist" on the West Coast who has heard of Death Valley anomalies like glass-like sand fusions.

At the same time, however, there isn't a single scientist who laughed at the question, "Do you believe in ancient atomic warfare?" Most have never heard of the theory and, believe it or not, are eager to learn more.

According to Hal Turner, Chief Archeologist for the Nevada State Department of Transportation, the problem in locating an ancient nuke site is the simple fact that history is written by mainstream historians instead of long-time Nevadans with firsthand knowledge of the state.

"The old timers who might have known about something like a patch of fused green glass in Death Valley are dead or have one foot in the grave," says Turner. "History continues to be lost." *—Jarret Keene*

Touring the Nevada Test Site

The "free things to do in Las Vegas" Web sites rarely list this tour, but if you play your cards right, you might gain entry to the Nevada Test Site, the location of hundreds of atomic bomb blasts. But you'd better plan in advance. In fact, you had better plan your trip around it.

The Test Site gives only eight or so tours a year, and there is a waiting list. Plus, you have to have a thorough background check, so be prepared to give all your personal information to Bechtel Corporation, the security company contracted to the Test Site. If you pass the background check, you will get a letter in the mail telling you the date of the tour you can attend. NOW buy your plane ticket.

The tour bus loads up early in the morning in front of the Atomic Testing Museum. Sixty-five miles later, you are at the Test Site's front gate. Beside the gate are two cages for activists who cross the line onto restricted land during frequent tree-hugger protests. The guide tells us that there are now two cages, segregated by gender, because when there was just one cage, there was a tendency for the protesters to "frolic." This tour is interesting already!

After passing through gate 100, you exit the bus at the town of Mercury, have your photo taken, and are issued a temporary access badge. Although the tour guides told us there would be no food available on the tour, there is a chance to get a snack and a cup of coffee at the Mercury cafeteria. Mercury was a community constructed for Test Site workers, both civilian and military. It had its own post office, bowling alley, and movie theater. In the Test Site's glory days, ten thousand people worked here and Mercury had housing for twelve hundred; CNN called it a "post-nuclear ghost town." Once you have your badge, it's back on the bus for a day of driving around the 1,350-square-mile "multi-use, open air laboratory" that is the Nevada Test Site. Some highlights:

News Nob: This is a row of benches where newsmen like Walter Cronkite sat for a close-up view of atomic bomb blasts. It conjures up images of a simpler, happier time when being within a few miles of an atomic bomb blast was considered a privilege instead of a danger.

Apple II Test Structures: We have all seen these; they are iconic American images. The federal Civil Defense Administration would build a "typical American town" and drop a nuke next to it to see what would happen. The films of these houses being blown to bits show up in almost every nuclear documentary. After the government blew up the houses, they built replacements for future tests. What was left is called a "survival town," which the Department of Homeland Security now uses for training exercises.

Priscilla Test Area, Frenchman Lake: Ever want to dangle a thirty-seven-kiloton nuclear bomb from a balloon and explode it seven hundred feet off the ground? It's been done, so think of something else!

The tour winds through the twisted and mangled

Left page: The town of Mercury. This page clockwise from top: Apple II Test Structure, Sedan Crater, and Priscilla Test Area.

structures that were part of Project Priscilla, a test to see what types of buildings might survive an air blast. A private company donated the bank vault, known as First National Bank of Frenchman Flat, that sits at ground zero. Other than the fact that the outer layer of reinforced concrete has been stripped off, the vault is intact—so breathe a sigh of relief knowing that in the event of a nuclear strike, your boss's money will be okay.

Area 5: The bus stops here, and someone else gets on and tells us that we are at a low-level radioactive waste dump . . . uh, Waste Management Site. He explains that things such as used radioactive equipment from hospitals are buried here.

Sedan Crater: This is the highlight of the tour. Sedan Crater is a result of Project Plowshare, an attempt to find peaceful uses for nuclear bombs, such as making ditches and mining. It turns out that using a nuke to make a big hole does work, but everything left in its wake is too radioactive to use afterward. It cost millions of dollars to figure this out, but at least it left behind "one of the largest man-made craters on earth."

Sedan Crater was formed when a "104 kiloton device" was exploded 635 feet below the ground. The crater is 1,280 feet wide and 320 feet deep. There is a wooden platform overlooking the crater, and it's the perfect place for a photo op, but . . . NO CAMERAS ALLOWED! Sedan Crater is presently the only part of the Test Site listed on the National Register of Historic Places.

Gate 700: At Sedan Crater, you are as close as you are going to get to gate 700, the back door to Groom Lake—or, as it is better known by UFO buffs, Area 51. The federal government still says this top-secret air base does not exist. Gate 700 is the checkpoint on the only paved road going into Area 51, the north end of the Mercury Highway.

Nine hours and two hundred and fifty miles later, you are back on the streets of Las Vegas, just a few blocks from the Strip. But wait a minute. Wasn't this a tour of an all-restricted area? Will you be glowing like the Strip's neon lights? National Nuclear Security Administration spokesman Kevin Rohrer reiterated that there is no place on the public tour that has more than the normal background radiation found in any other place in Nevada. Oh, by the way, the Web site notes that "Pregnant women are discouraged from participating in test site tours," but not for the reason you might think. The site warns that "the long bus ride and uneven terrain" are the only true danger. For information about Test Site tours, call Brenda Carter at (702) 295-0944.—*Tim Cridland*

Enola Gay Monument

Nevada loves its nukes. Las Vegas was once known as Atomic City because of its proximity to the Test Site. However, Wendover lays claim to being the place where the bomber unit that dropped the first atomic bomb was trained.

In September 1944, Colonel Paul W. Tibbets, under the direction of the Manhattan Project, selected Wendover Air Force Base as the training area for the 509th squadron, which would eventually drop atomic bombs on Japan and end World War II.

The mission was top secret; the squadron had no idea what their mission would be until the last minute. Tibbets is quoted as telling them, "Don't ask what your job is, that's a surefire way to be transferred out. Never mention this base to anybody. This means your wives, girls, sisters, family."

On August 6, 1945, the *Enola Gay* dropped its atomic cargo on Hiroshima. Three days later *Bock's Car* did the same at Nagasaki. Japan surrendered two days later.

Wendover Air Force Base now sits abandoned on the Utah side of the border. It was declared "surplus" in 1976. But the hangars that once housed the *Enola Gay* are still standing, and there is a museum and a self-guided tour.

On August 25, 1990, the city of West Wendover unveiled a monument dedicated to the 509 Composite Group and the "First Atomic Bombardment." It stands in the middle of the welcome center on Wendover Boulevard. A Harry Truman quote is engraved on the front:

> THE ATOMIC BOMB IS TOO DANGEROUS TO BE LOOSE IN A LAWLESS WORLD . . . WE PRAY THAT GOD MAY GUIDE US TO USE IT IN HIS WAYS AND FOR HIS PURPOSES."

Journey to the Edge of Area 51

Area 51 is a top-secret military base located approximately 85 miles northwest of Las Vegas. The site is called by many names: Dreamland, Paradise Ranch, Watertown, and Groom Lake to name a few. Although

not much is known about what actually goes on at the base, it is known that several high-tech aircraft have been developed or at least tested there. Perhaps the thing that Area 51 is best known for is

being a sort of Mecca for UFO hunters and researchers. The area began to draw attention from those interested in UFO activity in the early seventies, when reports of strange lights and objects flying over the area began to circulate.

Over the years, the legend of Area 51 continued to grow. Some have speculated that it is the place where the craft and aliens that crashed in Roswell, New Mexico, were brought for examination.

In the mid-nineties, the state of Nevada actually renamed State Highway 375 (the only highway that runs directly past the restricted area) the Extraterrestrial Highway and posted signs complete with flying saucers announcing the name change. (See *Roads Less Traveled*.)

It has become a popular quest for UFO enthusiasts to get as close to Area 51 as possible. There is a well-maintained dirt road, unofficially known as Groom Lake Road, that will lead you to the base. However, if you venture too close you will be detained by the security force in charge of the perimeter to the restricted area. One cannot discuss Area 51 without including the small town of Rachel. It is the closest town to Area 51 and has actually been home to many employees of the base.

Rachel has a population of only about 100 (the sign welcoming you states,

POPULATION: HUMANS—98, ALIENS—?).

Rachel was founded in the early seventies and was populated mostly by employees of Union Carbide in the Tempiute tungsten mine. Once the mine closed, most people moved on. Those that have stayed behind have made the best of their town's reputation as "The UFO Capital of the World." The main attraction in town (and one of the only permanent structures) is the Little A'Le'Inn [pronounced alien] bar and grille. The Little A'Le'Inn was featured in the blockbuster film Independence Day, appeared in a two-part episode of "The X-Files", and has been the backdrop for several documentaries.

One of the first things you see as you approach the Little A'Le'Inn is a 'Flying Saucer' being towed. At first glance, the Little A'Le'Inn is the kind of place you could just drive by and not even notice. The sign in front advertises a motel. In front of the A'Le'Inn, I noticed a strange-looking monument. Upon closer inspection I learned that the makers of *Independence Day* buried a time capsule to be opened in the year 2050. The plaque reads:

ON THIS EIGHTEENTH DAY OF APRIL, A.D. 1996,
TWENTIETH CENTURY FOX HEREBY DEDICATES
THIS TIME CAPSULE AND BEACON
FOR VISITORS FROM DISTANT STARS,
TO THE STATE OF NEVADA AND THE
"EXTRATERRESTRIAL HIGHWAY."
THIS TIME CAPSULE WILL SERVE AS A BEACON,
TO BE OPENED IN THE YEAR A.D. 2050,
BY WHICH TIME INTERPLANETARY TRAVELERS
SHALL BE REGULAR GUESTS OF OUR PLANET EARTH.

GOVERNOR BOB MILLER OF THE STATE OF NEVADA
TWENTIETH CENTURY FOX FILM CORPORATION
THE FILMMAKERS AND CAST OF INDEPENDENCE DAY

I had a nice lunch at Little A'Le'Inn, then started off for Groom Lake Road, a road that doesn't exist and is not on any map (except the homemade map I paid 33 cents for back at the inn). Even though I was alone and couldn't get a signal on my cell phone, I was perfectly at peace. The area is so awe-inspiring that I can see why, if aliens do exist, they would want to visit here.

Finally, I was actually at the edge of the famous Restricted Area. For the final half-mile or so I had been driving on some winding roads that brought me through a ravine. It was obvious that if someone had wanted to prevent me from leaving here, it would be a perfect place for a roadblock (or ambush). Remember, putting all the UFO folklore aside, this is the edge of the most secretive military base in the free world. Not wanting to get myself in any trouble I kept far from the markers—there is no fence or wall here, just signs and orange posts. If you go past one, you will be arrested and fined. If you go too far, they claim the right to shoot you.

After looking around for a few minutes, I took one more walk around the perimeter, then it was back down the long, lonely roads that lead to Las Vegas. Did the experience answer any questions or unravel any of the mysteries that surround Area 51? No, but that was not the purpose of my adventure. This adventure was about seeing a piece of pop culture and modern folklore up close. It was a wonderful experience that I highly recommend. *—Henry C. Conley, PMP*

The Venusian of Lake Mead

"Good evening, I am Valiant Thor, and I am from Venus." –*Val Thor, speech at Salmon Arm, British Columbia, Canada, July 22, 1994.*

The legend of Valiant Thor started as a word-of-mouth phenomenon in the 1950s. It was the height of the cold war, the beginning of a new age of space exploration, and a time of UFO hysteria in America. Sci-fi movies of alien invasions and little green men from Mars permeated the public consciousness. Rumors began to spread of a mysterious man who claimed to be from Venus who was walking among us. Some said he could walk through walls; others claimed he had no fingerprints. Speculation on the location of his ship (in which, according to rumor, he lived) ran rampant. It was the beginning of a mystery that after more than half a century still persists.

In the 1950s, a handsome, charismatic man began to appear at conventions of UFO enthusiasts. He claimed to be an emissary from the planet Venus and wowed the crowds by being able to speak any language or dialect any member of the crowd could throw at him. And, he said, he was not just any Venusian, but the commander of all the Venusians on Earth. The man's name was Valiant Thor.

According to Thor, he came from a race of beings who lived within Venus, not on its surface. They were sent here to protect us from ourselves, and their number one mission was to make sure nuclear war never occurred.

When Val arrived on this planet, he immediately went to visit President Eisenhower to offer his assistance in solving all of Earth's problems. He was refused by Eisenhower and Vice President Richard Nixon, but claims he did briefly meet with the Secretary of Defense. After that, he was held by a government agency within the Pentagon, where he was questioned and studied.

The story and message of Valiant Thor has been perpetuated by many, but most notably by one Dr. Frank Stranges. Stranges claims that agents of Mr. Thor escorted him into the Pentagon in 1959 to visit with Val. Since then, he has been periodically visited by Thor. He reports seeing Thor's brother, Donn, walk through solid matter. He also claims that Val, during their first meeting, showed him a strange spacesuit made of an unidentifiable fabric that could not be destroyed and that sealed itself without buttons or zippers, merely a wave of Val's hand over it. Stranges has gone on radio and TV talk shows and given lectures for years, attempting to perpetuate the legend of Valiant Thor. Also a religious preacher, Stranges believes Val and his shipmates are a race of people created by God before Adam, who never suffered the fall from God's grace that humankind did.

These days it is said that Valiant Thor's ship, *Victory One*, remains hidden somewhere near Lake Mead, just outside Las Vegas. The ship is home not only to Val, but also Donn, crewmates Thonn and Teel, and a medical officer known simply as Doc. Though he periodically returns to Venus, Thor always winds up back here on Earth, where he and his shipmates live a quiet life beneath the Nevada landscape. He spreads his quasi–New Age messages worldwide, through Dr. Stranges, in an effort to better the human race and prevent us from destroying the planet. He has chosen not to reveal himself to the masses yet because he is working on a very specific timeline, which has not yet reached the point of public appearances.

Is Val Thor really a Venusian superhuman being responsible for maintaining peace on Earth? Is he even real, or just a figment of Frank Stranges's imagination? It seems no one is sure.

Unexplained Phenomena

We take a break from our usual chapter introduction to present you with a short quiz.

Who is most likely to be an alien (space, that is . . .) in Las Vegas:

> a. Those guys who hand out the flyers for the prostitutes and sex shows
>
> b. Wayne Newton
>
> c. The person in charge of keeping hot things hot and cool things cool at the buffet
>
> d. The Mafia
>
> e. Every other blackjack dealer

And the answer is . . . any one of them. Because Vegas—really the entire state of Nevada—provides the perfect universe-away-from-universe. Think about it.

You're in space. You miss home. You pull up to a nice blue planet and find a bright, loud city in the middle of a desert, a city that shines and dazzles and doesn't seem to close shop, ever. And the people there are so busy with machines and tables that nobody really pays any attention to you. It's perfect. You could look like someone out of the cantina scene in *Star Wars* and still blend right in.

The *Weird* team found stories from Vegas and all around the state, many of which involve direct contact with UFOs and aliens, and some could be standing next to you right NOW. And we've got other stories about skyfalls, toads in rocks, and strange lights in the night. Which might all be influenced by aliens too. You never know.

Nevada UFO Roundup

On June 24, 1947, the modern era of UFOs was ushered in when pilot Kenneth Arnold, while flying near Mount Rainier, Washington, witnessed a formation of nine boomerang-shaped craft which moved "like a saucer would if you skipped it across the water." A journalist bastardized his description of the crafts' movements, and the term "flying saucer" was born.

Nineteen forty-seven was a banner year for strange objects in the Nevada skies. Everything from "flying saucers" to "flying washtubs" and "flying Cardinals' hats" were reported. A mere four days after Arnold's sighting, air force F-51 pilot Lieutenant Armstrong, flying thirty miles north of Lake Mead, claimed he spotted a formation off his right wing of five or six white disks flying at an altitude of 6,000 feet. Three weeks earlier a reddish UFO had been sighted above Las Vegas. Witnesses claimed it emitted a flash of light before shooting heavenward. Newspapers ran sensational articles speculating that the UFO flap was the result of atomic testing in the Pacific.

On June 24, 1950, three years to the day of Arnold's sightings, something extraordinary blazed across Nevada's night sky. The saga began when two United Airlines pilots, their crew and passengers spied an object "somewhat cylindrical or dirigible-like" in shape. Captain E. L. Remlin, First Officer David Stewart, and Captain Sam B. Wiper, along with dozens of passengers aboard the UAL Mainliner agreed upon a description:

The cigar-shaped UFO had a bluish center, a bright orange tint, and was flying horizontally at about 20,000 feet, considerably faster than the plane.

The pilots logged it with CAA ground control at the Silverlake checkpoint just north of Baker, California, at 8:08 p.m. The "ship" was also reported by two military planes and sighted by at least four other commercial airliners. Two of the CAA operators at the checkpoint watched the object in disbelief for ten minutes. The pilot who made the initial report described it as gunmetal gray, with an appearance of heat radiation near the rear, which he could make out when the object jolted west.

Dozens of civilian pilots and hundreds of spectators watched the craft from all over the state. In Tonopah, a pilot watched it moving back and forth in its vapor trail. In Lovelock, pilots watched it shoot north at a terrific speed. In Fallon, a woman told her husband, a reporter, that she witnessed a brilliantly intense light moving at an "unbelievable speed" in the northeastern sky. In less than a minute's time, it created a huge, circular "smoke trail," which other witnesses described as luminous and corkscrew-shaped. An hour after the initial report was made, the object had winged its way over northern Nevada. Witnesses in and near Ely watched as the sky was lit up by the spiral trail, which remained in the air for half an hour.

President Harry Truman created the Nevada Test Site on January 11, 1951. The first atomic test, Operation

Ranger, was conducted on January 27, when relatively small bombs were dropped over the desert. In February, UFO researcher Donald Keyhoe predicted that A-bomb tests there would lead to an increase in the activity of these unknown objects. The following year the air force initiated Project Blue Book, to investigate reports of UFOs, and, indeed, two of the three Nevada cases that the project officially listed as "unknown" occurred in the summer of 1952. On April 17, a group of circular UFOs buzzed Nellis Air Force Base. Checking up on the test site, perhaps?

U.S.A.F. Captain D. A. Woods reported another sighting on August 26, 1952, at Lathrop Wells near Nellis Air Force Base. The captain saw a lone round and very bright object with a "dark cone" in the center that left a V-shaped contrail. It flew rapidly and hovered before making an instantaneous ninety-degree turn, accelerating gently, and rocketing into space.

Five years later Project Blue Book ran into an embarrassing problem. At 6:30 on the morning of November 23, 1957, First Lieutenant Joseph F. Long had a close encounter with four classic flying saucers. Long was in his car about thirty miles west of Tonopah when his engine died. While trying to restart it, his ears were assaulted by a high-pitched droning hum that emanated from four disk-shaped craft resting on the ground

between three and four hundred yards from the highway. Curious, Long walked to within fifty feet of the identical objects, which he estimated were fifty feet in diameter, between ten and fifteen feet high, with a dark ring around the outside. Each was capped by a transparent dome and rested on three hemispherical landing legs.

As he approached, the objects retracted their landing gear and rose fifty feet into the air, traveling slowly north across the freeway and disappearing behind some small hills, leaving behind a depression, but no evidence of heat. The encounter lasted twenty minutes. Upon returning to his car, Long found that it started with no problem and ran perfectly. He drove on to Indian Springs Air Force Base and reported the sighting to the base security office. A memo in the Blue Book files outlined the air force's problem:

> The damage and embarrassment to the Air Force would be incalculable if this officer allied himself with the host of "flying saucer" writers, experts and others who provide the Air Force with countless charges and accusations. In this instance, as matters now stand, the Air Force would have no effective rebuttal, or evidence to disprove any unfounded charges.

The sighting had to be explained or at least explained away. A psychologist was contacted, and the best he could do was suggest it was "road hypnosis," that the lieutenant had hallucinated while driving. Untenable as that may seem, the official Blue Book explanation lists the occurrence as "physiological" in nature, thereby ensuring no further investigation. Over the years, many investigators have noted the credibility of the case. When Jack Webb produced the TV series *Project UFO*, he based one of the episodes, "Incident in the Nevada Desert," on Long's case.

Secret UFO Crash at Ely

During the 1950s, reports of flying saucers or UFOs were common throughout Nevada, but not all the stories made the news.

According to an Ely tale, a young woman was entertaining dinner guests on an August evening in 1952 when she happened to look out at the horizon just in time to see a flying saucer crash to earth. It didn't take long for those who were first on the scene to realize that the strange craft was not of this earth and that all of its occupants were dead. Apparently the space travelers had been killed on impact.

Before more could be learned, a highly secret team sent by the government rushed in and confiscated what was left of the strange vehicle and all the bodies of the space aliens on board. Ely's UFO crash was soon forgotten by outsiders, though some residents still watch the sky.

The Ely event outshines pretty much every reported UFO crash for sheer extraterrestrial body count. It's said the crash yielded sixteen humanoid corpses, which were presumably whisked off to the deep freeze storage at Wright-Patterson Air Force Base in Dayton, Ohio. Serious UFO researchers have uncovered no further information on the crash.

Ely Times editor Kent Harper acknowledged the event's fifty-year anniversary with a modest attempt to uncover the truth. "We had an individual who lived here who isn't necessarily an ufologist, he doesn't believe in flying saucers from outer space visiting us, but he had an

extreme interest in what the air force might be doing at Area 51," Harper writes. "He had talked to one individual who was a night watchman at our copper mine that had told him that he had seen the crash and then was interviewed by government people that told him to forget about it afterwards in the interest of national security." The eyewitness claimed to have seen a glowing object fall out of the sky and crash into a mountain.

In his article, Harper recalled a conversation with an old-timer in a local bar. "Back in the early '50s," the old-timer told him, "an Air Force jet crashed on South Ridge overlooking Copper Flat and U.S. 50." He said a radar station was built atop the mountain afterward.

Did the military try to cover up the crash with a terrestrial explanation? The *Ely Times* verified the story by heading out to Highway 50. "There in the dark in the middle of the valley midway between Robinson Summit and the Ruth turnoff was a chilling sight. High atop one of the mountains was the flashing light of the radar facility."

So was it a UFO or a jet that crashed? And what about that body count?

The 1962 Las Vegas UFO Crash

In the wacky world of UFOs, few events are harder to explain away than those of the night of April 18, 1962. There were reports of a blinding light moving above. According to the *Los Angeles Times,* Reno residents described seeing a "vivid greenish light that flashed across the skies and then disappeared over the mountains traveling from west to east." Reno resident Homer Raycraft described it as "a big fireball." It was also said to be a dazzling white light that changed to green, orange, and red. Witnesses in Reno saw an object that made a "sweeping turn to the south" toward Las Vegas.

Flash back about thirty minutes earlier. An object was reported traveling in the skies from Oneida, New York, all the way to California. Over one thousand witnesses reported seeing the object over Utah, Montana, Idaho, New Mexico, Wyoming, Arizona, and California.

From New York, it was described as a glowing red ball, heading west. Over Utah, it was described as either a blue light or as an incandescent, white-yellow ball with a bright yellow flame trailing behind it. Many witnesses claimed loud booms accompanied it. Its fiery trail was tracked by the North American Air Defense Command, and air force bases were put on alert across the country.

Bob Robinson and Floyd Evans ducked under their pickup truck south of Eureka, Utah, when the object touched down nearby with a brilliant white flash. Robinson claimed he could make out small windows through the almost blinding haze. The object knocked out power in the area, and parts of Utah and Nevada were briefly lit up bright as day.

Project Blue Book tried to pass the object off as a rare, exceedingly bright type of meteorite known as a bolide, which seems impossible when you look at the facts. Meteors don't show up on radar, but this object was tracked by radar and scrambled jets in two locations. The pilots of at least two airplanes reported the object traveling beneath them. No meteor could sustain such a flight path for thousands of miles. And meteors cannot change their trajectory!

Captain Herman Gordon Shields was questioned at Hill Air Force Base in Utah, and reported that his "cockpit was illuminated from above . . . the light intensity increased until we could see objects [on the ground] as bright as day for a radius of five to ten miles." When the light decreased, the pilot saw "this object which . . . was illuminated. It had a long, slender appearance comparable to a cigarette in size, that is, the diameter with respect to the length of the object. The fore part, or the lower part of the object was very bright . . . The second half, the aft section, was a clearly distinguishable yellowish color."

The morning after the sightings, the *Las Vegas Sun* reported, "a tremendous flaming sword flashed across the night sky and heralded the start of a search for a weird unidentified flying object." The object seen, according to the *Sun,* was "traveling almost northeast of Las Vegas until a final explosion and column of brilliant smoke rose from the direction of Mesquite." The Clark County sheriff's office led a search for wreckage, first by jeep and then by air. Nothing was officially recovered. Author Kevin Randle debunks dozens of reported incidents in his book *A History of UFO Crashes.* The Las Vegas crash is one of the very few he deems positively authentic. In print, he has called it "the best evidence" of extraterrestrial craft visiting earth.

In *A History,* Randle concludes, "The Air Force offered a series of explanations ignoring the facts. They ignored the information that didn't fit with the bolide theory. But the witnesses know the truth. They saw something from outer space, and it was not a meteor. It was a craft from another world."

Johnny Sands and the Men in Black

*It was late at night and I was speeding along
In the Desert in Nevada and I was all alone.
I was tired and hungry and I was Vegas bound
When out of the sky came a light with no
sound.* —Song by Johnny Sands

Johnny Sands has had an interesting life. He has been on TV and in movies. He is a country singer and a stuntman. He has driven a motorcycle on the "wall of death," performed on a Ferris wheel with dynamite strapped to him, and been sealed in a coffin underwater for charity.

Some people still remember the day that he met some aliens on the Blue Diamond Highway outside Las Vegas. Sands was returning from Pahrump around ten thirty p.m. when he noticed a cigar-shaped aircraft that looked "like the Goodyear blimp, only longer" following him. He did not pay much attention to it until his car suddenly died. When he got out to look under the hood, he saw the craft hovering a thousand-feet above him. He noticed that it had a ring around the middle and a series of round portholes.

The craft landed and two strange-looking men walked toward him, clad in black-and-silver uniforms. He tried to move but was paralyzed. They were about five feet seven inches tall and were hairless, lacking even eyebrows or eyelashes. Their mouths were small and never opened, and they had "pugish" noses. Their eyes were black with white pupils. Later Sands would say, "the eyes remind you of a flashlight, they shine right at you when they looked at you." The beings' strangest feature was what seemed to be gills under the ears.

They spoke to him through speakers on their chests.

The humanoids told Sands that their thoughts were translated into English via the devices. One of them asked him what he was doing there. He told them he was an entertainer and was going to Las Vegas to do a show. He was then asked why there were so many people in Las Vegas. Sands told them that it was a tourist destination and that people came from all over to visit.

Next they asked a question that confused Sands, "What is your means of communication?" Sands told them that he did not understand, which caused the humanoid to blurt irately, "Answer the question!" Sands repeated that he did not understand. With this, the humanoid stared blankly at his companion and then suddenly turned, touching Sands's left hand with his own. He told him not to tell anyone of their encounter and that "we will be watching you, we will see you again." They walked away and vanished in a flash of light. The whole encounter had lasted ten minutes. Sands's car restarted, and he drove on to Las Vegas.

Sands did not keep quiet about his experience for long. The front-page headline of the January 31, 1976, *Las Vegas Sun* screamed, UFO CREWMEN GRILL MUSICIAN.

Sands says, "I wanted to see if it was some kind of experiment. I called the Air Force Base there in Nevada. They told me to contact APRO (the Aerial Phenomena Research Organization) in Tucson, Arizona." The air force told Sands they had closed Project Blue Book, but APRO was following up things like his sighting.

Sands is somewhat reluctant to talk about the events that transpired afterward.

"I really didn't want to promote it. I don't think to this day it was worth the time and trouble. It certainly wasn't any help to me as far as going to Vegas, because . . . if you're talking about aliens from outer space, the majority of the people think, Well, he's a little wacko, I don't know if we need to work [with] him."

Hearing Sands, now entering his sixties, tell his tale you can't help but be taken by his sincerity. Though he doesn't speak much of his experiences with the aliens these days, recently Johnny did grant *Weird Las Vegas* a rare interview in which he told us his story.

"Now [APRO] asked me if I would be willing to submit to a voice analysis, a stress test, and a Polygraph test with a hypnotist of their choice. And I said, "Well, I don't have no reason to hide nothing.

"They had a doctor, Leo Sprinkle from the University of Wyoming, fly in to give me some tests there in Vegas. He asked me five or six questions. He asked me did I see what I believed to be aliens in the desert, and I said yes. He asked did they talk to me, not using their mouth, but through a mental-telepathy type situation, through the intercom on their belt, and I said yes. He asked me what they looked like, were they pale and did they have gills and a nose, and I answered yes. When I got done with all the questions, I went out of the room, and he looked at the men who were there waiting, and he said, "He's not telling a lie about any of it, every word that he has told me is true." He said the voice analysis says so, the stress test says so, and he passed the polygraph test one hundred percent."

Some people think that Sands's story may have been suggested to him by the movie *Men in Black*, but Sands maintains he'd never heard of the Men in Black before his encounter. And the creatures he met looked nothing like the movie men. He eventually left Las Vegas and returned to his native North Carolina, in part to escape the unwanted notoriety his experience had brought him. He has seen a few more UFOs since his Vegas encounter but never saw another humanoid or MIB. Presently, when he is not working the fair and carnival circuit, he lives in a small town in Georgia near the Florida border.

McDermitt's Mysterious Lights

The mysterious lights of Marfa, Texas, are world famous. Oddly enough, such lights have been reported from one end of the country to the other, and theories as to just what causes them abound. At the Nevada–Oregon border in the high desert region, people in McDermitt have been seeing mysterious lights for over a hundred years.

The McDermitt lights were first brought to the attention of those living in other areas of the country in an article entitled "Phantom Lights in Nevada." The

story appeared in the 1948 debut issue of *Fate* magazine and was written by Kenneth Arnold, the pilot who was the first person to report a UFO, or flying saucer, sighting.

In his article, Arnold told of incidents in which the lights actually encircled a group of people and frightened horses and dogs. Anyone hoping that fame might come to the town as a result of the mysterious lights was disappointed. Eventually, McDermitt's mysterious lights were forgotten by most people, but those who lived in the tiny farming and mining community on Highway 95 continued to witness the strange show.

Depending upon whom you talk to, the lights are

described as being orange fireballs, or twinkling red or fluorescent yellow disks. Some say they look like car lights or someone swinging a lantern in the distance. Most people say the lights hover a few inches above the ground; some have seen them racing across the sky. Apparently more predominant in the summer months, McDermitt's mysterious lights have been seen on the highway and in the canyons. Recently, or so the story goes, the lights were seen at a nearby ranch.

One witness says, "I was driving home from school one night and was coming by Orvada when I looked out and saw an orange ball of fire on the horizon."

Another person describes the lights as UFOs. "Sure, it could have been an airplane I saw, but I don't think so. Those were some sort of UFO lights."

There are few city lights in a town the size of McDermitt. Light pollution is not a problem here as it is in Las Vegas. This is the high desert. There are no swamps or excessive moisture to blame for the phenomenon. Nor is there a steady stream of cars traveling along the highway. The lights remain a mystery. But motorists driving down Highway 95 at night still continue to catch glimpses of the strange lights sparkling in the darkness of the desert near McDermitt.

Amazing Kreskin Predicts UFOs in Vegas Desert

In March 2002, the Amazing Kreskin predicted, on FOX news, there would be a dramatic UFO sighting in the desert of Nevada, minutes from the Silverton Casino. The Amazing Kreskin claims he is not one to write things off as cosmic coincidences, but even he was at a loss to explain what happened to him on June 6, 2002.

At eight that evening, the World's Foremost Mentalist had performed a free show to over five hundred people. During the performance, Kreskin planted a posthypnotic suggestion in the minds of dozens of people in the audience, telling them that when he dropped a white handkerchief, they would see UFOs in the sky above them.

Kreskin offered $50,000 if his prediction of UFO sightings on that night did not come true. Of course he has been performing for years, and it's a fair prediction that he has never given away fifty grand nor that he ever plans on giving away that kind of money. The trick is in basic semantics.

"A sighting can be many different things. It's simply something in which people direct their attention and 'believe and see' that something is there," offers the amazing one.

Later that night, Kreskin showed up in the desert for the event he'd set up, attended by, he says, about 1,800 people. In the crowd were local townies, visitors, and various alien/Kreskin believers who came to see the UFO show he'd promised. After a brief chat with the audience, he dropped his handkerchief, and according to the master showman, forty-one members of the crowd had very animated reactions to what they perceived as UFOs.

To the hundreds who were not under Kreskin's spell and saw nothing in the skies above, the reaction ranged from annoyance to dismission. Kreskin claims this stunt was to make the public aware of the power of mass psychological suggestion and to warn America of the possible disastrous consequences if this power were used in the wrong hands.

According to a witness of the event and member of the advisory board for the National Institute for Discovery Science, John B. Alexander, Ph.D., "he [Kreskin] had demonstrated that with only minutes of preparation, he had been able to make people see objects that undeniably were not physically there. Therefore, if that could be accomplished with little effort, there is an urgent need to understand the implications of what can be done with intense programming."

The weird side note to this story is that at 11:03 the same night, a number of devoted UFO seekers and local NBC news cameramen were still in the desert, and all observed a green luminous form passing across the dark desert sky, followed by a second object less than one minute later. The forms made no sound but were broadcast live on KVBC TV.

Says Kreskin, "For the first time in history, thousands of viewers [witnessed] a live UFO sighting."

Amazing.

Little Bonnie Claire Playa Rocks

Not every unexplained thing in Nevada is extra-terrestrial. Some of the weirdest stuff is truly down-to-earth. Take the state's mysteriously moving rocks.

The best place to see them is at Racetrack Playa inside Death Valley. But Little Bonnie Claire Playa, about a hundred miles north of Las Vegas, is the next best. There, the rocks are smaller and the effects are more subtle, but the location is much more accessible. It's just a few miles off Highway 95, next to a paved road that leads to Scotty's Castle, a major tourist attraction. In peak months, thousands of tourists pass by this rocky bit of weird Nevada without realizing there's anything special about it.

Even if you know what to look for, the evidence of movement is not apparent at first. Then suddenly you'll notice a trail behind a rock in the dry lake bed and know you are in the right place.

Once you see the first rock, they all begin to pop out. Most are the size of a fist or smaller, and some are VERY mobile. The ones that move are clustered in certain areas of the dry lake bed, and their "slug trails" become very evident. The rocks seem to have been moving willy-nilly, even bumping into each other.

Joseph Crock, a miner from Fallon, first noticed the more famous moving rocks of Racetrack Playa in Death Valley in 1915. They fascinated his wife, who placed stakes next to

them and verified that they were, in fact, mobile. The rocks have had limited study in the decades after the initial discovery. Their movement is usually attributed to a combination of high winds, slight rainfall, and varying temperatures.

Thomas Clements, a professor of geology at the University of Southern California, visited Racetrack Playa in 1950. He speculated that if there was one dry lake bed with moving rocks, there must be others and conducted a survey of other playas in the area. He visited Little Bonnie Claire for the first time in January 1952. It had just rained, and he noted three rocks that had left trails. He returned that March for a detailed study, which was published later that year in the *Journal of Sedimentary Research*. The day after a light rainfall, Clements noted much evidence of movement. He wrote that "some trails were straight, some were gently curved, a few had right-angle bends and a few were serpentinous."

Stepping into the playa today, you can still see the trails, but more evident are the tire marks of dirt bikes. Some of the rocks have been arranged into circles for campfires. The humans who move the rocks doubtless do not notice, or care, about their bizarre mobility.

An airstrip was built in the middle of Little Bonnie Claire Playa in the 1960s as a possible emergency landing place for the X-15 rocket plane. The X-15 never touched down there, but something else did. In May 1998, two rocks discovered there were found to be meteorites, extraterrestrial rocks cavorting with the ancient rocks of Nevada.

Bizarre Beasts

There are many strange beasts in the Silver State, and not all of them are the two-legged, one-armed-bandit–pulling variety. Despite the arid conditions in most of the state and the lack of flora to hide behind in the desert, Las Vegas and the rest of Nevada have beasts aplenty. Some swim; some fly; some dash across highways and are seen only in the flash of a headlight before they disappear into the dark desert night. Some of them smell REALLY bad. Are these beasts indigenous to the land or some freakish result from a nuclear test gone awry? Your guess is as good as ours.

Lake Monsters

Lake Lahontan once covered 8,000 square miles of northern Nevada and California. The size and depth of the inland sea fluctuated over a span of 60,000 years in prehistoric times, leaving plenty of freshwater remnants, including Pyramid and Walker lakes, both outside Reno in the western part of the state. Also left behind was evidence of the creatures that once swam or slithered through these prehistoric deeps. In fact, remains of ichthyosaurs, sort of a cross between a pleisiosaur and pterodactyl—toothy, flippered, and seventy feet long—are Nevada's official state fossil.

Walker Lake Monster

Considering that the Silver State is the driest in the nation, it might seem jarring to discover that Nevada is home to a trio of well-documented lake monsters. Take Cecil, the mechanical serpent who does double duty as Hawthorne's goodwill ambassador and high school mascot. Cecil is no public relations pipe dream. Indian legend says that when Lake Lahontan began to dry up, a pair of serpents were forced apart. The male made his way to what became Walker Lake, while the female burrowed north into the land, creating Sand Mountain.

Historically, the Walker Lake monster has Nevada's strongest record of sightings, and we don't count the one in Hawthorne's annual Armed Forces Day parade. When white settlers founded the town on the south end of Walker Lake in 1881, they noted a strange absence of fishing boats—the local Paiutes refused to traverse its waters. According to the *Hawthorne Arsenal*, it was "believed to have been the only lake in the country near which resident Indians had no boats, and they had no desire for any." Traditional teachings said one or more huge serpents lived in the lake.

John Keel is a disciple of the legendary Charles Fort, who made a career of recording strange events. Keel says that "early Indian settlers around the lake became annoyed because the monster occasionally dined on members of the tribe. They decided to launch a major effort to trap and kill the creature. But somehow the swimming sneak overheard the plot, surfaced, and held a pow-wow with his pursuers. A bargain was struck. If the Indians promised not to kill him and turn his hide into moccasins, he would promise to eat only white men."

In the summer of 1876, the whites of the territory, ignoring this old tale, launched a small steamer. It was quickly decommissioned, and the natives weren't surprised. Whatever the sailors saw out on that lake, they didn't want to see it again. And Samuel Pugh, superintendent of the Walker River Indian Agency, apparently rethought what he had chalked up as Indian superstition after "several white men claimed similar visions" of the serpent.

The *Walker Lake Bulletin* reported in August 1883 that settlers

near the lake were "awakened by a horrible, soul-shrinking screech" when a pair of monster pythons, writhing in battle, took their fight ashore. The loser's corpse collapsed on shore and was measured at exactly "seventy-nine feet, seven inches and a quarter in length." The victor slithered back into the lake—but, like many of his brethren, was fond of sunning himself lakeside. A quarter century later, local businessman E. J. Reynolds told the *Goldfield Daily Tribune* that the uncoiled beast was seen "wallowing" on the sand, and he estimated its length as at least seventy feet.

After a highway was built around the lake, "respectable" tourists and locals reported seeing "a huge monster, wholly unlike any fish inhabiting the waters of the lake, swimming about." As recently as 1956, a couple from Babbit wrote to the editor of Hawthorne's newspaper, claiming to have seen "something moving in Walker Lake at a terrific speed"—it actually outpaced their automobile. It performed an aquatic hundred-yard dash before plummeting below the surface.

Lake monsters are perennial fodder for tall town tales. One old coot claimed May 15, 1964, as Serpent's Night at Walker Lake. He told the *Nevada State Journal*, that every hundred years on the dot the serpent surfaces and seeks his prey. "He never fails, the old timers say he is as regular as the Capistrano swallows and far more dangerous."

Luckily, the creature continues to elude capture.

Tessie, the Lake Tahoe Monster

Lake Tahoe straddles the Nevada–California border and has fascinated white settlers since John Fremont laid eyes on it in the winter of 1844. Mark Twain described it as "a noble sheet of blue water lifted 6,000 three hundred feet above the level of the sea, and walled in by a rim of snow-clad mountain peaks that tower aloft a full 3,000 feet higher still!" Tahoe is the second deepest lake in the Northern Hemisphere, with seventy-one miles of shoreline, portions of which remain deeply forested. No wonder it is a place of perennial legend.

The local Washoe Indians told many tales of creatures and spirits inhabiting the Tahoe region. The most persistent is that of the Big Fish, a water-dwelling monster now nicknamed Tahoe Tessie. Tales of the beast made it into local papers almost as soon as whites began inhabiting the shores of Tahoe and persist to this day. How many lake monsters can claim a best-selling children's book (*Tahoe Tessie: The Original Lake Tahoe Monster*, by Bob McCormick) and a mention on *Lifestyles of the Rich and Famous*?

Today the creature is most often associated with McCormick's friendly Tessie character, but the Big Fish was notoriously nasty in the 1800s. The *Carson City Daily Index* of May 11, 1883, relates an encounter with a monstrosity that is anything but cute and cuddly: "He suddenly rose in front of the steamer *Governor Stanford* and disputed her passage . . . the fish leaped upward, and snapping off the bowstrip, went away with it in its mouth." Captain Lapham, builder of the *Stanford*, told the paper he thought "there is just as much probability" of something huge dwelling in the lake "as a huge saltwater fish in the bottom of the sea." He even built a small schooner and sent for "hook and line that is strong enough to hold 1,000 pounds . . . forever on the alert to capture what I positively believe exists."

Reports were so numerous that the beast was nicknamed Lizzie Ann in the '30s, and hunting parties were organized to capture what would surely be the ultimate fishing trophy. But it continued to outsmart its would-be captors.

"The thing that strikes me as most interesting," says McCormick, "is that most of the stories are the same. They describe something very large and very lethargic. It doesn't jump out of the water like a trout. It's black, very dark, with smooth skin like an eel. It's huge and slow and strong. It acts like a fish, because it doesn't rear its head like the Loch Ness monster, but it sounds like a nightmare from the movie *Anaconda*."

In July 1984, two local women spied the creature as they were hiking above Tahoe's western shore. It had a humped back and seemed to surface in a "whale-like" manner; they stated emphatically it was not a "log, diver, or ripple."

"A big hump" was how Reno police officer Chris Beebe described Tessie. In June 1982, Beebe and another police officer were waterskiing on the deepest part of the lake when something resembling "the top of a Volkswagen Beetle" paced their boat from roughly six feet away. It was so massive that water was sucked down around it. "I knew that whatever it was, it

was alive, and I knew it was bigger than my boat," Beebe said, estimating its length at eighteen to thirty feet. "My immediate reaction was that I would stop moving so that I didn't lose any of my feet." Luckily for them, Tessie—or son of Tessie—seems to have given up its old habit of taking chunks out of anything that floats. Beebe never returned to the lake and eventually quit his job and moved away from Tahoe because of the publicity he

received after his report.

Skeptics claim that most likely the beast is a huge sturgeon, a fish that can live to be one hundred years old and have no natural predators. One sturgeon found in the Sacramento River measured over twenty-two feet long and weighed over a ton. In 1888, a seven-foot-long sturgeon was caught in Pyramid Lake, which is connected to Lake Tahoe by the Truckee River. Perhaps the monsters trade lakes from time to time, using an underground river system to facilitate their aquatic time-share agreement.

But witnesses' descriptions don't sync with a hypothetical "Mother of All Sturgeons."

According to McCormick, "Sturgeon have very noticeable, rough scales. What Beebe and others have claimed to see is smooth like an eel." He adds, "I'm convinced there's something big out there, and it's not natural to Lake Tahoe. But if it's not a sturgeon, what the hell else could it be?"

Aerial View of a Lake Monster

My family and I took one of those helicopter trips to the Grand Canyon from Vegas when we were there in May 2001. We were on our way to the canyon and we were flying over Lake Mead. My mom and I were gazing out the window when I saw something in the water. It was a long creature—it had to be at least 50 feet long—and what appeared to be the head was above water. The rest of the body came above the water and then went below. The creature had a white tint to it, and at first I thought it was a boat pulling a skier or something like that. Then all of a sudden it disappeared under the water so I knew it could not have been a boat. My mom and I both observed this. There were no boats or anything near it. It was truly amazing. —*Anonymous*

The Pyramid Lake Monster

Sand-colored tufa spires ring Lahontan's deepest remnant, Pyramid Lake, lending it a sense of alien antiquity. Surrounded by barren desert, roughly thirty miles northeast of Reno, the lake is named for the massive tufa rock formation in its center. The Northern Paiutes, within whose reservation the water lies, have passed down stories for hundreds of years about a serpent living in the lake. According to legend, a native girl who violated the tribe's moral code was banished to the lake's island. Her death was attributed to the monster, and the island was named Anaho in her postmortem honor.

The first published sightings by white men occurred in 1869. According to the *Elko Independent*, Indians pleaded with a man named Spence, who was there to assess the

lake for borax, to forgo his mission. They claimed the monster "had the power to draw everything within a mile of its head into its mouth." The no-nonsense captain urged his crew into the middle of the lake, where their boat nearly capsized, thanks to something huge dozing on the lake's surface.

"Stopping within a hundred yards of the monster . . . it was about 300 feet long . . . its scales appeared to be black and white, with a tendency to copper color," Spence reported. On closer examination, he claimed the thing to be "an agglomeration of millions of worms of a species never before seen by him." Evidently, the worms were clever enough to fashion a head for their collective "monster." Spence, not surprisingly, soon left the area.

Commercial fisheries harvested one hundred tons of trout at Pyramid between the winters of 1888 and 1889, and along with fishermen came fish tales. The creature was blamed for blockading fish at the mouth of the Truckee River, which feeds into Pyramid. It was described in the *Reno Evening Gazette* as "having the body and tail of an alligator, with the flippers of a seal . . . [and] the mouth of a frog, which enables the animal to scoop in a wide streak of fish when he strikes a school." A well-known fisherman went on to claim the monster would often sun itself along the island's shore after gorging on trout.

"White hunters and trappers claimed to have seen something in the lake that closely resembles the serpent," asserts a 1925 *Los Angeles Times* article, as the monster was blamed for depleting the lake of fish as well as visitors. The article continues:

> Though reports of its visage are inconsistent and various theories have tried to explain it away, the Pyramid Lake monster was officially recognized by the Nevada state assembly in 1959. A bill, introduced by Democratic assemblyman Don Crawford, was passed by overwhelming majority and prohibits "hunting, molesting or capturing" the beast, its nest, eggs, or young.

Lake Mojave's Giant Prehistoric Minnow

Sometimes in the world of weird beasts, everything old is new again. A local Indian caught a sixty-pound "prehistoric" minnow in Lake Mojave in Novembe 1952. By the time the United States Fish and Wildlife Service came calling, the Indian and his compadres had scaled, skewered, and kabobed it. But enough was left unmangled that a ranger determined it was of a species thought extinct for hundreds of thousands of years.

Exactly a decade later a sports fisherman from Las Vegas caught a sixty-two-pound specimen of the same creature. The longtime angler was baffled by Nevada's

version of a landlocked coelacanth and brought it to the Fish and Wildlife station to be identified. They told him it was a rare prehistoric fish. They were overjoyed to see that the previous catch was no anomaly and promptly assured the man they'd preserve the fish and send it on to Washington for study.

He told them to stuff it like he had planned to do to the fish. It was going over the mantel of his den's fireplace. While the ichthyologists dreamed of their piscatorial prize, the sports fisherman went to court and demanded the return of his catch.

The judge sided with the fisherman—after all, he was properly licensed to catch the thing, ergo, he was entitled to keep it. The case was appealed twice. Ultimately, the fisherman trotted off with his well-preserved prize, and presumably had it stuffed and mounted over his den in Las Vegas.

The Ong—Tahoe's Big Bird

Giant birds, or Thunderbirds, are staples of Native American legend. Modern sightings span the country. These airborne monsters occasionally pluck humans from the ground; the most famous case involved a ten-year-old Illinois boy carried off in 1977. The Washoe Indians know this avian monstrosity as the Ong.

The Ong was described as huge, "bigger than the houses of the white man," with a body like an eagle's and the face of an Indian brave. It was covered in feathers and impenetrable scales, and had a wingspan that eclipsed the tallest pine tree. Its clawless feet were webbed.

Apparently amphibious, the Ong nested deep at the bottom of the Washoes' Lake of the Sky. The lake's undercurrents drew anything caught in them into the mesh of its nest, providing food for the creature.

But the Ong was not content to nibble on trout. The bodies of the drowned were also sucked into its subaquatic lair; this is how the Washoe explained the fact that drowning victims often didn't return to the lake's

surface. In time, the Ong developed a taste for human flesh and circled the lake looking for people to eat. Swooping down from behind, the huge creature would pluck a victim from the shore. With powerful feet, it would carry the struggling unfortunate high above the center of the lake and drop him to his death. The corpse-snack would be waiting in its nest when the Ong returned to its roost.

One season, as the Washoe held their final hunt, the chief promised his daughter to the tribe's most daring warrior. The lucky man would be chosen at the great council fire before the Washoe left the area for the winter. But the chief's daughter was in love with a brave too young to have had many heroic adventures. He went out to the cliffs overlooking the lake and prayed to find a way to prove himself.

Soon the dreaded Ong began to circle overhead. The brave jumped up to attract the big bird's attention. He soon found himself clutched by giant webbed feet. As the Ong flew high above the lake, the brave unwound a buckskin cord and tied himself to its leg. The Ong let go, but the cord held, preventing the brave from tumbling to his death. Still airborne, the enraged bird beast contorted itself in an attempt to bite him. With each thrust, the brave threw poisoned arrowheads into the Ong's gaping mouth.

As the poison began to take effect, the Ong dived into the water, which foamed as the Ong flapped its wings wildly and struggled for life. The buckskin cord held fast and prevented the creature from escaping.

As darkness fell, the Indian was presumed dead, and the council fire went on as planned. Stealing a canoe, the chief's daughter paddled to the center of the lake in search of her love, but her absence went unnoticed until long into the night.

In the dawn hours, an empty canoe floated to shore. The tribe assumed the worst, until they saw the rigid body of the Ong floating lifeless in the lake. Then the strangest sailing vessel the Washoe had ever seen approached the shore. It was one of the Ong's dismembered wings, with the tip of the other wing fashioned into a sail. Riding upon it were the chief's daughter and the young brave, arm in arm.

The name of the brave was Tahoe, and the Washoes' Lake of the Sky was named in his honor. The Ong's nest is still at the bottom of the lake, trapping the bodies of all who drown in Tahoe.

Considering that the fossilized remains of the prehistoric *Teratornis incredibilis*, a condorlike bird with a sixteen-foot wingspan, have been found in Nevada, it's possible the Ong tale is the result of distorted memory. Perhaps the prehistoric bird's descendants survived in Nevada into the era of human habitation. Perhaps some kind of giant bird still travels the skies of Nevada, preying on wildlife.

In April 2005, a man identified as "Monroe" from Wenatchee, Washington, told radio host George Noory that years ago, while flying a Cessna over northwestern Nevada, he saw a giant bird with an estimated wingspan of fifteen to twenty feet.

The theory that Thunderbird sightings are just misidentified California condors is preposterous. America's largest known soaring bird, these endangered raptors have a ten-foot wingspan, long hooked beaks, and a vaguely prehistoric air. They are protected and under close scrutiny. The last remaining California condors were captured to initiate a breeding program in the '80s. Only eighty-five exist in the wild today.

Was It a Wahoo?

Some stories that we hear of weird creatures may be accounts of real beasts, distorted by the fanciful tale-telling of the papers of their time.

In the late 1800s, the newspapers of northern Nevada entertained the populace with reports of a unique creature given the whimsical name of the Wahoo. The first description was furnished to the *Reno Weekly Gazette* by a local bank agent named Richard Smith, who had returned from a hunting trip in the vicinity of Halleck and Deeth, now ghost towns near Elko. The locals told him of the Wahoo, so-called after the sound that it made.

Although he did not see it himself, Smith's brother allegedly had obtained a tanned hide of the creature. The legs were short, with large paws and long claws. The body was long and slender, with a medium-length tail that curved up over the back. It was covered with long, fine hair, mostly black with white spots. The beast was larger than a coyote, weighing between fifty and seventy-five pounds, and from a distance could be mistaken for a large dog.

Tales multiplied, and people headed out to hunt the seemingly not-so-elusive beast. "Was it a Wahoo?" asked the *Gazette* in 1880. A "strange and strong-smelling animal" killed in Modoc County (at the time within Nevada territory) measured

five foot three inches from one track to the other, its tail about the length of its body, with a bunch of red hair on the tip; a stripe down the back about four inches; deep red stripes running with the ribs; his ears shaped like a hog's, standing straight out; two tusks two inches long, on each side of his mouth above and below.

The creature was said to be very vicious, growling at two hunters as they approached, and one impaled it with a hayfork when it leaped at him. The creature mutilated the other hunter's foot and tore up his pants. "The scent of the animal was very offensive, and we could not save his hide," the hunter said.

The aforementioned *Gazette* article recalled accounts of Wahoo sightings from Idaho to Montana. Its September 4, 1879, issue described A. A. Adams's encounter with a doglike creature that perched atop the fence outside his house at midnight. "Was it a Wahoo?" the paper asked. It had claws for climbing and

red eyes that "glowed with unnatural brightness; looking more like hot coals than visual organs." Adams did what any reasonable homeowner would do: He turned the hose on the thing. The creature was unaffected, turning its snout toward the spray and holding its position without protest. Adams retreated to his house and locked the doors and windows. In the morning, he found no trace of the beast.

So, was the Wahoo real? Maybe it was. Certain Native American tribes have a legend of doglike beasts called the Shunka Warak'in, the "carrying-off dogs." Ross Hutchins's book *Trails to Nature's Mysteries* tells of the killing of a "wolflike beast" described as being "nearly black and having high shoulders and a back that sloped downward like a hyena." The stuffed corpse was displayed at a museum in Henry Lake, Idaho, near the Nevada border. The museum dubbed it a Ringdocus.

Loren Coleman, an expert in the field of cryptozoology, the study of creatures unknown to mainstream science, believes the description of the Shunka Warak'in is identical to that of a Pleistocene hyena-like dog known as Borophagus. The present location of the specimen is unknown, but photos of the Idaho exhibit demonstrate that the tales of a strange, doglike creature having been-grounded in reality.

Bigfoot in Vegas and Nevada

Does Bigfoot exist? The federal government thought so. The army Corps of Engineers once listed Sasquatch as part of the natural fauna of Washington State. Sightings of a hairy manlike beast date back to the 1800s in the Pacific Northwest, while the "Idaho Wildman" chased cowboys in the 1860s. In that same decade, in Nevada,

bloodhounds refused to track something big, hairy, and smelly, possibly a member of what primatologist Grover Krantz believed to be a perfectly normal species of higher primate native to certain parts of North America.

By most accounts, the nocturnal, omnivorous, and shy but inquisitive bipedal Sasquatch—or Bigfoot, as the creature came to be known after a huge footprint was discovered at a construction site in California—has been seen all over the Silver State, including Las Vegas.

Prints have been found close to the Owyhee River drainage wilderness near the point where the borders of Idaho, Oregon, and Nevada meet. Most tracks are solitary, and researchers believe the uniform stink that accompanies so many Bigfoot sightings is given off by the males as a pheromonal signal to keep them at a huge distance from each other. The idea that there's no wilderness left to hide a huge animal is absurd. Nearby, Nevada's Humboldt National Forest covers roughly 7,935 square miles, with only one unpaved road cutting through it. By some estimates, it could contain forty undisturbed Sasquatches. Although Lake Tahoe is a popular tourist destination, there are 14,000 acres of undeveloped forest on its northeastern shore.

In August 1973, two couples wrote to the *Reno Evening Gazette* about their "frightening experience" on Tahoe's shore. While driving up Kingsbury Grade one July evening, they saw what they thought was a black bear, until they got closer and discovered it standing on two legs. It was shiny, about seven feet tall, and had a face they described as "flat, like a gorilla's."

In 1984, two women hiking on the east side of the Sierra Nevadas above Lake Tahoe were told by two teenage boys they would encounter a "monster" if they proceeded farther up the trail. They ignored the boys, of course, and went on gathering pinecones for a school project—until they were met by a seven-foot-tall creature covered in fur "the color of dry pine needles." His approach was preceded by a foul smell, and at first glance, they thought it was a "guy in a bear suit." His arms hung "nearly to his knees" when he walked, and after the women fled, they could still see him crouched on a boulder, staring in their direction.

In 2001, two friends were riding on a dirt road near Telegraph Summit, ten miles off Highway 93 in Ely. When they stopped for water, they smelled something like "rotten garbage." As dusk approached, the rocky, mountainous area was ringed with "weird howls." They mimicked the sounds, like nothing they'd ever heard before, for about ten minutes and then decided to leave. When they did, they saw a brownish "apelike" creature between seven and eight feet tall dash into the trees.

Bigfoot was sighted and prints were found in the Diamond Mountains near Eureka in the 1960s, and it was seen "climbing a cliff" in the Black Rock Desert in the '90s. "A large greying/brown man-shaped thing" over ten feet tall was spotted by a security officer near Gold Hill in 1980. When security guys start sighting the beasts, you've got to pay attention.

Bigfoot at the Nevada Test Site?

In January 1980, wire services picked up on a report of Bigfoot being seen at the Nevada Test Site, about seventy-five miles outside Las Vegas. It was spotted crossing the Tippipah Highway between the site's control point and Area 12 camp, smack in the middle of the 1,350-square-mile testing ground, whose borders can be crossed only by those with security badges. The stunned employee who witnessed the creature

hightailed it to the test site command post at Mercury, where he reported it as being "somewhere between six and seven feet tall, standing erect and walking like a man, with dark hair completely covering its body." Bigfoot as a threat to national security? The incident would've never made the news if the NTS employee who spoke to the witness hadn't contacted the *Las Vegas Sun*.

Dave Jackson, the NTS public information officer at the time, recalls the incident well. "I called and got a hold of security, and one guy said, 'Yep, we had a report of Bigfoot.' I said, 'Come on, you're pulling my leg.' And he said, 'Oh, no.' This driver, who was a Mormon bishop from a little town in Utah, was driving on his daily run. He had been at the test site for many years, never drank . . . he was not the kind of guy to be a practical joker. He said he saw this big hairy beast go across the road in front of him."

The security officer Jackson spoke to was adamant. "There were big footprints that went out across the desert and absolutely disappeared!" Jackson got calls from disc jockeys and reporters from all over the country. "And then I got a call from a Bigfoot researcher from somewhere in the Northwest. I described the thing to him, and he said, 'That's typical.' And I said, 'Well, what about the footprints disappearing?' And he said, 'Oh, that's typical.'

"And then I got a call from a guy who said, 'You're not going to believe a word I tell you.'" The man asked which direction the footprints were headed. "East, into the desert," Jackson told him. "He had already passed a pretty good desert to get there. And the guy said, 'Well, whenever we have a sighting of a Bigfoot heading east, there's going to be an earthquake within twenty-four hours.' The next day there was a 6.8 earthquake in the Owens Valley."

Bigfoot Captured Near Battle Mountain

In the summer of 1999, 169,608 acres of northern Nevada were burned in what came to be known as the Battle Mountain Complex Fire. With thirteen separate fires sparked by lightning, it made '99 the worst fire season on record for the state. Before it was contained, an anonymous government employee made a report to the Bigfoot Field Research Organization, claiming that a Sasquatch had been injured in the blaze.

Firefighters tranquilized the creature, which had multiple burns to its hands, feet, legs, and body. The reporting party claimed it moved "on all fours, not like a bear, more like an ape." He estimated the creature to be "approximately 7.5 feet tall, with human-like arms and legs, face not like man or ape but mixed between," with hair covering most of its body. He noted it had human opposition of thumbs, and that it tried to communicate with the emergency personnel "once it realized they were attempting to care for it."

In his book *The Locals,* researcher Thom Powell followed up on the incident by speaking to the witness. While some researchers believe the whole thing to be a hoax, Powell disagrees. "I have a real problem with the suggestion that a person could concoct such a highly detailed fabrication and build it around a completely verifiable wildfire within two days of the fire's beginning."

Local Heroes and Villains

Las Vegas might just boast the most unique and unusual array of characters of any place in the United States, or perhaps the world. Where else can you find snake charmers, murdering mobsters, porn star politicians, and even psychotic boxers ranked among the honored and celebrated?

It's not always easy to discern who are the heroes and who are the villains in Vegas. For example, should Bugsy Siegel be considered a villain because he was a psychotic killer and underworld thug? Or should he be remembered as a hero for his foresight in envisioning the city of Las Vegas that we know today? We're not the sort to draw those distinctions; we'll leave that up to you, the reader, to decide. Hero or villain, though, one thing can be said about the Nevadans who dance to the beat of a different drummer from the rest of society. They do it Vegas-style, with plenty of flash and showmanship!

Bugsy: Father of Vegas

Among the many things Las Vegas owes to mobster Bugsy Siegel are the city's trademark palm trees. Before Bugsy arrived in the then small desert town, there were none. He liked them so much that he ordered several sent here from California and started a Vegas horticultural fashion statement.

Benjamin "Bugsy" Siegel was born of humble beginnings on February 28, 1906, in Brooklyn, New York. A natural lawbreaker, he started his criminal career at the age of nine, setting vegetable carts on fire, in a sort of primitive protection racket. By the time he was a teenager, Siegel had earned the name Bugsy, which in the vernacular of the day meant "crazy."

Crazy he may have been, but Siegel liked the high life and was always attracted to big money and glamour. In the late '30s and early '40s there were few places as profitable and glamorous as Hollywood. Bugsy Siegel went to Los Angeles in the early 1930s and in no time at all he was turning millions of dollars in profits, making a name for himself and pleasing the syndicate in the process.

And there were other benefits. Bugsy's rugged good looks and genuine tough guy persona were catnip to the Hollywood ladies. One of the most intrigued—and intriguing to Bugsy—was actress Virginia Hill.

Hill is said to have been as treacherous as she was beautiful. She may have been an actress by trade but her real fortune was made by threatening to expose, the secrets of many of Hollywood's closeted homosexuals. Blackmail was a good business for Hill. It was this intoxicating combination of splendor and duplicity that Bugsy Siegel found irresistible.

During his occasional drives back to the East Coast, the good-looking gangster would pass through Nevada.

According to popular myth, Siegel pulled over in the small gambling town of Las Vegas to take a bathroom break, and had a vision of converting the tiny, barren betting berg into a wagering wonder-land. Watching people engaged in the pursuit of winning, Bugsy was fascinated by the amount of money gamblers were willing to risk. There was money to be made in Las Vegas, and Bugsy wanted his share.

Bugsy believed the high rollers would flock to the desert if he provided them with the right combination of glamour and gambling, and he managed to convince his mob bosses to foot the bill for a hotel venture. Unfortunately, Siegel might have been an excellent gangster, but he lacked business acumen. Worse, he liked to spend money, especially on horses, dining, and beautiful women. The club he set out to construct finally got built, but at a cost of over $5 million. The Flamingo (Bugsy's pet name for Hill, due to her impossibly long legs) opened for business on December 25, 1946. It was a startling change for Las Vegas. Notably absent was the cowpoke look of the other establishments in town. The decor was modern, up-to-the-minute swank "class" as interpreted by Benjamin Siegel. No bolo ties, boots, or plaid shirts. Top Hollywood entertainers were booked for the clubs. Bugsy and staff were attired in formal wear. But luck was against Bugsy. A freak storm kept the high rollers away on opening night, and the ones who did arrive found their rooms only half finished. In the months ahead, the club struggled to survive, dribbling away money like so much desert sand. Siegel's mobster buddies were furious with him. They were out millions, and they were sore losers.

The end came in Hollywood on June 20, 1947. In Las Vegas, Bugsy had surrounded himself with bodyguards. His suite in the Flamingo was locked behind a steel reinforced door. The windows were bulletproof, and in the closet was a secret ladder that would allow him to escape to a getaway car.

Unfortunately for him, no such safeguards were in place at Virginia Hill's rented Beverly Hills home.

Bugsy and a friend had returned from an early dinner and settled onto the sofa. The mobster casually glanced at his newspaper and switched on a reading lamp. The killers silently crept up the long driveway to the mansion. The target was in full view, relaxed and unaware. . . . They took aim . . . a hail of gunfire smashed through the manor's windows and five bullets penetrated the skull of forty-one-year-old Bugsy Siegel. His shattered, bloody corpse slumped on the colorful chintz sofa.

It would not be the end of the casino, only a change of management. Within hours of Bugsy's death, things were back to normal at his beloved Flamingo. While five mourners gathered for Siegel's funeral, gamblers eagerly tossed their money into the Flamingo's coffers.

But Las Vegas has not forgotten Bugsy. It remembers that his vision paved the way for southern Nevada's hotel-casino industry. In celebration of its fiftieth anniversary, the Flamingo commemorated its founder by putting his likeness on its $5 chips. And he is a popular feature at the local museums. The Nevada Historical Society in Lorenzi Park has an exhibit of some of the gangster's personal items, including the security door to his penthouse at the Flamingo.

And rumor has it that Bugsy is still around Las Vegas, or at least his restless spirit is. For more on that, see the "Desert Ghosts" chapter.

Guy McAfee and the Las Vegas Strip

The glitzy thoroughfare known as the Strip is actually a four-mile length of Las Vegas Boulevard South. It has also been called U.S. Highway 91, Salt Lake Highway, Arrowhead Highway, and the Los Angeles Highway. But its most famous and lasting appellation is the Strip.

It was so named by Guy McAfee, a shady Los Angeles captain of vice who fled L.A. in the late 1930s amid a new mayor's tough stance on vice and corruption. McAfee wound up in Vegas and liked what he saw—gambling, lots of it, and it was all legal. Eager to get in on the easy money, McAfee bought the Pair-O-Dice club three miles out on Highway 91 and renamed it the 91 Club.

One night as McAfee drove along Highway 91, or so the story goes, he felt a sudden pang of homesickness for Los Angeles and the Sunset Strip. Thus inspired, he began calling the highway the Strip. It would take years for the name to catch on, but once it did, that portion of roadway would be known as nothing else.

In 1946, McAfee opened the Golden Nugget in downtown Vegas and for a time was a major player in Sin City's gambling operations. Today he is best remembered for having named the Strip. In 1991, Congress implemented a program to recognize the nation's roadways. Roads that are important for their cultural and historical significance are designated as American Byways. Not surprisingly, the Strip was one of those so designated. Guy McAfee would be proud.

Ronald Reagan, Sin City Headliner

Long before he strode across the White House Rose garden to the strains of "Hail to the Chief," Ronald Reagan earned his living as an actor. But in 1954, less than a decade after Bugsy Siegel bit the dust, Reagan was finding acting jobs to be few and far between. So he did what other entertainers were doing; he starred in his own Las Vegas lounge act. He is the first and only U.S. President ever to have done so.

Unfortunately, his show was a flop. The future fortieth President and his First Lady, Nancy, posed for countless publicity shots at various Las Vegas locations to encourage casino show-goers to give his act at the Last Frontier a chance. Reagan was certainly debonair in his sophisticated black tux. And he was wise enough to surround himself with a comedian or two, a troupe of chimps, and a bevy of busty beauties. But the act lacked oomph.

After his show was cancelled, Reagan left Sin City and headed back to Hollywood, *Death Valley Days*, and a two-term stint as governor of California. Eventually, he ended up doing a two-term gig at the White House. Not bad for a failed lounge performer!

Las Vegas may change its look at the drop of a showgirl's G-string, but the city does pay homage to those it holds dear; Ronald Reagan fit this category. When the former President died in 2004, the lights of the Las Vegas Strip were dimmed in his honor. Others who have been so honored include President John F. Kennedy, Frank Sinatra, Sammy Davis Jr., and George Burns.

Ronald Reagan in fabulous Las Vegas Frontier Hotel in 1954.

Graceland Chapel

The rest of the world might think that Elvis Presley is moldering in his Graceland grave, but here in Las Vegas he is alive and well. The rock singer, of course, was one of Vegas's biggest stars, so big in fact that he continues to be an attraction even after his death. Fans may see Elvis or a reasonable facsimile on just about every block on the Strip.

There are two things that separate Brendan Paul from every other greasy D.A. combing, sideburn-wearing, sequined-cape–attired Elvis impersonator in this glittery hamlet: his height and his sense of self.

"I'm six feet four," he deadpans, "six feet seven with hair." It's the kind of joke that even though he probably uses it as often as he brushes his teeth, Paul delivers with the charm and aplomb of a seasoned stage veteran.

Paul is not only an Elvis impersonator, he's a businessman. "The Elvis thing is great, but you can't do it forever. Forty-five, fifty years old, and when it's over as Elvis, what are you going to do then?" In 2003, he bought the famous Graceland Wedding Chapel.

As one can imagine, a person who makes a living dressing up in rhinestone-studded jumpsuits and crooning rockabilly love songs to nervous brides and grooms has a number of stories to tell. He's seen people who met at the craps table and got married after knowing each other for two hours. "Where do you guys live?" he questioned a soon-to-be-groom. "The guy says, 'I live in Chicago,' then turns to her and asks, 'Where do you live?' She tells him Seattle. He's like, hmmm, I guess one of us is going to have to move."

When asked if he's ever tried to dissuade a couple from getting married, Paul grins. "My wife has a moral code. She's had talks with people sometimes, but to me, if the check clears, they're hitched."

A fair number of musical celebrities have had their

checks clear and gotten hitched at the Graceland Chapel. Jon Bon Jovi married his high school sweetheart here. Roger Glover of Deep Purple pledged his eternal love in front of the ersatz hip-swiveling showman. The Thompson Twins took the plunge, as did Aaron Neville and Donald Trump's little brother, Robert.

You may have planned your special day for years or found your soul mate a scant few hours earlier over martinis and blackjack losses. Whichever, you're sure to have a wedding you won't forget at the Graceland Wedding Chapel. Brendan Paul promises your betrothed will always love you tender, never return you to sender, never ever step on your blue suede shoes, and will always be your lovin' teddy bear.

The Chapel is located at 619 South Las Vegas Boulevard. Thank you very much.

Elvis-a-Rama Museum

Legend has it that in 1975, Dave Hebler refused to accept a brand-new $14,000 purple Lincoln Continental Mark IV from Elvis Presley. Hebler told the King he was still enjoying the Mercedes that Presley bestowed upon him not long before. According to Hebler, a former member of Presley's inner circle (the Memphis Mafia), Elvis's famous sneer turned sinister. Quick as a wink Elvis whipped out a gun from a holster beneath his jacket, took careful aim at his now frightened buddy, and threatened to "blow [his] head off" unless he reconsidered the gift. Needless to say, Hebler acquiesced and accepted the car. Elvis chuckled as he reholstered his weapon, and Hebler lived to tell the tale.

Elvis was fond of cars and guns, and plenty of both can be found at the Elvis-A-Rama Museum. In one day alone, Elvis gave away thirteen cars, at a personal cost of over $140,000 dollars.

Sitting in one glass case in the Elvis-A-Rama Museum are at least a half-dozen guns, including a gold-plated .38 Smith & Wesson that was his "TV shootin'" gun. Elvis had a penchant for pulling out his piece and busting a cap in any television that dared show Robert Goulet's face.

Also in the same display, next to a number of police badges and a can of mace Elvis kept in his briefcase, is a wooden plaque given to Presley by the Shelby Sheriff's Department. Elvis was licensed to write citations to law-breaking citizens in Memphis. In fact, Elvis kept a blue light in his car and would occasionally pull people over, but instead of issuing tickets, the good-natured Rock Cop would sign an autograph.

There is about $5 million of King collectibles to be found here. No self-respecting Elvis shrine would be complete without a bunch of high-collared sequined jumpsuits, guitars, and movie posters, but this place has his army trunk, the famous blue suede shoes he wore, his karate robe complete with black belt, and Elvis Aaron Presley's authentic Social Security card. The price of admission also covers a nice short concert by an Elvis impersonator, and the gift shop should satisfy most fans' desires for all things Elvis, from Elvis baby bibs and sippy cups for the young, to the Elvis clock with the swiveling hips that act like a pendulum.

The building, located at 3401 Industrial Road, is a must-see for both the diehard and the casual Presley fan. Visit the museum. You may not get a brand-new purple car, but on the plus side you won't have a gun aimed at your head either.

Mr. Showmanship

Liberace was born and raised in Milwaukee, but to Las Vegans he was one of their own. The entertainer's Tivoli Gardens Restaurant on East Tropicana was a favorite with locals, and he built the famous Liberace Museum in the same strip mall. Decades after his death, the museum remains a top spot for tourists.

Liberace lived on Shirley Street, a few blocks from the museum. His place was in a neighborhood of middle-class homes, and when glimpsed from the outside it doesn't appear to be very remarkable. On the other side of the threshold, it's a different matter entirely. Two houses have been combined into one for 20,000 square feet of unbelievable luxury. In decorating his Las Vegas home, Liberace demonstrated his exquisite taste and appreciation of antiques and *objets d'art*.

Because he had so admired the Sistine Chapel ceiling on a visit to Vatican City, he hired a direct descendant of Michelangelo's to paint a replica of it on the ceiling of his master bedroom. The one-of-a-kind painting is valued at well over $1 million. The master bathroom featured a custom designed sunken marble bathtub that came with a $65,000 price tag, two-thousand-year-old Grecian marble pillars, and $25,000 Baccarat crystal chandeliers.

A caring man, Liberace remembered the importance scholarships had played in his rise to the top. With an aim toward helping others just starting out in the entertainment industry, in 1976 he founded the Liberace Foundation for the Performing and Creative Arts. Since that time, 1,400 scholarships have been awarded.

When he died in 1987, the flamboyant entertainer owned seven homes. Those in the know say that the Shirley Street home was his favorite. Today that building is operated as Las Vegas Villa and is available for wedding and party rentals.

A Visit to the Liberace Museum

If you're a man's man, undoubtedly gambling plays a big part in any decision to visit the Oasis in the Desert. Eating more shrimp cocktail than any human has ever consumed in a single sitting at the seafood buffet may also be part of your plot. Lying to your wife, girlfriend, or both, about how you never left your cramped hotel room when you weren't at that "lame-ass" convention would have to be an absolute must.

It seems highly unlikely therefore that you have given a tour of the Liberace Museum any consideration at all, but let's examine this memorial to the master of musical showmanship before you dismiss the idea.

Do you like tricked-out cars? This guy owned a number of classics, and he spared no expense making his rides as sweet as they could be. The 1962 Phantom V Landau Rolls-Royce is a serious chick magnet. The British royal family had one, but Liberace's is covered in thousands of tiny etched mirrored tiles. Chicks dig mirrors.

You know what the ladies like more than a guy who owns one Rolls-Royce? That's right, buster, a guy who owns two of them. Liberace had his 1954 Rolls-Royce Silver Dawn convertible sedan painted in a stars-and-stripes motif, and he drove it while wearing a red jumpsuit and a white feathered cape with blue lining. The ladies love a guy who knows how to accessorize.

Another thing the fairer sex loves is bling, and nobody did bling like Liberace. This dude owned a piano-shaped wristwatch draped with diamonds, emeralds, sapphires, and rubies. He also had a matching piano-shaped ring to complement his watch. It's a little white- and yellow-gold number with no fewer than 260 diamonds, and it went really well with his white llama-fur coat.

Ever tried seducing a woman with your expensive sound system or maybe even by whipping out your old acoustic guitar? Ya know what probably would have worked better? An antique French Pleyel piano formerly owned by some guy named Chopin. It's just one of eighteen pianos in the museum. There's another one once owned by this person named George Gershwin, and still another to match that mirrored Rolls-Royce. Yeah, your boom box and beat-up old six string is looking kind of tired in comparison.

Finally, power is just one more attribute that women admire, and Liberace had that as well. Just weeks before his death, at age sixty-four, Liberace not only had the fortitude to perform in front of a packed house, he did it in a two-hundred-pound outfit. That guy was no sissy.

So the next time you're heading out this way, you might want to stop at 1775 East Tropicana Avenue and check out the Liberace Museum—a monument to a true Vegas-style hero. Liberace: He was the man!

Howard Hughes's Deep Pockets

Like countless others, Howard Hughes loved Las Vegas. Unlike them, he had the financial wherewithal to change the city. When the eccentric billionaire decided to leave California, he chose Vegas as his new city of residence. In the fall of 1966, Hughes and his entourage moved into the penthouse suites at the Desert Inn. You'd think the management would have been thrilled to have a rich guy like Hughes calling room service. But instead, they panicked after a few months and asked Hughes and his party to leave. Seems they needed the suites for their high rollers.

But Hughes had no intention of moving; he whipped out his checkbook and bought the Desert Inn. As the owner, he could damn well sleep where he wanted to—if only that sleep wasn't being interrupted by the gaudy spinning high heel sign at the Silver Slipper across the street. Each revolution of the heel sent light sparkling through Hughes's window. Didn't they realize how annoying that could be? There was nothing to do but purchase the Silver Slipper and tear the insidious sign down. And so he did.

He also schmoozed the Nevada Gaming Commission into giving him a gaming license without making the personal appearance required of other mere mortals. Once a licensed owner, there was no stopping

him. Like a mall shopper gone mad at a moonlight sale, he started purchasing every hotel-casino that his aides could lay their hands on. Among his newly acquired properties were the Sands, the Castaways, and the Landmark.

Howard Hughes may have been Vegas's knight in shining armor. As the owner of so many gaming properties, he lent an air of legitimacy and changed the way such establishments were operated. The mob was supplanted by his corporations, and skimming became a thing of the past. Under Hughes's watch, the bean counters and bottom liners could account for every nickel. The Bugsy Siegel days were over.

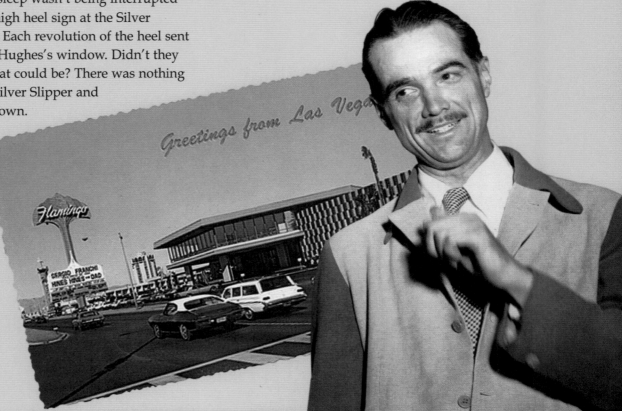

Mike Tyson

Las Vegas has been home to many world-renowned celebrities, but in the late 1980s there were few more recognized and none more feared than "Iron" Mike Tyson. At twenty years and four months old, Tyson was the youngest fighter to ever be crowned the Heavyweight Champion of the World. His rare combination of amazing hand speed, impenetrable defense, and brute strength made Tyson the "Baddest Man on the Planet."

Las Vegas has been the backdrop for much of Tyson's adult life. It was here that he wrestled with his five-hundred-pound pet tiger until the beast was so exhausted it fell asleep for several hours on top of the pugnacious pugilist. It was at the MGM Grand, in 1997, that a frustrated Tyson twice bit Evander Holyfield during a boxing rematch, taking a serious portion of Holyfield's ear in one of the maulings. Las Vegas was also slated as the city in which Mike Tyson was to attempt to regain the heavyweight belt, then held by Lennox Lewis. Tyson whetted the public's appetite for that fight when he announced to Lewis on camera immediately after a tune-up fight, "I want your heart. I want to eat your children. Praise be to Allah!"

During a press conference in New York to hype the Vegas match, Tyson bit Lewis on the leg. After that, the competition was moved from the home of the All You Can Eat Buffet, Las Vegas. It was obvious Tyson had acquired a specific appetite, but it appears the Nevada Boxing Commission has a two-bite limit on humans. The bout was relocated to Memphis, Tennessee.

Nowadays Tyson is no longer interested in making a living as a boxer. After earning and losing hundreds of millions during his career, a seemingly sedate and relaxed Mike Tyson still occasionally throws punches in Nevada clubs. In September 2006 he made an appearance at the Aladdin/Planet Hollywood.

The crowd was probably only a few hundred strong when Tyson finally entered the makeshift arena, forty minutes after the announced time. The fighter did not exactly electrify the crowd, but it didn't seem as if he were putting any effort into doing so.

This was not the Mike Tyson who once said, "I'm on Zoloft to keep me from killin' y'all. . . ."

This Mike Tyson was here to do a quick appearance, pick up his paycheck, and go back to his room and chill. This Mike Tyson even seemed to apologize for the behavior of the old Mike Tyson. When asked at the contractual question-and-answer period with the audience if he would consider doing a reality TV show, Tyson did not hesitate, "Oh, man, I've made a big enough fool out of my life. I don't need to do that anymore," and later added, "I did a lot of things—was a weird guy back then."

We at *Weird Las Vegas* saw our segue, so we asked the former champ what was his weirdest Las Vegas experience. Tyson paused, took a deep breath, rolled his eyes, and laughed to himself, as if he had just censored the first fifty memories that popped into his head. He then got very serious and thoughtfully reflected.

"When Tupac Shakur died, that was a very blue period in my life. It was a very odd moment in my life,

Maybe it was our generation, maybe we just had a little too much success in our life."

Tyson answered a few more questions after that, but it was obvious he wasn't enjoying the spotlight, so twenty minutes before his scheduled departure he matter-of-factly announced, "I'm out of here," and abruptly exited, along with a small entourage.

As Tyson disappeared into the multitude of spectators, it dawned on us that there still is some magic left in Las Vegas. After all, one of the most feared and wealthiest warriors in the history of boxing has transformed himself

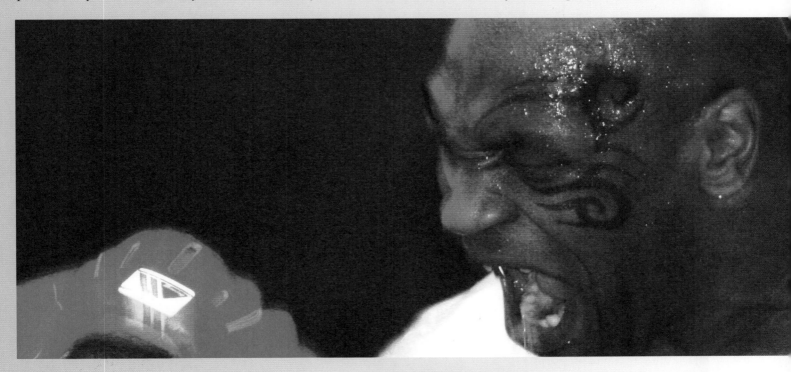

so I don't know . . . I just thought the eighties were magic . . . Whitney [Houston] was magic, Bobby Brown was magic, New Kids on the Block—everyone was magic. Everyone was a big star; there just wasn't enough room.

into a humble, self-effacing working stiff who's just trying to make a buck. To paraphrase former Tyson promoter Don King, "Only in Las Vegas."

Medusa Sedusa

While she admits it is not her legal name, it is the only name she gives. Brazilian born, Medusa Sedusa is one of Las Vegas's more colorful characters. The home page of her Web site (www.medusasedusa.com) clues you in to that fact right away, and while animal acts are not unique in this town, Medusa certainly is.

The crack staff at *Weird Las Vegas* set up an interview with this enigmatic snake charmer, who welcomed me into her home and immediately placed me in front of a television set. She turned on the televish and proudly popped in her DVD.

As the show begins, Medusa, sword in hand and wearing what resembles a Princess Leia slave-girl outfit, prances about, barefoot on the hot desert sand. She begins an ancient ritualistic-looking dance with her nine-foot albino python. The performance is not rehearsed, and Medusa boasts to me, "I just do what comes naturally, and I dominate the snake with my body."

It's hard to argue with her. At various times during the filmed ceremony, this zaftig entertainer is on her knees, suggestively straddling the giant serpent, hips thrusting. At other times, she is licking the head of the reptile. While the film is not likely to win any artistic awards, there is an absolute can't-turn-away factor to the performance. I silently wonder if the snake is hypnotized or, like me, simply staring blankly in utter disbelief.

As the video ends, I start to ask Medusa her life story and how she learned to control these giant reptiles. After an hour of questioning, I find her reluctant to speak about anything. For a woman who dresses so dramatically and poses so salaciously on her Web site, Medusa is shy and hesitant to share stories about her snakes and her powers over them.

Not getting much in the way of quotable dialogue, I look around the room in hopes of an icebreaker. Spotting a book on the life of Clara Bow, I ask if she's a fan of the ingenue from yesteryear. Medusa perks right up and speaks passionately on the subject of Clara Bow, and swears Ms. Bow has protected her from many an unscrupulous character.

"Clara Bow always looks out for me. She does not like it when people try to take advantage. One time an ex-boyfriend was leaving my house, and Clara Bow told me to check in his socks. I told him he could not leave until I look in his socks, and then I find hundreds of dollars in there. Clara Bow is my angel."

Clara must have given Medusa a spectral thumbs-up indicating that I was a good egg, because shortly after telling that story Medusa asked me if I'd like to see the giant python. Truth be told, I'm not a big fan of even the tiniest snakes, so I wasn't thrilled at the prospect of viewing this scaly gargantuan, coiled up and hissing defiantly from inside its glass tank. I did figure, however, that Medusa looked like she was finally ready to chat, and like her slithering pet, I needed to strike when the time was right. I'll get the interview, I thought, ask her for a couple of eight-by-ten publicity shots for the book, and I'm out of there before you can say, "One slick snake slid up the stake."

Unfortunately, nothing in Vegas is that simple. It turns out Medusa doesn't have any photos left, but she offers to release the snake and pose with it in her living room. Anything for art, I chant to myself, and before you can say, "One silly scribe was swallowed by a snake," it's just Medusa, the snake, and me.

Medusa's living room is roughly twelve-by-sixteen and no matter how you do the math, a nine-foot deadly reptile is always within striking distance of a nervous writer with a camera. My very life was in the hands of a woman who believes the ghost of a dead actress stops sticky-fingered lovers from making off with her hard-earned cash. It was at that instant that I realized I should have held out for more money to do this book.

Joyously, Medusa danced and swayed, firmly holding the yellowish snake just below its head. At times, it seemed the snake wanted to wrestle Medusa for dominance, slinking inch by inch above her hold. It set its glare upon me, flicked its tongue, and reared its head back to strike. I started looking around the room for Clara Bow, but she was nowhere to be found.

After taking a few jittery photos, I informed Medusa I had all I needed. She lured the elongated monster back into its home, but before I could leave, she took my palm in her hand and started to read it. She smiled, and just as she was about to tell me my fortune, her phone rang. She needed to get it, and I needed to go. Not that I had anywhere specific to be, but I had to specifically be somewhere without giant snakes.

As I was making a beeline to my car, I shouted to Medusa that I had a great time. Shouting back, she asked if I would spread the word that Clara Bow needs help finding something she lost when she was among the living. Considering myself lucky that I was still among the living, I told Medusa I'd put that in the story, and maybe someone would contact her at her Web site and help Clara and her out. So if you happen to find anything that once belonged to Clara Bow, click on to Medusa. Me, I spent the rest of the afternoon calming my jangled nerves in the closest non-snake bar. Thankfully, there are plenty in Vegas. *–Joe O.*

Card Stacking with Bryan Berg

He concedes he doesn't play cards very well, but Bryan Berg is a world record holder when it comes to playing WITH cards. Stacking cards, to be more precise, has been Berg's passion since he was in third grade.

Berg reminisces, "I started when I was about eight years old. Between card games, my grandfather would build these one-deck constructions. Sometimes they'd get as high as three stories, but they'd always come down, and he'd curse, and then he'd start playing cards again."

These childhood experiences led to a lifelong interest in engineering, and a degree from the Harvard Graduate School of Design. Although Berg holds a genuine fondness for architecture, he has little interest in making it a forty-hour-a-week vocation. "I have no desire to sit in an office and design strip malls or shopping malls or gas stations or office parks, because it's kind of like same song, different day."

Berg is in the *Guinness World Records* for both the tallest card structure (over twenty-five feet tall, using 1,700 decks) and for the World's Largest House of Cards. That structure is a replica of Cinderella's Castle, which he constructed at Walt Disney World.

The iconic Vegas sign WELCOME TO FABULOUS LAS VEGAS NEVADA seemed a natural project for a man who makes his living handling cards. Berg says the full-scale model is made up of over nine hundred decks, plus a good amount of poker chips and dice. This is the first time he has ever used glue on one of his creations. According to Berg, "So far this is my only 'permanentized' work. . . . The downside is gluing takes forever and makes it more labor-intensive. These things already take up to a month to do."

Berg's four-hundred-and-fifty-pound Vegas sign is not just a one-dimensional copy of the original; his version has a honeycomb-like depth to it. Says the artist, "There's a definite art to wallpapering, but I wanted to show off the 'builtness' of it." (Wallpapering is a two-dimensional representation in which no glue would be needed to hold the design together, as gravity would do that.)

"We loaded that sign into a truck and drove it over some very rough terrain. Some of the poker chips from the word 'fabulous' fell off." Pressed to deliver his piece before the start of the World Series of Tournament Poker at the Rio hotel and casino, Berg reconstructed parts of the sign while en route. "All told it probably took about four hundred and fifty hours to make, and took about two years off my life."

Factoring in those trials and tribulations, life is treating Bryan Berg pretty well. He makes a good living doing what he wants, has no boss, and travels around the world being paid for what he loves. All in all, the deck is stacked favorably for this "weird" architect.

Weird Entertainment

With gambling and prostitution not only legal in Nevada but also among the state's principal industries, it's no wonder that Las Vegas has earned the nickname Sin City. The town has another moniker, though, which it also richly deserves—Entertainment Capital of the World.

Vegas is the number one vacation destination in the United States, where more than thirty-five million visitors flock each year. And, believe it or not, they don't all come for the gambling and the girls. They come to see the shows, experience the spas, and enjoy the restaurants and shopping.

Of course, just about any city in the United States offers this kind of recreation. So Vegas has to up the ante if it's going to attract customers out to the middle of the desert. It does this by making its entertainment a little bit flashier, a little bit trashier, and, well, just a little bit weirder. Sometimes these giddy thrills are not what you'd call wholesome activities, but hey, this is Vegas we're talking about and you know what they say: "What happens in Vegas stays in Vegas." It's probably best that way.

Star Trek Wedding

Tales will surely be told, and songs will certainly be sung, of the glorious day when all the known races in the galaxy were united in celebration. Normally emotionless Vulcans joyfully raised their glasses in toast with the often adversarial and fierce Klingons. The sometimes opportunistic but always cunning Romulans danced merrily with the ordinarily double-crossing Ferengi. The Cardassians, being Cardassians, naturally vied for the dominant position at the gathering, and the crystalline Tholians, whose bodies are not accustomed to temperatures less than 404 degrees Fahrenheit, felt perfectly at home in the sweltering heat of the Las Vegas desert.

They traveled from every corner of the known universe, from as far away as the frozen regions of Denver, Colorado, to the battle-scarred terrain of Oakland, California, all to bear witness to this momentous occasion. On this day in June, they came to see humanoid and avid *Star Trek* fan Richard Huzieff not only kiss a real-life woman (the lovely former Deb Mitchell), but also actually marry her.

In news that may stun as much as any phaser beam, every year there are dozens of other *Star Trek* fans who get to not only kiss a living breathing girl, but also marry her on the bridge of the U.S.S. *Starship Enterprise* at the Hilton.

The Hilton offers a number of *Star Trek* wedding packages. Some arrangements offer a brass plaque memorializing the date of the nuptials for proud display. Others offer "genuine intergalactic music" to be played as the bride and groom boldly walk down the aisle, and more than one wedding party has narrowly escaped a fate worse than death as they evaded assimilation to the Borg Collective just before the blessed union, thanks to the special effects–laden thrill ride, the Borg Invasion 4D.

Guests are encouraged to dress as their favorite *Star Trek* character from throughout the generations. Sometimes unrelated alien life forms such as the occasional Wookie and Predator have beamed up for the promise of a good party. "We're both big fans of the show," stated the (actually very cool in real life) groom Richard Huzieff minutes before the ceremony. "We like the show and feel there's a positive message behind every episode."

His new bride, (the also cool) Deb, added, "We've been together forever already, and we figured it would be fun to get all our friends to Vegas and just have fun."

The happy couple may not have been together "forever," in the sense of the space-time continuum, but they have been together long enough to have grown children and even grandchildren. So much for the theory that Trekkies don't get any.

The moral for this particular adventure is, if you ever get the chance to attend a *Star Trek* wedding—go! Chances are you'll be up partying until the twinkling starlight of thousands of years prior fades and gives way to the earth's one sun as it comes up and blinds your disbelieving eyes. You WILL have fun at a *Star Trek* wedding and reception. Resistance is futile.

Stratosphere Thrill Rides

If the prospect of losing your life's savings on a single roll of the dice isn't enough to get your heart palpitating, you might want to try a few amusement park rides. The Stratosphere Hotel takes thrill rides to a new height.

At 113 stories and 921 feet high, the Stratosphere is said to be the tallest building west of the Mississippi. The 1,800-feet-per-minute elevator ride to the observation deck alone is enough of an adrenaline rush for some people, but that's not even the tip of the iceberg—which the tip of the Stratosphere's tower itself is. You can travel to the very tip-top if you have the price of admission, the heart of an adventurer, and an empty stomach.

It would be impossible not to have second thoughts as the attendant straps you into the Big Shot—a 160-foot rocket launcher—and seconds later, you are blasted well over one thousand feet above the sparkling Las Vegas skyline. Thoughts of, what was I thinking? What if this thing comes undone? and finally, Whoa, this is cool! may enter your mind.

Of course, those thoughts happen within a span of 2.5 seconds, because that's as long as it takes for you to hit the peak. The next sensation you're aware of is momentary weightlessness, and then a free fall. The ride isn't over, because as you near the bottom you are whooshed up again, and plummet again, repeatedly. Each time is mercifully a little less intense, until the missile finally lands for good.

Before your brain settles back down inside your skull, another insane thought pops into your still shaky cerebellum: Let's go on Insanity. You may have the heart of an adventurer, but you also possess the mind of a lunatic.

Insanity the Ride is a green-and-purple mechanical five-tentacled octopus of excitable madness. Each tentacle, which holds two people, is affixed to one massive metallic arm that, once you are buckled up, proceeds to swing you sixty-four feet over the edge of the tower. When you look straight down, there is nothing but nine hundred–something feet of very light air, followed by a whole lot of very hard-looking ground.

Scared yet? Too bad . . . because it's just starting to get frightening. As you spin faster and faster until you reach speeds of three G's, the angle of your seat slowly turns on you. At one point your stomach seems almost parallel with that very hard-looking pavement. If you can keep your eyes open, it's a swirling psychedelic view of neon and traffic you can experience from only this unique vantage point. As the tentacles close back to their original position, the revolving mechanical beast slows down and swings you back to safety.

Arguably the scariest ride at the Stratosphere is X-Scream, an eight-seat toboggan car perched perilously close to the edge of the tower. There's nothing but a roll bar to hold you in this time, and you wait anxiously for the teenage attendant to send you racing over the edge. A button is pressed, and your car jolts to life with a ferocious kick. At the speed you are traveling, it doesn't take long to come to the end of the eighty-six feet of track, but when you do, powerful magnetic brakes make sure you stop just before physics and gravity make you just another car sitting in traffic on the Strip, 113 stories below.

The view is breathtaking as you sit motionless. Then, as you breathe a sigh of relief, your stomach muscles tense and you realize you have been had once again. This time, the entire car, track and all, quickly drop at a mind-blowing angle, and just as before, you're viewing that very hard pavement from a distance and perspective you never imagined. Suddenly the track adjusts itself and you roll back to safety, but you should know the pattern by now: Zzzooooommmmm, you fly out over the perimeter again, Whoooooooaaa, you get dropped again, you get pulled back again, you get zoomed again, until finally the pimply-faced kid at the switch decides you've had enough.

There is one thing to take into consideration before going anywhere near these rides. Make sure you do not have a stomach full of buffet food.

Fremont Street Experience

At one time, not very long ago, when people who had never been to Las Vegas imagined the city, the vivid neon images that came to mind were those of Four Queens, the Horseshoe, the Golden Nugget hotels, and of course the fifty-foot-tall waving cowboy, Vegas Vic, and the equally large and leggy cowgirl across the street, Vegas

Vickie. These were, after all, the visions that would blur before our eyes as we watched the requisite car chase or lonely, drunken midnight walk that took place in any pre-1990s Vegas movie or TV show. And it all happened on Fremont Street.

The very first gaming license was issued to the Northern Club, on Fremont Street, in 1931. It was the beginning of a tradition of brightly colored lights on this storied thoroughfare. More hotels and casinos opened on the street, and big-name entertainment was easily lured in. What was once a sleepy little stretch of roadside gambling halls became an illuminating beacon for investors with lots of money to make and tourists with money to lose.

But during the '70s, the once shiny new Vegas began losing some of its radiance. Street hookers, conmen, panhandlers, and various other ne'er-do-wells began to populate Fremont Street just as another area, the Strip, was coming into its own. By the time the early '90s rolled around, Las Vegas Boulevard was looking more like Disneyland. The more volcanoes and pirate ships they built, the more out-of-state visitors flocked in, never giving the now tacky Fremont Street of Old Vegas a second thought. Vegas was family friendly, and Fremont Street was considered the wrong side of town.

In order to compete for gambling dollars, Fremont Street's casino owners came up with a number of ideas to win back the tourists. Early plans included a system of canals, à la Venice, Italy, but eventually they decided on the Fremont Experience.

Car traffic is closed for five blocks, and an environment is created that is best described as part light show, part gigantic strip mall, part gambling mecca, and part strip joint. Starting around eight p.m. every night, all the lights outside the casinos are turned off, and the

ever-changing and surprisingly riveting six-minute music-and-light show begins.

Completed in 1995 and refurbished and improved in 2004, the Fremont Street Experience is 1,500 feet long and 90 feet high at its tallest. A giant, curved metallic awning shades Fremont Street from the harsh desert sun by day and provides the oversized television screen for your viewing pleasure during nightfall.

At the outset, the display, which contained 1.9 billion lightbulbs and a sound system putting out 350,000 watts, was controlled by thirty-two computers, but the recent improvement now features a 12.5 million LED (light-emitting diode) display for sharper resolution, and the sound system was raised to 550,000 watts. All of this is now controlled by only ten computers.

Of course, if you miss the gritty charm of Old Vegas, you always have options. You could walk about four or five blocks east on Fremont, where you stand an excellent chance of being propositioned for sex, hit up for spare change, and/or getting mugged!

Lions in the Casino

The pitch meeting probably went something like this: "I want ideas, and I want them now!" blustered the brash boss. "Mendelson, what do you think would bring more people into our fine hotel and casino here at the MGM Grand?"

Looking around the room, Mendelson fidgeted in his seat, before blurting out the first thing that came to his mind. "Um . . . lions, sir?"

"Ferocious, lions in a wildly popular casino, Mendelson?" the boss would incredulously inquire.

"Um . . . yes, sir. I believe that's pretty much the only kind of lions I've ever heard about," the jittery middle manager would say, gulping.

The domineering head honcho would then remove the pricey cigar from between his clenched teeth. The master of all he surveyed would take a step, then spin around on his fine Italian heels, and once again and skeptically pry, "Are you telling me, it's your opinion that to attract more people to our hotel—elderly women and tiny children stay here, mind you—you suggest we throw a couple of eight-foot-long, man-eating African lions right smack dab in the middle of thousands of patrons?"

"Um, yeah," a sweaty Mendelson would answer.

"I love it!" exclaimed the boss. "Mendelson, I'm promoting you to head idea guy. Richardson, you're fired! You never thought of lions in a casino! What kind of head idea guy are you anyway? Get out of my sight. You disgust me."

And now here are some actual facts about the Lion Habitat at the MGM Grand:

At this time there are thirty-four different lions, which rotate in and out of the habitat. The lions live on an eight-acre ranch in town called the Cat House.

Each lion is given a special bath and shampoo to prepare for its visit to the casino. If a lion is "acting up" during bath time, owner and trainer Keith Evans does not allow that animal to travel to the casino that day. The lions are never inside the MGM casino habitat longer than a few hours and spend a number of days at the ranch in between appearances.

Adult male lions weigh on average more than five hundred pounds, and the biggest lion at the MGM is just over six hundred pounds.

The glass "cage" the lions are displayed in is made of bulletproof Plexiglas, which is so thick the lions cannot smell the various restaurants or the edible people inside them, nor can they hear the constant clanging of the slot machines.

The temperature is controlled at a constant seventy to seventy-five degrees with fifty percent humidity, which is much more to the lions' liking than even their native Africa. Lions sleep from eighteen to twenty hours a day, or about the length of time most first-time visitors to Vegas stay at the same roulette table that has been beating them all day.

Dixie Dooley and the Houdini Séance

On the evening of October 31, 1926, world-renowned illusionist Harry Houdini shed his mortal coil, but left this plane of existence promising to his beloved wife, Bess, that if there were a gateway to the world of the living, he would find it and contact her. Bess was to know it was her late husband by a secret code the couple had decided upon.

For a full decade after the great entertainer died, Bess held a séance every Halloween night, the anniversary of her beloved's death, in hopes that Houdini would be able to communicate to her from the other side. Finally, in 1936, after exactly ten years of every spooky vaudevillian charlatan in the business having falsely claimed to have heard the secret message, Houdini's wife announced, "My last hope is gone. I do not believe that Houdini can come back to me — or to anyone. The Houdini shrine has burned for ten years. I now, reverently . . . turn out the light. It is finished. Good night, Harry!"

While it may have been finished that night for Bess Houdini, the desire to be the first one to contact Harry Houdini has never entirely diminished. Las Vegas's own Dixie Dooley is living proof. Dooley is not just a Houdini enthusiast, he is also a magician who has modeled his "close-up" magic act after history's most famous illusionist. For over twenty years, Dooley has been holding the Houdini séance in Las Vegas. Attendance is open to the public, and audiences have grown from twenty attendees to five thousand.

Dooley admits his views on the afterlife differ slight-

Bess Houdini

ly from those of his idol. According to Dooley, while Houdini never claimed spirits didn't exist, he also never saw any evidence that they did. Dooley, on the other hand, claims to have felt and experienced some contact with the unexplainable other side.

"I was holding a séance for Elvis [Presley] at the Greek Isles Hotel," he offered. "You know how it hardly ever rains in Vegas; well, this was just another bright sunny day, and we have this pretty unusual crowd, fans of the occult, fans of Elvis, and just curious people. At the very moment I called on the spirit of Elvis, this lightning bolt comes out of the sky, and there's a huge thunder crack, and it starts pouring rain. This is one of those older buildings in Vegas, and since it never rains, you don't know if the roof needs repair until it leaks on you. Well, it was dripping rain on everyone for the whole séance, and when I finished up, we went outside, and it was bright and sunny again. That was something. The Elvis fans and the occult fans determined the lightning bolt was Elvis's symbol. He used to wear a necklace of a lightning bolt, and it said TCB — Taking Care of Business."

When asked if he ever had that kind of success when trying to make contact with Houdini, Dooley admits that so far he hasn't and has come to grips with the fact that he may never, but that doesn't stop him from trying. He won't, however, stoop to the same type of cheap parlor tricks that Houdini spent much of his later years exposing.

"Houdini hated mediums, because he felt they were taking advantage of grieving people who lost their loved

Dixie Dooley, left, channeling Houdini

ones during World War One," Dooley explains. "Fortune-tellers and mediums were a big fad back in those days, kind of like reality TV is today, but the difference is people would give over their life savings for the chance to contact a lost relative. . . . [Houdini] wanted to make it a law that mediums would have to be licensed by the government and have a certificate posted." Dooley has re-created many of Houdini's tricks onstage over the years. He has escaped from straitjackets while suspended eighty feet in the air, been buried under three hundred pounds of ice, and performed Houdini's famous Milk Can Escape. Nowadays, though, Dooley's magic shows are lighter in tone. He now infuses a little humor and has attractive assistants.

"It's nice to be serious," he says, grinning, "but I like to clown around too." Dooley then proceeds to tell a very funny story about a fellow magician who betrayed their friendship while competing for a job at a casino. The punch line is that Dooley and a number of his magician friends got even with the double-crossing diviner by urinating in his water tank before his opening night show.

"It was a long time ago, and I haven't told that story in a while, but when he [the rival magician] went underwater, my friends and I were all hooting. We gave him a standing ovation."

When asked if he felt Harry Houdini would have approved of the prank, Dooley never hesitated. "Houdini used to play tricks on fellow magicians all the time. I have no doubt if Houdini were alive, he'd have unzipped his fly and joined in."

To inquire about Houdini collectibles or to find out where Dixie Dooley is scheduled to perform, visit his official Web site at www.houdiniexperi-ence.com.

Mermaid Bar

If you were on Jeopardy and the answer given as a clue was, "These are the top four things men want to do when they're not gambling in Las Vegas."

Your question in response would naturally be, "What is drink alcohol, watch sports on TV, look at sharks, and ogle pretty young mermaids swimming in a 117,000-gallon aquarium, Alex?"

The Mermaid Restaurant and Lounge is the exact place to enjoy all of these activities. If Aquaman were a gambling sort, this is no doubt where he'd hang. The lounge is in the Silverton Casino on Blue Diamond Road, about three miles off the Strip.

The ambiance here is underwater chic, complete with menus shaped like seashells, a jellyfish tank that subtly changes colors, tasty food, and high-back mermaid fin-shaped chairs with such nautically inspired names as Nemo, Moby Dick, Flipper, and Craig.

Who's Craig? Who cares. We're not playing *Jeopardy* anymore, we're talking about this excellent bar, the centerpiece of which is the enormous fish tank. It is the desert home to over eight thousand brightly colored exotic fish, including three species of sharks, three species of stingrays, and a bevy of undulating mermaids.

As it turns out, the mermaids aren't actually mermaids at all. They're just very pretty Olympic-medalist synchronized swimmers wearing mermaid costumes. At least that's what one of the bartenders told us when, after one drink too many, we asked why real mermaids would need a breathing apparatus during the show.

The show was excellent, and we bet if Aquaman ever was able to make the trip, he'd agree.

Throwing Voices with Ronn Lucas

Ronn Lucas is an extremely talented ventriloquist. He has performed for various U.S. Presidents, had his own TV variety series in England, and continues to do his family-friendly act to sold-out crowds everywhere he travels. He is among the masters of his craft. *Weird Las Vegas* caught up with the headline after a show and asked him for a few of his *Weird Las Vegas* Tales.

Ronn: One of the weirdest things that ever happened to me was when I pulled this guy from the audience to do this thing I do in my act. I put a mask over the person's face, and the mask is animated from the nose down, and the jaw opens and closes kind of like a dummy, and we get to see him panic, as I put words in his mouth, from the nose up.

Now this guy is huge, and I'm already thinking this is going to be funny because of the dichotomy of him being almost seven feet tall, and me being five foot five.

I ask, "What is your name?" and he says, "Vladimir," and he's Czechoslovakian and speaks almost no English. So I'm very respectful, and I say, "Okay, I'm going to have you wear this mask," and started the act. [Ronn pulls a string on the back of the mask, which activates the mechanism, and the "mouth" moves up and down.]

Well, we started to get laughs, but he tries to leave the stage. Finally, after two or three more jokes, he takes the mask off and very politely hands it to me and whispers something in my ear, and I don't know what to do. Because what he told me was, "I'm in a witness protection program."

I felt bad for a moment but then thought, Wait a minute, he'd had a mask on.

Weird Las Vegas: Well, still he is a seven-foot Czech. They're easy to spot in Vegas with or without the mask.

Ronn: Good point.

Weird Las Vegas: Anything weird ever happen to you when you first started playing Vegas?

Ronn: When I first started playing here, I was in this little tiny nightclub. One day a group of stock car racers came in, and they were so much fun. They were just laughing and drinking like crazy, and there was this guy up front who was obviously the winner of the race, so I had my puppet start picking on him like crazy.

I said, 'What's your name?' and he said, "Larry," and suddenly Larry stood up, and he was smiling and grinning. He walked forward, and he goes, "I've had enough of you," and rears back his fist, and starts to punch the puppet. This was a wooden puppet too, and I just thought it was hysterical that the guy has so much booze in him that he's pissed at the puppet.

Weird Las Vegas: Do you have any good stories about any Vegas celebrities?

Ronn: Okay, I'll give you this one: I used to have a costume, very '80s. It had the padded shoulders—I was opening for Joan Rivers at Caesars—and it had stripes, almost like epaulettes going through the shoulders, and I thought it was pretty cool. I used to walk through the audience to get onstage, and I'm walking through as Joan introduces me, and Alan King was sitting in the front row, and he grabs me by the shoulders, just seeing the side of me, and he goes, "I ordered another drink!"

Well, that's when I got rid of that costume. I thought it was cool, but apparently, I just looked like a very well-dressed maître de.

Weird Las Vegas: Well, I guess Alan King went thirsty for a few more minutes. Great talking to you, Ronn. Ronn's website is www.ronnlucas.com.

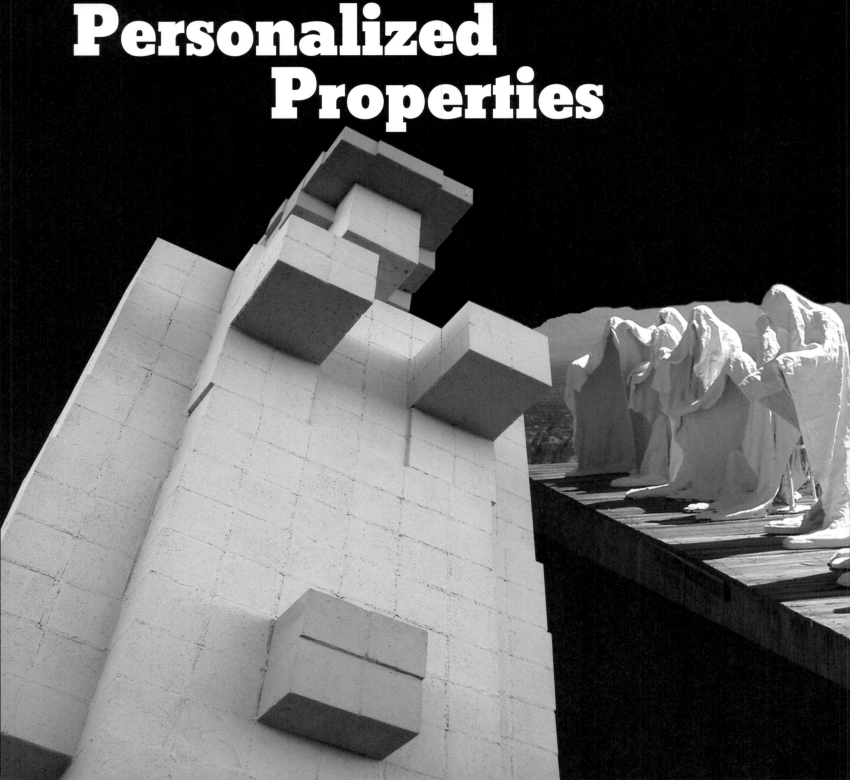

Personalized Properties

When it comes to personalizing property, Nevadans do it best. In fact, we've been doing it since back in the day, when we started making houses out of bottles—a technique that then caught on in other, less creative, places. Our state is something of a mecca for those seeking weirdness in general, and they won't be disappointed when they look past the larger-than-life casinos and hotels to the homes of ordinary people. Ordinary for around here, that is!

Houses built to look like Homer Simpson's, a full-blown medieval castle in the middle of the blazing desert, rooms decorated with coffins, or Bugsy Siegel's toilet—they're all normal for Nevadans. And if you're buying a home here, don't forget to ask if it has any secret entrances. It might just be built on top of an underground fortress meant to withstand a nuclear holocaust.

In fact, while wandering around Vegas and beyond, it's not unreasonable to bet that any weirdness that catches your eye might be somebody's front yard. So take in the scenery and admire the view—there really is no place like home!

Dr. Hammargren's Home of Nevada History

I couldn't help but feel a bit like Charlton Heston in the final scene of Planet of the Apes. There she was, directly before and above me, as she was with Heston earlier. Mocking my very eyes in the distance—the Statue of Liberty.

It wasn't the real Statue of Liberty, and as it turns out, it was only the hand holding the torch, severed just below the giant wrist. I slowed down, realizing it stood

this book you are now reading, he agreed to allow me into his home.

I showed up a little early, hoping to grab a few photos of the front of Hammargren's home, Castillo del Sol. In 1969, this four-bedroom home was just one of a few dozen other domiciles in this suburban Las Vegas tract. Over the years, Hammargren bought the houses on either side of his, connected them to the original dwelling, and added second and third floors to each building. He also added a mini-planetarium and had an

among a cacophony of colossal collectibles peeking from the backyard in this otherwise normal suburban neighborhood. There was an abandoned space capsule of some sort; a paratrooper caught on scaffolding and twisting in the wind; a rocket sled poised to jump over the roof; Popeye, Sweet Pea, and Olive Oyl rowing a boat, and a sign that read THE HAMMARGREN HOME OF NEVADA HISTORY.

His name is Dr. Lonnie Hammargren. I called, the good doctor answered, and after a brief explanation of

observatory constructed on his roof.

All this might seem a bit "over the top," but it is just the beginning, as Dr. Hammargren is the former lieutenant governor of the state of Nevada, a respected neurosurgeon, and an amateur archaeoastronomer (a combination of archaeology and astronomy). He has been called the Physician to the Gladiators, a title he proudly accepts. He's treated motorcycle-stunt daredevils Evil and Robbie Knievel, and just about every boxer, famous or otherwise, who ever suffered from head trauma while plying his trade in this fair city. He is also, without question, a first rate packrat.

The front of the structure is a pastiche of styles and elements. Lonnie Hammargren's front yard is the only one on his block that has a replica of the *Venus de Milo,* a stairway to the top of a Mayan pyramid, a facsimile of the space shuttle, and personified trees with faces on them—some happy, some angry, but all showing emotion.

Hammargren, a large, powerfully built man, greeted me at the door. For a moment, I was taken by his relaxed folksy manner and almost forgot why I was there. That's when, through a giant porthole in the den, I saw Abe Lincoln sitting down . . . underwater. Not the real Abe, but a reproduction of the statue at the Lincoln Memorial. But instead of the Lincoln Memorial, he's in the Parthenon. Underwater. Why? I don't know for sure. I know Dr. Hammargren told me, but when you're in this house, your mind focuses on so much so quickly it's hard for a mere nonarchaeoastronomer to keep everything together.

The tour began in the backyard. An avid supporter of the space program, Lonnie had a mural of the crew of the *Challenger* painted in one pool, while his other pool is home to the actual submarine from the TV show "Sea Hunt." There's also the $1 million mechanical fire-breathing dinosaur from the David Cassidy musical *EFX,* a working train, the first jail cell doors in Clark County, a huge Fabergé egg doorway from which Liberace made appearances, a life-size cartoon-style mannequin of President Bush (the elder), and the marquee of the old Showboat Casino. Actually, you could name just about anything and there's a fifty-fifty chance it's in Hammargren's backyard.

My mind was still trying to organize the contents of the place when it came time for a little music. Dr. Hammargren is nothing if not a consummate showman. We went inside, and the doctor sat down at the white-

sequined honky-tonk piano once owned by Liberace. The endearing eccentric started banging away on the ivories. Sensing that the audience was in the palm of his hands, Hammargren switched instruments to his own creation: the Carryoke.

The Carryoke is a working guitar shaped like the state of Nevada, with a karaoke player inside. As we continued to explore the house, overwhelmed by the sheer size of the collection, I saw the holy grail of Vegas artifacts. There it is, in the bathroom in a hallway: Bugsy Siegel's toilet, a pistachio-green porcelain throne rescued from Siegel's private apartment in the Flamingo Hotel.

Hammargren owns one of the original George Barris–created vehicles from the popular 1960s TV series

Batman. Hammargren had promised me that we'd see it, but we had a lot more to visit, including the Tomb.

This ominously named spot is through the garage, but this is Hammargren's garage we're talking about, so instead of lawn mowers and tool benches, we passed the original balloon basket from the movie *Around the World in 80 Days*, a couple of 1936 Rolls-Royces, and an honest-to-goodness iron lung. I was led to yet another secret passage. As I held on to the good doctor's belt loop, we wandered in the dark through a tiny labyrinth, until we were where we needed to be—in a mock Egyptian tomb. The hieroglyphic paintings on the walls and ceiling depicted neurosurgery from 5,000 years ago, but the closed sarcophagus was a mystery until Hammargren pulled on a rope to reveal an armored German Messerschmitt car, complete with machine gun bolted to the driver's-side door. The car was a gift from Evil Knievel, who had the good sense to paint the American flag and emblazon his own name on both doors.

The friendly physician next asked if I'd like to check out the observatory, and we ascended to the top of his house. I know the brilliant doctor said a lot of intelligent things about astronomy and astrology while we were up there. But if Underwater Abe messed with my mind when I just walked into this place, there was no way I was going to comprehend, let alone recall, anything that required actual thinking on my part. And I never did get to see the Batmobile.

Every year around Nevada Day (the last Friday of October) the community-minded M.D. invites the general public over for ice cream. Castillo del Sol is located at 3196 South Maryland Parkway. *—Joe O.*

Laughter and Tears at the Clown Motel

Driving into Tonopah from the east, the first thing you notice is the Clown Motel. People either love this place or they loath it. It is on a "best place to stay" list for people heading to the Burning Man festival. One Web site calls it the "most terrifying hotel in the world," which it would be if you have clown-a-phobia. The themed motel has clowns all over the place. Out front, a clown on a Harley beckons BIKERS WELCOME. Stuffed clowns, ceramic clowns, and paintings of clowns overwhelm the lobby. "We do have people, especially kids, who won't come in because of the clowns; they're scared of them," says Bob Perchetti, the motel's current owner.

But it is not just the clowns that creep some people out. It's the fact that the lobby is adjacent to the Tonopah historic cemetery. Step one way, and you are heading to your motel room; walk the other way, and you enter a Wild West–looking cemetery, complete with weathered wooden grave markers.

The cemetery was active from 1901 to 1911. It was in that last year that it became the final resting place of the victims of the Tonopah-Belmont mine fire, the most tragic event in the town's history.

So how did the motel end up next to the cemetery? According to Perchetti, a man named Leroy David bought the property in the 1970s for sentimental reasons. His dad, Clarence H. David, was one of the miners who died in the 1911 fire and was buried in the cemetery.

The younger David decided to put a motel on the land. "He had a collection of clowns he had bought from a man in Vegas," Perchetti says. "Then one day, he just came up with the idea: 'I've got a motel and I've got all these clowns, so I'll put clowns in the rooms and clowns in the office . . . and make them pay for themselves.' So he built the motel around the clown theme."

Since Perchetti took over the motel, he has added to the clown collection, amassing things from all over the world. He now says he has over five hundred clown-related items at the motel.

Sometimes guests donate a clown to his collection. Sometimes a clown just shows up in the mail, with an accidentally taken room key tied around its neck.

If you want to stay at the only clown-themed motel located next to a graveyard or just want to send Bob a clown to add to the collection, the address is Clown Motel, 521 North Main Street, Tonopah, NV.

Coffin It Up in Pahrump

The neighbors don't talk to Bryan and Dusty Schoening, owners of the Coffin House in Pahrump, who live a life based around death. Their front yard has a cemetery; their collection of hearses is parked in the driveway. They have built and installed a coffin-shaped gazebo in the front yard. The house's interior is adorned with death images and custom-made coffin-shaped furniture.

The house doubles as the headquarters of Coffin It Up, where you can buy yourself an old-style coffin, either for decorative purposes, functional, or both. Remove the shelves from one of the bookcases, and you have a burial coffin fulfilling all the legal requirements for human interment.

For those unschooled in the finer points of the funereal culture, a coffin is different from a burial casket, which has become the standard in the United States. A casket has straight sides, while a coffin has widening "shoulders" at the top. Coffin It Up is one of the few places in this country where you can purchase a classic coffin.

Bryan creates and builds all the coffins, whether intended as furniture or a final resting place. Dusty takes care of the financial end of the business. The death-obsessed couple met in Los Angeles when they were teenagers; they have been an item ever since. They married at a young age and recently renewed their vows in a ceremony in Las Vegas, where the minister was dressed as the grim reaper. They moved from Oregon to Pahrump in 2002, bringing with them a U-Haul truck full of coffins. Dusty felt, from a prior trip, that Pahrump would be a good place to die, and he liked its proximity to Death Valley. They started Coffin It Up later that year. Word of mouth spread the business at first and still plays a big part, along with their Web site, coffinitup.com.

Clients have included many professional people: psychiatrists, forensic scientists, coroners, lawyers, and even a clown. We asked Dusty if the clown was looking for a very small coffin and wanted to see how many dead clowns could fit inside. She said he just wanted furniture.

Some people request burial coffins for religious reasons, such as conservative Jews, who require a very plain coffin for a traditional burial. Some foreigners are looking for the style of coffins used in the old country. But all kinds of people have planned ahead for one of life's certainties. Some are looking for unique styles of coffins. Some request interior compartments for keepsakes from life. And some, like Bryan and Dusty, share the death obsession: Bryan has installed coffin-shaped kitchen cabinets in a private home in Las Vegas. His ultimate plan is to build a house in the shape of a coffin, including a rooftop that hinges and moves like a coffin lid.

Currently, the coffin house has another function; aside from a home and a business, it is also a church. The Church of the Coffin was formed on October 31, 2005, and became a legal house of worship in July 2006. Bryan had become a Universal Ministries ordained minister five years before the church was formed. The congregation meets once a week, on Tuesday evenings. The coffin represents the unity of humanity, a reminder that life is short and that whatever our differences, all of us will eventually be humbled by death.

Goldwell Art Park at Rhyolite

A sure sign that you are traveling on the correct road en route from Las Vegas to the ghost town of Rhyolite is the figure of a prospector standing next to a giant penguin. The twenty-four-foot-tall rusted steel sculpture is part of the Goldwell Open Air Art Museum. The sculpture was created by Belgian artist Fred Bervoets in 1994. The prospector is said to represent Shorty Harris, the man from whose gold strike the town sprouted. The penguin represents the artist, who felt as incongruous in the desert as an Antarctic bird.

The museum took root in 1984, when Albert Szukalski, a renowned Belgian sculptor, selected Rhyolite as the location for his next work.

Back then, a small group of people lived in the former train station, which was also a gift shop and casino. Jim Spencer, Rhyolite's "mayor," granted Szukalski permission to put his sculpture in the town, partially because he hoped that this would be the start of an art colony.

Szukalski was fascinated with America and found its deserts "fantastic." His original sculpture for Rhyolite was *The Last Supper*, a depiction of the biblical scene of Jesus and the twelve apostles. The figures are all ghostlike empty shrouds retaining the shape of the people who once filled them. Szukalski felt that many people had their last supper in Rhyolite while seeking their fortune in the desert and said that his sculpture "is an homage to those who made it." The counsel general of Belgium was in attendance at the October 27, 1984, dedication ceremony

where Szukalski was presented with a letter from the lieutenant governor saying in part "how fortunate for us, that during your travels last year, you saw in our desert a resemblance to the Holy land."

The Last Supper was originally in front of the old train station, the main building in town at that time. Today it has been moved to the entrance to town, now the official location of the 7.8-acre sculpture garden. Three other Belgian artists added additional sculptures over the years, and another was created by Beatty resident David Spicer.

When Szukalski died in January 2000 at age fifty-four, his business partner took control of the property and in March 2000 arranged to donate it to a nonprofit organization. Charles Morgan and Susan Hackett, who have been involved in the project since 1994, could be said to be the museum's curators and caretakers. In 2005, when *Lady Desert: The Venus of Nevada*, a cinder block sculpture made by Hugo Heyrman, was looking a little rundown, Susan organized a makeover. The all-female Pink Lady Paint Party wore pink bandanas as they cleaned and repainted the Lego-looking nude female effigy. The team also repaired *The Last Supper* and built a new platform for it. Their caring maintenance makes it likely that the sculptures will be enjoyed for generations to come.

Underground House, Complete with Backyard

In an exclusive neighborhood in the southeast side of Las Vegas, twenty-five feet beneath a fashionable home, there is an underground house that is a throwback to the days when every family was going to have their own fallout shelter.

Known as the Flintstone House, Las Vegas's underground house is the creation of Girard "Jerry" Henderson. Henderson was a businessman who made a lot of money from, among other things, serving on the board of directors of the Avon Corporation. This wealthy East Coast businessman who, spurred on by the Cuban missile crisis, believed nuclear war was inevitable. He formed the Underground World Home Corporation and brought the concept of underground living to the 1964–65 New York World's Fair.

In 1969, Henderson moved his headquarters from New Jersey to Las Vegas. In 1971, he built a home that was partially underground, but it was not until 1978 that he would create his own completely subterranean home.

What he built was something worthy of a 1960s-era

movie spy. An iron fence surrounded some boulders and trees. If you approached a certain boulder and knew what to do, it would slide open, revealing a door to an elevator that would take you twenty-five feet down. There you would find a 16,000-square-foot home that showed that you could survive the apocalypse in style. A 1,900-square-foot living room was designed for entertaining. The decor included many mementos from Avon (the company that had made Henderson most of his money) and a necklace that once belonged to Elizabeth Taylor. No doubt Jerry's wife, Mary, a former Beverly Hills hairdresser, contributed to that display.

But it was the "outside" of the house that everyone remembers. The backyard had a heated swimming pool, a waterfall, Astroturf-style "grass," a mini-golf course, and "trees" that grew up into the ceiling. One of the artificial tree trunks concealed a vent for the barbeque grill. The faux outdoors had controlled lighting that changed from daylight to sunset and nighttime. At night, distant cityscapes glowed and twinkled, thanks to the mercury, from broken streetlights, painted into the walls.

Jerry Henderson died of a heart attack in November 1983, and the house ended up in the ownership of a distant relative. In the 1980s, the boulders on the surface were removed and a regular-style house was built on top of the secret underground lair.

For a time, the new owner contracted an events-planning company to manage the subterranean house and would rent it out for corporate functions. That was about the only way a member of the general public could see the underground manor. The property has recently changed hands, and this owner is not renting it out or giving tours. Perhaps it now belongs to Bruce Wayne!

The Simpsons' House

Today the house at 724 Red Bark Lane, in the Henderson subdivision called Springfield, doesn't look much different from the other homes that surround it. But in 1997, when it was first built, the house was painted in bright cartoon colors and thousands of people a day would walk by it just to get a glimpse.

The home is a replica of the house from the TV show *The Simpsons,* built to celebrate the show's tenth year on the air. The house was the prize of a contest sponsored by Pepsi-Cola and the Fox network: the winner was to receive a real-life version of the Simpsons' cartoon tract house.

The building company Kaufman & Broad Home

Corporation had its employees watch a marathon fifty-six episodes to familiarize themselves with the layout of the cartoon home. "I watch TV shows and try to figure out how the [floor plans] work anyway," architect Mike Woodley told the *Las Vegas Sun,* "so it was natural for me to do this."

It turns out that transforming a cartoon house into reality is not as easy as you might think—cartoon houses don't have to have things like load-bearing walls! Also, the Simpsons' home had no closets whatsoever. However,

a true-to-cartoon detail in the real house is a "mystery door" in the living room. This door, which can be seen in every episode, goes nowhere and is never opened.

When the public first toured the house in August 1997 it was painted orange, green, and canary yellow. Reminders of the Simpsons were scattered around, from empty cans of Duff Beer to painted-on oil stains in the driveway. Costumed Marge and Homer characters gave tours to hordes of fans. In mid-September, *Simpsons* creator Matt Groening made an appearance. He spray-painted EL BARTO WAS HERE on the garage and made a portrait of Homer in wet cement on the walkway.

Sixty-three-year-old Barbara Howard, a retired factory worker from Richmond, Kentucky, won the contest and got the house.

By now, the house has been painted to match the rest of the neighborhood. The Simpsons memorabilia that once filled it are long gone; but peek up the walkway (remember, it is private property) and you will see Homer's face still etched in the cement.

Stokes Castle

As you enter Austin on Highway 50, you may notice what looks like a castle turret on a hillside overlooking the highway. You've seen correctly: The turret is part of Stokes Castle, the product of a time when Nevada was ruled not by royalty, but by silver mining.

Anson Phelps Stokes commissioned the castle in the 1890s. He was a wealthy East Coast businessman who built the Nevada Central Railroad and who also had bought into a few local mines. The castle would be the perfect place for his family to live whenever he came out west to keep an eye on his mining concerns.

Work on the castle began in the fall of 1896 and was completed the following summer. Stokes spared no expense in the building of his home. A hand-operated winch was necessary to hoist the heavy hand-hewn granite walls into place. A water line was put into the home from the Austin city water system, and a master carpenter was hired to install the floors, stairway, and interior woodwork.

The castle has three stories. The first contained the kitchen and the dining room, the second the living room, and the top story had two bedrooms. With north-side fireplaces on every floor and south-side balconies off the living room and bedrooms, the home was built to ensure its dwellers' comfort regardless of season. The roof was an outdoor living area with curtains to shield the wind and an awning for shade.

Despite the extravagance and expense involved in the project, the Stokes family occupied the castle just three times. The first time was also the longest: one month in the summer of 1897, soon after it was completed. They returned that October, but only for a few days. When they came back again, in the summer of 1898, it was to sell off Stokes's interests in the area mines.

The castle sat unoccupied for decades and slowly fell apart due to the ravages of the elements and vandals. In the 1950s, word got out that someone was planning to buy the building and ship it piece by piece to Las Vegas. Molly Magee Knudsen, a relative of Anson Stokes, would not stand for this. To keep it in the family and in Austin, she purchased the castle and the property in 1956. She then put up a chain-link fence to keep out vandals.

Placed on the National Register of Historic Places in 2003, Stokes Castle is easily accessible by a dirt road that goes up the hill just off Highway 50 near the west side of Austin's city limits. While everyone is free to drive up and gawk to their heart's content, admission is not permitted. Take some photographs, enjoy the sixty-mile desert vista, and keep an eye out for the ghosts that are said to reside behind the old castle's stone walls.

Chief Rolling Mountain Thunder's Monument

I remember when I first saw Thunder Mountain Park. I was heading east on Interstate 80 when I caught a glimpse of it as I sped by. What little I saw was enough to make me do two U-turns to get back to see what I had missed.

Curious travelers who pull off the highway, as I did that day, will find themselves wandering a deserted area filled with houses and shacks made of all manner of salvage, statues, screeds criticizing the U.S. government and its treatment of Native Americans, and some piles of plain old junk.

Thunder Mountain Monument is the creation of Frank Van Zant, of Okmulgee, Oklahoma. Van Zant was a man who loved telling stories and often blended fiction with fact. He seems to have joined the military in World War II, was injured, and after the war he moved to Yuba City, CA, and went into law enforcement. He ran for sheriff but narrowly lost, and was a private investigator.

In the fall of 1968, Van Zant took his ex-stepchild and new wife on a trip across Nevada. For some reason they stopped, and stayed, at a desolate site just east of the Imlay exit on I-80. Legend has it that Van Zant's car wouldn't let him leave. He got it on the road,

and it started running badly; then he turned it back around, and it started running better. "I was just going to drive away and leave it. Only I couldn't get away. I got forced back with a full load, and there was a car sittin' there on the prairie. It was the guy who owned the property. And he offered me such terms that I couldn't turn it down," Van Zant–Chief Thunder told a reporter in 1975.

From 1968 on, Thunder rarely left the spot. He built a unique environment from materials which included stones from the area, typewriters, car parts, farm

equipment, bottles, TVs, windshields, and just about anything else. The only time Thunder left was to get bags of cement to hold it all together. There are statues of Indian icons like Sitting Bull and Sarah Winnemucca, but also odder sculptures—like one devoted to Lyman Gilmore, an aviation pioneer who made the dubious claim that he had beaten the Wright brothers at heavier-than-air flight.

The first building was constructed around a travel trailer. A roundhouse, a storage shed, a hostel house, an underground room, and a guest cabin joined the budding village.

Somewhere along the way, Van Zant had become Chief Rolling Mountain Thunder. Like everything in his life, he told different versions of how it happened. He claimed to be at least a quarter Oklahoma Creek Indian, although some have disputed that he had any Native American blood at all.

Just to keep things clear, there was another Rolling Thunder in northern Nevada. Also known as John Pope, this Rolling Thunder was a Cherokee medicine man who had a commune in Carlin. That's not the guy we're talking about.

Our Chief Rolling Thunder totally transformed himself into an Indian shaman persona. He attracted nomadic hippie types, who might pull off the road and stay for months. The visitors helped with the construction of buildings and sculptures. Thunder Mountain became a hippie commune. The chief raised his family on the grounds, giving his offspring the Indian-style names Obsidian Lightning Thunder, Thunder Mountain Thunder, and True Brave Eagle Thunder.

But as the years rolled on, things changed.

The hippies faded away; Van Zant's wife left him, taking the children with her. Some of the houses had burned or collapsed. For these, and reasons known only to himself, in early January 1989 Chief Rolling Mountain Thunder committed suicide in the roundhouse.

After his death, the encampment fell into further disrepair, with curious travelers still pulling over for a look—and perhaps a souvenir. The property ended up in the hands of Daniel Van Zant, Chief Thunder's son from his first marriage. Daniel fixed up the place a bit and got the state of Nevada interested in preserving it. Eventually, it was declared a state historic site and a national monument.

These days there is no one there and many of the buildings are fenced off—but it is still viewable and still a very weird place. *—Tim Cridland*

Roadside Oddities

There was a time in our not so distant past when there wasn't much more than one game in town. So a couple of neon signs protruding from the desert landscape was all it took to guide bleary-eyed motorists across the burning sand to the glowing promise of big jackpots and all-you-can-eat buffets. Nowadays, however, with competition for tourist dollars at an all-time high, businesses in Las Vegas and elsewhere in the state have had to turn to ever more eye-popping forms of advertising to capture potential customers. Fake cityscapes of New York and Paris have sprung up side by side with cheesy re-creations of the world's ancient wonders, like the Great Pyramid of Giza and the Sphinx.

Fortunately, such attractions are not always the exclusive property of the big corporate casinos and hotels. Just about any business, great or small, that can be seen from the road will visually hawk its respective wares—from wedding chapels to brothels. And roadside oddities are not limited to just kitschy advertising. Some serve no commercial purpose whatsoever, making them true head-scratchers.

These curious creations not only speak volumes about who we are as a culture. They also distract us during those mind-`drives through the desert, making our trips a little easier to bear and sometimes even a journey to remember.

Pinball Hall of Fame

Once upon a time, when a teenager wanted to get away from the mundane routine that was his life, he could escape to a place populated by superheroes, cowboys, aliens from outer space, and girls in bikinis. It was a wonderful land, full of carbonated soda, dazzling colors, and a cacophony of beeps, dings, and rock and roll music. Admission to this magical world was free, but if you had five bucks in your pocket, you could be king of this universe for hours. Hours that would be forever wasted if you were stuck back at your parents' house doing homework.

If you haven't figured out the location of this adolescent Shangri-la by now, you were likely frittering your time away on trigonometry and sweating to get into the college of your choice. The rest of us, however, the truly smart kids, understood the allure that is pinball, and we're better equipped to take on the world for it.

The pinball arcade has all but vanished from today's modern culture, but thanks to Tim Arnold, owner of the Pinball Hall of Fame in Las Vegas, and his trusty sidekick, the Hippie, new generations of kids of all ages have the chance to congregate and learn the fine art of pinball.

Arnold is a fifty-something self-described "long hair," who hasn't had a non–pinball-related job since he was fourteen. He is well versed in the history of the pinball machine. He should be, as over the last fifteen years he has bought, restored, and now owns over a thousand of the flashy table games.

The nonprofit Pinball Hall of Fame donates all its gains to the Salvation Army, but at least for the moment, the Salvation Army will have to continue to employ street-corner Santas to help pay its bills. "We're open from eleven to eleven seven days a week, but we're barely making ends meet." Arnold sighs. "People love the place; we get maybe two hundred people on a good day, each spending a buck or two, but the only reason there's any profit at all is because the Hippie and I basically work for free."

The Pinball Hall of Fame houses over two hundred games, with another eight hundred in various states of repair in a ten-thousand-square-foot warehouse in Arnold's backyard. If you're nostalgic for a certain game, chances are you'll find it at this fine institution. Pinball has always reflected pop culture, and a stroll down the aisles here can tell you a lot about the social mores of America. Arnold informs us, "You can tell the era based on the clothing, hairstyles, and the physical attributes of the women [portrayed]." As for the history of the machines themselves, Arnold and the Hippie try to include a detailed placard on each. These handwritten signs are as informative as one can expect, espe-

cially given that many of the companies are now defunct. Nevertheless, you can find facts, such as the year the device was manufactured, the artist, and which parts were replaced and when.

When asked if it was a risky decision to house machines that will not "pay off" in a town known more for slot machines than pinball, Arnold answers, "No. The quarter has virtually no value anymore. The quarter is what the nickel used to be. . . . The nice thing about this place is you can still walk in free and have an evening's worth of fun for four to five dollars."

The Pinball Hall of Fame is located at 3330 East Tropicana, and Arnold encourages anyone who ever played a mean pinball to help out a worthy cause. Besides, what are you going to do that's more fun? Homework?

Neon Museum

Museums in Italy proudly display the work of such Renaissance men as Botticelli and Da Vinci. Artists Toulouse-Lautrec and Claude Monet are sources of great national pride in the finest galleries in France. And the Las Vegas Neon Museum immortalizes the work of the Young Electric Sign Company (YESCO) and its contributions to the world of art, like the cute neon milkman with the oversized head and the giant genie lamp

that lights up.

The word "museum" frequently conjures up images of pipe-smoking, erudite men in tweed jackets, cocking their eyebrows as they search paintings for meaning the artist never imagined. There is little of that going on at the Neon Museum, and at the risk of sounding boorish, that sounds like one more reason to prefer Vegas to Paris.

This museum is not a traditional repository of treasures. Instead, the artwork is on display outside the many tiny souvenir kiosks and low-cost luncheonettes that make up much of the real estate on Fremont Street.

The nonprofit organization was started in 1997 when town historians realized that much of the neon kitsch that made Las Vegas so appealing was starting to vanish. New hotels with enormous million-color computer screens were swallowing up the smaller hotels and their seemingly outdated glowing signs.

Today the Neon Museum has restored about a dozen signs and icons. They include the Aladdin's Lamp, which was originally installed in 1966 at the old Aladdin Hotel, and classic signs like the one from the Flame Restaurant, a Vegas twenty-four-hour steak joint that thrived during the Rat Pack era.

Melanie Coffee, media coordinator at the Neon Museum, would love to be able to revive every incandescent guidepost that ever lit up in the dark desert sky. "Las Vegas is known as an oasis of light in the middle of the desert," says Ms. Coffee. "The signs are the history of Las Vegas, and the Neon Museum's restored collection on Fremont Street is one of the few places that tell that story."

So the next time you're contemplating a sophisticated sojourn to some fancy European gallery, consider instead the Neon Museum. Sure, the Louvre has the Mona Lisa, but chances are you can't get a ninety-nine-cent foot-long hot dog anywhere near the place.

Vegas Vic and Sassy Sally

Vegas Vic is Las Vegas's best-known celebrity. He has appeared in more movies than any other Las Vegan. He starred with, among others, Elvis Presley and Ann-Margret in *Viva Las Vegas,* Sean Connery in *Diamonds Are Forever,* and Robert De Niro in *Casino.* He has battled giant humans, such as the *Amazing Colossal Man,* and legend has it that he once rumbled with Lee Marvin.

Vic was once THE symbol of Las Vegas. Back in his glory days, the brightly garbed, forty-foot neon cowboy could be seen from miles away on Boulder Highway, enticing and directing would-be gamblers with his enormous automated arm to the Pioneer Club on Fremont Street. Locals used to joke that while Vic's mechanical voice box would welcome passersby with a friendly, "Howdy,

Podners," his flickering wink was actually saying, "Howdy, Sucker."

Vic was originally commissioned as a cartoon character by the Las Vegas Chamber of Commerce in 1947. Salt Lake City graphic artist Patrick Denner designed the mechanical and neon version of Vic, and the famous Young Electric Sign Company built him at a cost of $25,000. He was placed above the Pioneer Club in 1951.

For a long time, Vic was the most prominent sign in Las Vegas, which has its advantages, such as getting in the movies. But it also has its disadvantages, like getting shot at.

In 2000, Vic got a total makeover, including a different shirt. In an interview he gave to the Las Vegas Sun in June of that year, he confessed that "I've had more work done on me than Cher, lemme tell ya."

In 1966, Lee Marvin was in Vegas during the making of *The Professionals*, a cowboy movie filming in the Valley of Fire. The cast was staying on the sixteenth floor of the Mint, directly across the street from Vic. Tiring of Vic constantly saying, "Howdy, Podner," into their windows, Marvin and other cast members took matters into their own hands. Using movie props, they fired steel-tipped arrows and, according to some reports, actual bullets, into the defenseless Vic. Sparks flew everywhere, the statue started crackling, and "Howdy, Podner" was heard no more.

Marvin's co-star Woody Strode writes in his autobiography that he was the one who did the deed while Marvin was asleep. But the police and newspapers blamed Marvin, who already had a reputation as a wild man, and he was only too happy to accept irresponsibility and the publicity that went with it.

Whether the complaint was made with words or arrows, this incident silenced Vic for decades. He would not speak again until the late '80s, and only a few years later he became silent again. Vic's waving arm went gimpy around the same time and has remained motionless since. Over the years, as his color began to fade and his neon lost its luminosity, Vic was covered by the long canopy that now envelops Fremont Street. To add injury to insult, the once popular Pioneer Club is now a gift shop.

In 2000, Vic got a total makeover, including a different shirt. In an interview he gave to the *Las Vegas Sun* in June of that year, he confessed that "I've had more work done on me than Cher, lemme tell ya."

Of course it's not all bad news for one of the city's most recognizable faces. Vic got "married" a few years ago in a highly publicized wedding to the beautiful and leggy former Sassy Sally, now Vegas Vicky. Vegas Vicky sits atop the Topless Girls of Glitter Gulch bar, right across the street from Vic's perch.

Vicky showed up on Fremont Street in 1980. Those who call her Sally do so because Sassy Sally's was the name of a casino that she was adjacent to. She was designed to kick a leg out over the street, but she never did manage to do this. If you stand in the right spot on Fremont Street, you can see Vic and Vicky side by side and imagine the time when downtown Vegas was the place to be.

It's said that some nights Vic will climb down from his roost, stroll over to his comely cowgirl wife high above the nudie establishment and engage his sensual supercolossal spouse in marital pleasures. It would be interesting to see a drunken Lee Marvin try to put an end to that.

Wendover Will

Most people do not realize that Vic is part of a tall neon family and that his relatives live in other towns in Nevada. Vic's big brother, Wendover Will, welcomes people to Nevada as they travel from Utah on I-80. Standing sixty-three feet tall and looking much like Vic with both arms moving, Will was once listed in *Guinness World Records* as the "world's tallest mechanical cowboy."

It is said that Will is named after William "Bill" Smith who in 1926, opened up a gas station and convenience store just off Highway 40 in Wendover. A solitary light on top of a pole in front of his State Line Service Station served as a beacon for weary travelers crossing the barren Salt Lake desert. When gambling was legalized in 1931, Smith's Service Station became the State Line Casino.

In 1952, Will showed up in town, a grandiose replacement for the single bulb. Will, like Vic, was designed by Patrick Denner and built by YESCO. But unlike Vic, Will had nothing to say, at least vocally. Over the years, the phrase "This Is the Place" could be seen at his base from the Utah side and "Where the West Begins" from the Nevada side.

The State Line Casino was sold in 2002, and the new owners of the property, the Nugget Casino, decided they didn't want Will. Rather than trash him in some neon boneyard, they offered him to the city of West Wendover (the town's official name since 1991). The town fathers were delighted to accept, and after acquiring Will, they gave him a major makeover and moved him to his present location on Wendover Boulevard.

Fixing up Will cost about $200,000. Money came from a grant from the Nevada Commission on Tourism as well as donations from businesses and individuals. YESCO, still sentimentally attached to its neon creation, also helped with the restoration.

"Wendover Will" Welcomes You To

WEST WENDOVER NEVADA

River Rick

Another mechanical cowboy, River Rick or Laughlin Lou, stands above the Pioneer Casino in Laughlin and looks out over the Colorado River. He showed up in 1981 when Margaret Elardi, who was an owner of the Pioneer Casino in Vegas at the time, bought the Colorado Club and changed its name. And installed Rick.

Rick is new to the game but is promoted as Vegas Vic's first cousin. He was built by YESCO and is based on Patrick Denner's design, although Denner was unaware of this. Rick's arm moved, and he vocalized the familiar "Howdy, Podner." In all, he seems more like a tribute to the original than anything else.

These Boots Were Made for Rustlin'

In the early days of the West, cattle rustling and horse thieving could put an hombre at the end of a rope quicker than a jackrabbit can jump across sagebrush. Times had changed by the 1920s; the automobile was fast becoming the preferred mode of transportation, Prohibition was the law of the land, and bootlegging was a crook's way to riches. So when two ranch hands who worked for the Utah Construction Ranch near Elko noticed that a couple head of cattle were missing on a regular basis, they were mystified. Especially since there were no horseshoe or boot prints that might help in catching the rustler. They scratched their heads in consternation and wondered just how cows could be induced to wander off on their own. Either that or an invisible rustler was at work.

Determined to solve the mystery, they decided to watch the cattle more closely. One afternoon the men noticed that two more cows were missing; they saddled up and followed hoof tracks into a clearing. Seeing the missing cattle nearby, the men knew they had finally got the drop on their rustler.

They hadn't reckoned on the ingenuity of Crazy Tex Hazelwood.

"Guess you got me!" Tex exclaimed as the ranch hands crept up on him, guns drawn.

"Didn't think you'd miss a few head o' cattle," Tex explained wearily. They had. More importantly, the men wanted to know how the no-account cowpoke had pulled the theft off. "Say, Tex, how'd you manage to—?"

Tex silenced him by pointing to his feet. Both men stared in amazement.

Fastened to Tex's boots with straps were shoes that he had cleverly fashioned using cow's hooves on the

bottoms. The only tracks he left were those of the hapless cow whose hooves formed the bottom of his rustlin' shoes.

The sheriff took Tex and his shoes into custody. Tex stood trial for cattle rustling and was found guilty as charged. For the next few years, he cooled his heels at the state prison in Carson City. Upon his release, the old cowpoke headed back to Elko, where he continued to get in and out of trouble. That is, until a bullet marked the end of Crazy Tex's days.

Anyone who wants to marvel at the ingenuity of the Elko cattle rustler can take a look at Crazy Tex's rustlin' shoes at the Northeastern Nevada Museum in Elko.

Neon Boneyard

It doesn't take much of an imagination to envision the spirits of Las Vegas of long ago when traipsing through the Neon Boneyard. More cool than spooky, this is the opportunity of a lifetime for lovers of old-fashioned Vegas kitsch.

Just a short distance from the Fremont Street Experience, the non restored historic signs sit inside a fenced and guarded three-acre lot and have been the backdrop to the Tim Burton movie *Mars Attacks* and at least one CSI episode. Here are the beautiful, gaudy, worn-out husks of such Sin City icons as the oversized Silver Slipper from the hotel and casino of the same name, the entrance sign to the Golden Nugget, and the original giant pirate skull from Treasure Island. The collection ranges from the 1940s to the present and could teach a history of signage over the last sixty years to anyone who takes the time to notice how the colors and typography have changed and evolved.

No one needs a degree in the graphic arts to appreciate the difference between the pre-neon World War II–era "Time to Swing to Standard Wholesale Supply" sign and the vastly more modern, post-neon "Burger King" symbol.

The Neon Boneyard is open by appointment only on Tuesday–Friday between 11:00 a.m. - 5:00 p.m. Other days and times are subject to staff and volunteer availability.

Little White Wedding Chapel's Tunnel of Love

How many times has this happened to you? You're driving around town with the love of your life, and you'd like to make that eternal marital commitment, but you don't have the time to deal with the hassle of pulling into a parking space, turning off the engine, and worst of all, getting out of the car and walking all the way to the front door?

Well, your worries are a thing of the past, because the Little White Wedding Chapel Tunnel of Love has just made matrimony even more accessible to the chronically lazy.

"I had always dreamed of a big fancy church wedding," admitted the newly blushing bride, the former Miss Becky Sitsalot, from the comfort of the passenger seat in her husband's red 1991 Bronco II, "but when it came right down to it, the whole walking down the aisle

thing just wasn't for me. Some of those aisles are like seventy-five feet, and if I wanted that kind of exercise, I'd join a gym. I just wanted to get married, not compete in some decathlon."

"Exactly," concurred bridegroom Barry Doeslittle. "This was cool because we were going to go to Mickey D's but that line was too long, so I noticed the Little White Chapel's Tunnel of Love drive-through was a lot less crowded. I was going to get down on one knee, but this guy behind us started laying on the horn, so instead, I simply looked into her eyes, but not for too long, because I didn't want to get into an accident and get my insurance all jacked up. Anyway, I asked her, 'Are you really hungry for cheeseburgers or would you rather order off-menu, and have a super size of me for the rest of your life?' "

Becky's eyes glistened as she recounted that magical moment. "Well, I started crying right then and there because he's always been a big romantic like that, and then I started screaming because Barry almost ran over this old lady."

"She just walked out in the middle of the street," Mr. Doeslittle interrupted. "I slammed on the brakes and thought, Oh, great, now my insurance is going to get all jacked up, but I've gotta give her credit, she jumped aside pretty quick for a woman of her age."

At this point, the bride produced an iPod and slowly scrolled to the folder entitled OUR WEDDING.

"Barry made this whole folder filled with love songs from sometime in the '90s, because that's when we met. Look!" she exclaimed, pointing, "Michael Bolton doing 'Love Is a Wonderful Thing,' the Proclaimers singing, '500 Miles,' and 'Chumbawamba' just because he knows

I love that song."

"Basically I just borrowed a friend's CD called 'Nineties Hits,' and downloaded them, because searching through all my CD's would have been a lot of work," offered Mr. Doeslittle.

"I love you, Mr. Doeslittle," said Becky apathetically.

"I love you, Mrs. Sitsalot-Doeslittle," retorted Barry in a lackadaisical manner.

"And we both love the White Wedding Chapel Tunnel of Love." They unenergetically spoke in unison, and then, as if on cue, they held hands, turned up the iPod, and serenaded each other, almost comatose, to Celine Dion's "When I Fall in Love," as they drove carefully but passively into the languid Las Vegas night.

Author note: I made up the entire preceding story. I tried to get an interview with an employee at the White Wedding Chapel but was told they don't give statements to writers. According to their Web site, www.alittle-whiteweddingchapel.com, the drive-through was added to the chapel in 1991 to make marriage easier for the handicapped, and it became such a novelty that many able-bodied people have exchanged their vows at the chapel's window. I still believe this story is not only plausible but "probably word for word truth."—Joe O.

Lock Your Love at Lovelock

"Fasten a lock on the chain and throw away the key, thus uniting your love for eternity."
—Lovelock Chamber of Commerce

Outside the historic Pershing County Courthouse, a newly constructed structure invites couples to symbolically affirm their devotion by placing padlocks on a chain fence. A billboard on Interstate 80 beckons:

**DON'T LET LOVE PASS YOU BY,
LOCK YOUR LOVE EXIT 106 TO MAIN STREET.**

This tourist attraction is the brainchild of representatives of the Lovelock/Pershing County Chamber of Commerce and the China Market. It all began when chamber members visited China and signed a sister province agreement between the state of Nevada and a Chinese province. To commemorate the event, Lovelock representatives presented a replica of a Lovelock Cave duck decoy to people of the province.

In turn, Chinese representative Limin Liu visited Nevada. Lovelock's name intrigued her, and she was amazed that no one had capitalized on it. She told Lovelock officials that people in the Yellow Mountain area of China have a tradition of placing locks on trees and other landmarks to symbolize their love, which served as the inspiration for the creation of the Nevada version of the Chinese tourist attraction.

The Lovers Lock Plaza was dedicated on Valentine's Day of 2006. According to a brochure given out by the chamber of commerce, Lovelock is now "the nation's official love-locking destination. It is said that as long as the lock remains on the chain, the love will endure."

The chamber of commerce sells official Lovelock locks, although you can bring your own. Downtown businesses sell locks and will engrave your name on them.

"Everybody who is locking their love has a great story to tell," says JoLyn Laney of the Nevada Commission on Tourism. Lovelock lovers can post their love stories on a Web site or drop them in the "lock box" at Lovers Lock Plaza.

Lovelock seems to be growing fast, but there is plenty of room for expansion, and Lovers Lock Plaza will likely quickly grow to dominate the park behind the courthouse.

Giant Flashlight at U.N.L.V.

In a town where things that aren't supposed to be big are huge and everything that's huge shoots its luminosity toward the skies, it's ironic that the giant flashlight commissioned by the University of Nevada, Las Vegas, doesn't.

Located in the plaza between the Judy Bayley Theater and Artemus Ham Hall, the thirty-eight-foot, 74,000-pound black steel flashlight does not give off the kind of beam you'd expect from a tool of that magnitude. The reason for this is quite simple; it was constructed so that the "lens" faces the ground.

The aptly named *Flashlight* is the creation of the husband-and-wife team of Claes Oldenburg and Coosje van Bruggen. In the late '50s, Swedish-born Oldenburg was a happening guy, prominent in the pop art scene. He and Coosje were known for making things like squishy, soft drum sets and giant erasers. The two had already made a few big outdoor sculptures when U.N.L.V. art professor Tom Holder met Oldenburg in the late '70s; Holder suggested that Las Vegas would be a great place for another.

The sculpture was quite controversial when it was first unveiled in 1981. It seems that many of the good folks of Nevada assumed they'd be receiving something along the lines of a nineteenth-century garden sculpture, even though Oldenburg's portfolio is filled with similarly giant everyday pieces. From clothespins to hamburgers, Oldenburg has built his reputation on making the utilitarian grandiose.

Lippincott, Inc., a North Haven, Connecticut, foundry, fabricated the sculpture, which is made of steel painted with

WHITE KING

ENTRANCE

polyurethane enamel. It was driven cross-country on the back of a flatbed truck, doubtless to the bemusement of late-winter travelers. *Flashlight* was erected at the U.N.L.V. campus on March 11, 1981.

Art critics have since pontificated that Oldenburg was giving a sly commentary on the glitz and neon of the casinos just a couple miles away from the hallowed halls of the university. Perhaps the artist is acknowledging that mere artwork cannot challenge the spectacle that is the Las Vegas Strip.

Although cities all over the world have commissioned the Oldenburgs' giant-size art, and his stature rose in 2000 when he received the National Medal of Arts from President Clinton, some locals still feel that *Flashlight* would be more at home with the gaudy lights on the Strip. If only it came with giant batteries.

World's Largest Polar Bear

The Commercial Casino in Elko is home to what it bills as the World's Largest Polar Bear. The ten-foot four-inch-tall, 2,200-pound stuffed polar bear has been in the casino since 1958. The Commercial Casino has an important place in Nevada history as the birthplace of big-name entertainment in casinos. You would expect that Las Vegas would have this distinction, but on April 26, 1941, the Commercial booked Ted Lewis, "High-hatted Tragedian of Jazz," and his orchestra for an eight-day run in its newly built lounge.

In 1958, the casino's owner, Red Ellis, brought the bear, named White King, to the Commercial. King is said to be the winning entry in a contest to bag the world's largest polar bear. An unknown Eskimo killed him in Alaska on an unknown date. What is known is that Ellis acquired King and brought him to Elko, where he has stayed in a specially constructed display case to this day.

Berlin Wall Urinal

It is surprising to notice how many people using the men's restroom at Main Street Station, a casino and hotel in downtown Las Vegas, are not surprised that they are urinating on, or a least in front of, a chunk of the Berlin Wall. Of course, they may be thinking about the game they just left and not their aim.

Numerous antiques adorn Main Street Station, including a chandelier from the Figaro Opera House in Paris and stained glass from Lillian Russell's Pittsburgh mansion. All of the *objets d'art* used to belong to a Florida-based antiques collector and businessman named Bob Snow.

In Orlando, Snow had created the very successful Church Street Station, an entertainment complex housing many different nightclubs, which had been THE place to go. Snow figured he could transfer the formula to Las Vegas, with the added benefit of a casino. He pulled every trick in the book, including using eminent domain, to acquire property and build Main Street Station. But what worked in Orlando did not work in Vegas, and Snow filed for bankruptcy in 1991, after less than a year of operation. The Boyd Group reopened the Station in 1996, after sinking $45 million into renovating it.

When they reopened, a three-ton, five-by-ten-foot section of the Berlin Wall was in place in the men's room. Bob Snow had purchased the chunk in 1990 for $17,500, and when Boyd bought out the Station, they got all of Snow's antiques and artifacts, including the wall chunk. A Vegas newspaper quoted Dave Brendmoen, then Main Street Station spokesman, as saying, "We get a lot of comments from people who think it's a fitting and appropriate end to the Berlin Wall—it was a thick, steel-reinforced piece of oppression."

A coating of clear sealant protects the graffiti-covered hunk of concrete from new graffiti and stray urine streams. So, if you're feeling angry, there's a place in downtown Vegas where you can literally piss on communism and get pissed off about eminent domain, or at least 50 percent of the population can. As the Main Street Station's brochure, "Guide to Artifacts, Antiques and Artworks," says, "Sorry, ladies."

Brothel Art Museum, Crystal

The disappointment of some experiences in life cannot necessarily be predicted by any amount of forewarning, like when you went to see that movie that everyone told you sucked—and you found out they were right.

Such is the case with the Brothel Art Museum. Its billboard in Pahrump has lured many a curiosity seeker some twenty-five miles up the road to the small town of Crystal, where the main industry is prostitution. The billboard makes the dubious claim that the Brothel Museum is "the Oldest Tourist Attraction in Southern Nevada." The minimal Web site promises equally astounding

things, such as "Paved Roads."

Perhaps this is the place to note that, although Nevada is the only state in the nation where prostitution is legal, this is not the case in Las Vegas and Reno. Prostitution is not legal anywhere in the counties in which these two cities sit: Clark and Washoe. This leaves Sin City officially without a brothel. But there are plenty within driving distance, as in the town of Crystal.

The first thing you will notice about the Brothel Art Museum is that it looks more like a bar than a museum because it is. The "museum" exhibits can be found on the walls of the Crystal Springs Bar and Restaurant. Most of what could be considered art is not about prostitution.

Instead, one corner is devoted to prints of cowboys (and not even real cowboys; these are all portraits of famous actors from western movies). There is a lot of stuff on the walls about prostitution, but it is mostly yellowed newspaper clippings shellacked onto stained wood. Some of it is interesting, though. If you are looking for information about Nye County's infamous brothel wars, you might come here instead of a library. Accounts of the fire bombings and arrests cover most of one wall.

"It was the Wild West out here twenty or thirty years ago," said Rico the bartender, who also plays the role of museum curator. "There were some bad people out here. They were basically shooting each other and blowing each other up." So much for historic detail.

The highlight of the museum is a skeleton, upright in a glass-fronted display case, next to the bar's small stage. She goes by the name of Agnes. The bartenders will tell you all kind of tales about this skeleton. One of the stories is that she was a prostitute who was caught stealing and had her hands cut off as punishment

(the skeleton is complete, except for hands). Another legend is that she was entombed in a wall and found years later. But the reality is that she looks a lot like the type of skeleton sold to schools for anatomy lessons.

One bartender told me that the museum has been around since the "early '70s" and that the man who owns the brothels in town also owns the bar . . . uh . . . museum.

That man would be Joe Richards. Richards has been the subject of scrutiny and controversy as of late, but one has to wonder if there is a brothel owner who hasn't been. He was recently brought up on charges of bribery, but what put Richards and Crystal in the national news is his deal with the infamous "Hollywood Madam," Heidi Fleiss. In November 2005, Fleiss announced that she was partnering with Richards to open what she called a stud farm: a brothel catering to women, providing male prostitutes. The old Cherry Patch Ranch, the building adjacent to the Brothel Art Museum, was its planned location. But the plans changed. Fleiss and Richards ended their business relationahip after one week, and some suspected the whole thing was a publicity stunt.

Or was it? In late 2006, Fleiss announced that construction of a new building for her brothel in Crystal had begun. If it does happen, it will bring some more traffic to the Brothel Art Museum. If you happen to drop by, please bring some brothel-themed art with you and donate it. I have seen better art in a whorehouse.

Broken Beech Beside Beatty Brothel

Drivers traveling through the small town of Beatty, ninety miles north of Las Vegas, can't help but notice a dilapidated airplane by the side of the highway a few miles north of town. The crashed and trashed plane sits in front of a dirt road heading to Angel's Ladies Brothel.

There are lots of stories about how it got there. To an outsider, it seems strange that an airplane would be there at all, but rural Nevadans know better. Many of the desert brothels have dirt airstrips nearby, complete with wind socks and landing lights. The red light outside a Nevada brothel is likely to be at the top of a tall pole as a signal to incoming private planes.

One of the stories about this particular plane, a Twin Beech, is that it belonged to a pair of high rollers who decided to drop in, literally, to the brothel. They were both drunk, and they crash-landed the plane. This did not stop them from spending the night at the brothel, however, and in the morning they got a ride back to Vegas, abandoning the plane.

But that's not how it happened. The real story is that the plane has been there since 1979, when the brothel was called Fran's Star Ranch. It's a remnant from a skydiving contest that was an annual event for some California skydiving clubs. Fran's gave out prizes to the people who could come closest to landing at a marked spot, one of the prizes being a half-hour freebie with a girl of your choice.

One year, after letting the divers off, one of the planes came down for a landing. A witness described it this way: "I remember thinking, 'Boy, Spike sure got down fast!' Then a long cloud of dust and the Beech was ninety degrees to line of flight. We landed close by, and the two female-type passengers got out laughing, asking 'Can we do that again!'"

The plane was totaled, but insured. The pilot stripped it and offered to have it hauled off, but Fran asked him not to. It was getting attention, so why not leave it out front? Over the years, it became a magnet for curious travelers, who might be lured into Fran's for free coffee and other things that are not free.

The brothel was sold in the mid-'90s to a couple named Mack and Angel Moore, who renamed it Angel's Ladies. And here's where things go from weird to weirder. The new owners were both born-again Christians who had sold their Oregon-based funeral business to become brothel owners. They didn't seem to find anything strange about this, but some people did.

Their story got national attention. An article in the March 2002 issue of *Harper's* magazine said, "Angel's is the closest anyone is going to get to a Christian brothel."

You can still see the crashed plane if you swing by the former Fran's. But you won't get any of that old-time religion while patronizing the world's oldest profession. The Moores have moved on to other things. They sold the business in September 2005 to a company called JBJ Ranch, Inc. Of course, the crashed Beech plane out front was part of the deal.

Shoe Trees of Nevada

Just three miles east of Middlegate, on Highway 50, the Loneliest Road in America, is a cottonwood tree adorned with hundreds of shoes, draped like Spanish moss across its branches. And like Spanish moss, the shoes have a romantic air to them, for they are said to represent reunited love.

In the early '90s, the story goes, a couple had just been married in Reno and were making their way back to their native Oregon. They had their first fight under the cottonwood tree, where they had decided to camp for the night. Words flew, and the bride threatened to walk all the way back to Oregon. The man took her shoes and threw them into the tree, saying, "If you're going to walk home, you're going to have to climb a tree first." After half an hour of cooling off at the Middlegate Station bar, he drove back to make up with her, but they could not retrieve the forlorn pair of shoes. In a show of unity, the husband threw his own shoes into the tree, and they continued home. One year later they returned, bringing their new baby with them, and threw a pair of baby shoes into the branches.

That is one version of the tale told by Rus and Fredda Stevenson, owners of Middlegate's only watering hole. The specifics of the story change, even in a town where the population totaled eighteen before Clark Cole, a resident of the town, died.

What is certain is that the Middlegate Shoe Tree has been "growing" shoes for at least twenty years. Locals have even seen skis, snowshoes, and diver's flippers hanging from its branches. The Shoe Tree has garnered so much attention that it was the focus of a June 2002 article in the *San Francisco Chronicle*, which describes it this way:

Dangling in the branches of the 70-foot cottonwood tree in a gully a few yards off Highway 50 are what looks like every type of footwear in existence—cowboy boots, tennis shoes, running shoes, sandals, ballet slippers, high-heeled shoes, even Rollerblades. Red, blue, yellow, green, black, striped, red-and-white, yellow-and-black. All sizes, all shapes.

They've all been tied together in pairs or clumps and flung high into the branches, with the lowest shoes at least 15 feet off the desert floor. Most hang from shoelaces, others are linked by bras or underpants. Stand beneath the tree, and you can hear the relentless Nevada wind rustle through the shoes and the leaves like a leather-and-cloth version of a muffled wind chime.

We had heard tongues wagging, claiming that this was not Nevada's sole shoe tree (get it?). A well-traveled Nevadan told us there was another, near Hawthorne, but that the last time he had traveled that way he could not find it. Eventually, we found a map listing an "Old Shoe Tree" on Highway 95 a few miles south of Schurtz.

The Old Shoe Tree ain't what it used to be. It is obvious that the tree had been pruned of its fruit and the branches cut down by some heel with a chain saw. Or perhaps the reason for the missing branches was that they could no longer bear the weight (or maybe the odor) of the shoes. Although it now looks almost dead, there is hope. Leafy new sprouts are blooming on branches, and a few shoe clusters have even reappeared on the old tree.

Giant Prospectors

There are a few big men still digging for treasure in Nevada. Motorists driving from Reno to Carson City via Highway 395 will pass by the Washoe Prospector, an eighteen-foot-high fiberglass man kneeling down examining a rock.

He was originally on the rooftop of the Claim Strike Casino in Sparks, which opened on July 2, 1979. The casino closed four months later, but the prospector remained for years. Eventually, the city council ran him off, claiming he was an eyesore. He now squats happily at his current location, outside Dan Salzwimmer's Chocolate Nugget candy store.

Motorists traveling on I-15 have another chance for a photo op with a giant gold panner. Just pull over at the Jean exit and head to the Gold Strike Casino. Two huge concrete prospectors watch over the entrance to the parking lot. The Gold Strike opened in 1990 and has changed ownership several times. A veil of corporate bureaucracy obscures the origins of these prospectors, but at least they get to keep their jobs with each new landlord.

And there is a grinning prospector at the east entrance to the Fremont Street Experience in downtown Las Vegas. He may be grinning not so much because of the glowing nuggets in his pan, but at the prospect of removing money from tourists' pockets.

From left to right: The Las Vegas prospector, the Jean gold panner, and the Washoe prospector.

Fitzgerald's Lucky Forest

Fitzgerald's Casino in Reno seems innocuous enough—a working class casino themed around Irish good luck charms. Like most casinos these days, it's owned by a corporation.

Lincoln Fitzgerald, the casino's namesake, had a less wholesome reputation. Relocated from Detroit, he opened up the Nevada Club in Reno in 1947. Fitzgerald was already facing bribery charges in his native Michigan, and suspicion about his connections to organized crime was intensified when, on November 18, 1949, he was the victim of a "midnight alley ambush."

A sawed-off double-barreled shotgun greeted the casino owner as he was leaving his garage. He was not expected to live, but Fitzgerald truly had the luck of the Irish and an incredible will to endure. Although the shotgun blast reportedly severed his spine, Fitzgerald survived with only a limp. He went on to open the Nevada Lodge, the Silver Dollar Casino, and finally, in 1976, the casino with his name on it. He died of natural causes at the age of eighty-eight in 1981.

Fitzgerald's Gaming Corporation took over the casino in April 1985 and added the tacky tourist enticement known as the Lucky Forest. Located on the building's second floor, the Lucky Forest celebrates superstitions of luck.

The addition of a skywalk in 1998 caused some clearing of the forest, noticeably diminishing the size of the wishing well, but most of the artifacts remain. Rub the belly of the statue of Ho-Tei, Buddhist god of contentment and happiness, rub the genie's lamp, rub the lucky horseshoes—it seems they want you to rub almost everything in the forest. A display case in the center illustrates celebrity superstitions, although some of the choices of personalities seem dated, even for the mid-'80s. For instance, Babe Ruth collected hairpins for luck, actor Robert Morley had a lucky Teddy Bear, Tony Curtis

BLARNEY STONE

THIS RARE STONE IS FROM BLARNEY CASTLE IN COUNTY CORK, IRELAND. THE ONLY OTHER STONES EVER PERMITTED TO LEAVE THIS LEGENDARY IRISH LANDMARK WERE USED IN THE CONSTRUCTION OF THE LUCKY FOREST EXHIBITS INSIDE FITZGERALDS CASINO/HOTELS. IN THE BEST TRADITION OF BLARNEY, RUBBING THIS STONE WILL SURELY MAKE YOUR DAY LUCKIER.

DEDICATED MARCH 17

believes white cats are bad luck, and Peter O'Toole has a lucky pair of green socks.

There is a pair of socks in there, but do you really think O'Toole would give up his lucky socks? They are a facsimile for display purposes. But other items, such as the horseshoes, are the real deal. Nineteen eighty-six Preakness Champion Snow Chief wore one of them, and horse-racing legend Secretariat wore the other.

The literal cornerstones of the Lucky Forest are from Blarney Castle and were acquired by the casino in March 1987. There is only one Blarney Stone, at the top of Blarney Castle in Ireland. It is said that if you achieve the difficult task of kissing the stone while hanging upside down and backward hundreds of feet above the ground, you will be blessed with eloquence. Although the stones at Fitzgerald's are (obviously) not THE Blarney Stone, they are genuinely from the castle, according to a letter from the Blarney Estate.

Although the tradition is to kiss the stone, Fitzgerald's once again asks you to rub them, perhaps because asking people to put their mouth on the corner of a building is not good for business.

SECRETARIAT'S SHOE
(Rub It For Good Luck)
He was, perhaps, the greatest three-year-old race horse of all time. In 1973, Secretariat became the first Triple-Crown winner in 25 years. He won the Kentucky Derby in a record time of 1:59 2/5 and took the Belmont by an astonishing 31 lengths for another track record (2:24). Both marks stand untouched today, and had not there been a breakdown in the timing equipment at the Preakness, he surely would have set that record as well.
(Horseshoe courtesy of Calumet Farm)

LINCOLN FITZGERALD
This gaming pioneer, who founded the Nevada Club, Nevada Lodge, Silver Dollar Casino and Fitzgeralds Casino/Hotel, thought this color forest was extremely lucky. Widely thought of his namesake for prosperity, he carried his passion for the Crown to costumes, decorations and even cards.

TONY CURTIS
Instead of avoiding black cats, veteran actor Tony Curtis feels that WHITE cats are a sign of bad luck.

PETER O'TOOLE
Green socks on Lawrence of Arabia make for Good Luck if they happen to clash with wardrobe. In the event the actor is a stickler over the dress code rule.

Roads Less Traveled

No matter what state you may call home, there always seem to be certain roads that are not quite right. These strange byways possess a special kind of aura that sets them apart from ordinary streets. Perhaps nowhere is this more true than on the strange roads that crisscross Nevada's rugged terrain. Throughout the state, we find supposedly cursed thoroughfares and hills where the laws of gravity just don't seem to apply. There is a highway where drivers need to be cautious not only of other motorists, but of extraterrestrial traffic too! Some other lost highways meander across the barren landscapes seemingly coming from nowhere and going nowhere else. Strange things happen out there on these seemingly endless expanses of desolate asphalt.

Over the generations, the tales of these bizarre byways have become part of our state's local lore. They have proved their potential to strike fear into people's hearts as well as inspire personal reflection in those who travel them. Whatever the reason, one fact is indisputable: There are some roads that possess a certain kind of indefinable, yet undeniable power. So gas up the car, pack plenty of potable water, and let's head out for a road trip on a few of them now.

Touring Nevada's Lost Highway

Nevada is laced with lonely roads. Empty two-laners stretching to endless horizons, shimmering in the relentless Great Basin heat. U.S. 50 may get the billing of the Loneliest Road in America, but for me, the three hundred miles of U.S. 6 are much lonelier. Today there are only two living towns along that entire three-hundred-mile stretch: Tonopah and Ely, and neither one is exactly a bustling metropolis. Highway 6 is the very definition of "the road that goes from nowhere to nowhere else."

One hot afternoon in 1991, I stopped at the truck stop and motel complex called Coaldale at the junction of 6 and U.S. 95, hoping to get a flat tire repaired. The place was sleeping deeply. I stopped in the empty restaurant-bar, and the bartender told me he'd lost his mechanic "a while back." Not surprisingly, I passed through again in the summer of 1998 to find the entire location abandoned. By the summer of 2006, the restaurant was burned to the ground and the rest of the location smashed, ransacked, and littered with junk cars. Will there be any trace of Coaldale's existence in ten years except on old maps?

Set the cruise control on 80 across the desert for another hour and you'll finally roll into Tonopah. The town is just a shadow of its early twentieth-century silver-boom self; its western approach is littered with abandoned motels, trailer parks, and gas stations. The once fabulous Mitzpah Hotel and Casino built in 1908 recently closed its doors for the last time. It remains the centerpiece of this dusty little town, a dark-eyed stone monster looming over the highway. On the eastern fringe of town is Bobbie's Buckeye Bar, a brothel. When I stumbled upon this cluster of tired pink buildings in 2004, I found the back door wide open and the interior only mildly ransacked and vandalized. The sexy black velvet paintings and pink-tiled heart-shaped tub were still intact, the back rooms still furnished and filled with clothes. Judging by the expired liquor license, the place had been abandoned less than a year.

Two years later, I found Bobbie's in the same condition and locked up tight with shiny new padlocks on the doors.

Climb back in the car and motor east along 6. In minutes, you're deep into the American outback. It's about fifty miles to Warm Springs and the junction of the Extraterrestrial Highway. Warm Springs is long dead, nothing but a handful of rickety shacks and empty one-room cinder-block buildings. It's odd that it's still shown on most current maps, because there's been no habitation here for decades. Perhaps the cartographers felt the need for SOMETHING to be here on this long and empty road, but it's more likely that no one bothered to check this remote location for any signs of life.

Because most tourists will turn off toward Rachel and Area 51 on State Route 375, the next hundred and twenty miles of 6 will be just about as isolated as you can get in the American West. Odds are pretty good that you may not see a single car over the next hundred miles, especially if you travel at night—which can be a surreal experience. It's easy to lose track of time and space. The endless stream of reflectors and white stripes slips by, your only source of visual stimulation. Highway hypnosis kicks in, and you may find your speed creeping up. Eventually, you'll need to pull off to the side of the road to have a stretch. Turn off the car and walk fifty feet. The silence will be deafening; the sense of loneliness palpable. Better crawl back in the car and get going before something weird happens. *—Troy Paiva*

Right background Tonopah, inserts left to right, Bobbie's Buckeye Bar, Coaldale, Tonopah airport

David Brenner's Magnetic Hill

David Brenner is a legend in the world of comedy. He invented "observational comedy," the style that put Jerry Seinfeld on the road to fame and fortune. Brenner has been a part of the Las Vegas scene since 1971, when Buddy Hackett booked him into the main showroom of the Sahara, after seeing him on *The Tonight Show*. Soon after he came to Vegas, Brenner found out about a strange stretch of road. He's been taking people out to see it ever since.

"I heard a rumor from some old guy who lived here that there was a magnet field on the way to Mount Charleston that literally, when you stopped your car and put it in neutral, as you took your foot off the brake, it would pull your car backwards, up what would be a slight upgrade, going backwards." Brenner thought it sounded like a tall tale, but it was real. "[The] old man took me out in a truck; he had a little pickup truck, . . . we went flying, up that hill, backwards!"

Now a believer, Brenner takes visiting friends out to the site. "I would show them this wonderful magnetic field, and people didn't believe me. And then some friends of mine figured out, 'You know what he's doing, he got his car rigged, so that when he puts it in neutral, he hits something, and it activates the reverse, and he's conning us, you know he's messing around, that's Brenner, making a joke.' So I said, 'Alright I tell yah what, you guys rent a car, and we'll go out there, and if the car doesn't go backwards by itself, I'll give each one of you fifty dollars and pay for the rental. But if it does go backwards, you'll each give me fifty dollars and you'll pay for the rental.' They said, 'Okay, you've got a deal.' So we went out in a rental car, and of course they rented a Cadillac, a big heavy car, and we went out there, and I won two hundred dollars."

Brenner was kind enough to take *Weird Las Vegas* out to the spot and did not even charge the $50 fee.

Finally we were there, about thirteen miles down Highway 157 off the 95 turnout. Brenner pulled to the side of the road, on what appeared to be a slight downward grade, put the car in neutral, and let off the brake. Sure enough, we started to go backward along the shoulder. He said that he had not taken anyone out to the spot in about eight years, and he seemed like a kid playing with an old toy as he showed us the effect. He made a U-turn to the other side of the road. "Now let's see something interesting. Let's see if it's on this side of the road if we put it in neutral, if we go forward. Here we go." Brenner put the car in neutral, and sure enough, it gained speed as it went "up" the road. He got very excited. "Look, we're going up, in neutral, 10, 12, 15 miles an hour, 20 miles an hour, 25 miles an hour . . . wait, wait, wait, we're hitting 30 miles an hour, and I'm in neutral . . . 30 miles

an hour . . . look at me now, 40 miles an hour!"

At some point, we seemed to have gone over the hump and were now going downhill. David turned the car around to see how far the "field" extended. We drove past the slight downgrade to a very steep downward slope a few yards beyond it. He put the car in neutral, took off the brake, and nothing happened—which is weird because we should have been rolling down the hill. David got really excited.

"We're not going down. I'm in neutral, and we are not going down! This is MAJOR down, and the car in neutral doesn't move, with a real steep grade down." And this was something to be excited about, as there was no way that this could have been an optical illusion, as some claim these "magnetic roads" to be.

Brenner did not discover the spot, but he is the person keeping its legacy alive, so we here at *Weird Las Vegas* have dubbed it David Brenner's Magnetic Hill.

Extraterrestrial Highway

If you are driving along the Extraterrestrial Highway (Highway 375) in southern Nevada late some night and happen to catch a glimpse of something mysterious in the sky, don't be alarmed. It's probably just another UFO. Sightings of strange glowing craft that speed across the night skies have been reported along this lonely stretch of road for several years.

Opinions are divided as to whether these UFOs are visitors from distant planets or our own government's secret aircraft tests. But no one is disputing the highway's reputation for being the place where UFOs are most often seen. In fact, State Route 375 was officially named the Extraterrestrial Highway on April 18, 1996

Travelers hoping to catch a glimpse of craft from far-

away worlds traverse the Extraterrestrial Highway, scanning the night skies. Much of the land beside it is unfenced public territory, so stargazers are free to camp and watch the sky to their hearts' content. Amid the myriad of sparkling stars, UFOs will be easily discernible here, some one hundred miles north of the bright lights of Las Vegas.

Aside from UFOs, the standard sights along the Extraterrestrial Highway are typical desert: sagebrush, sand, and rocks. A few cattle ranches are scattered across the landscape of the highway, which connects U.S. 93 to U.S. 6. As it winds its way across the Tikaboo, Sand Spring, and Railroad valleys, the ninety-eight-mile-long highway is in open range; cattle sometimes wander out onto the road and can cause serious accidents. So designate a driver to keep a eye on the road while you search the Extraterrestrial Highway for something from out of this world.

Highway of Death

Las Vegans have been sharing tales of strange happenings out on Blue Diamond Road for years. During the '40s and '50s, the area near Blue Diamond was desolate and forgotten, a favorite out-of-the-way location for mobsters to dump the bodies of their victims. People who regularly drive the highway claim to have seen some strange sights here: a ghostly man who frantically attempts to flag down cars and a woman who wanders aimlessly in the middle of the road, only to vanish when a vehicle swerves to avoid her.

The Blue Diamond Road (Route 160) is the fifty-mile length of highway that runs from Las Vegas to Pahrump. Locals have dubbed it the Highway of Death, and for good reason. With a speed limit of 65 mph, the once rural road is now congested and dangerous. Recently seventeen people died in a six-month period. Blue Diamond is being widened in certain locations, and highway engineers are looking into the feasibility of lowering the speed limit. But some Las Vegans believe the road is cursed and that people will continue to meet death on it regardless of the speed limit.

One of the most famous people to die in a car crash on Blue Diamond was Las Vegas resident and retired porn star Anna Malle (Anna Hotop-Stout). Malle perished in an accident when the car in which she was riding attempted to make a U-turn and was smashed into by an oncoming vehicle. Sadly, Ms. Malle was not wearing a seat belt, and she joined the ranks of those who have met their fate on the Highway of Death.

Highway 50—The Loneliest Road in America

Nevada is one of the fastest-growing states in the nation. Both the Las Vegas area and the Reno area have been experiencing unprecedented growth for a number of years. In spite of this, there are still many open areas. While Nevadans find this open space appealing, others tend to look at the deserts that cover most of the state and see nothing but loneliness and monotony.

In 1986, *LIFE* magazine dubbed the 287-mile stretch of Highway 50 that crosses central Nevada from Fernley to Ely the Loneliest Road in America. It still is. Traffic has increased significantly since then, but odd as it may seem, motorists on Highway 50 can still cover a lot of asphalt before seeing a gas station, roadside diner, or another vehicle. Refugees from the congested freeway systems of big cities, relax. It's just you and the road that stretches on and on and on. Lonely or lucky depends on your viewpoint.

An American Association of Automobiles spokesperson once blithely claimed that Nevada's section of Highway 50 was empty and devoid of points of interest. Not so! Historians know that the Loneliest Highway in America not only parallels the original pony express route but was also part of the Lincoln Highway, built in 1926 to encourage motorists to travel from one end of the country to the other.

Every fifty miles or so, travelers on the Loneliest Road will come upon a small city: Fernley, Fallon, Lovelock, Austin, Eureka, Ely. Each offers something unique to the explorer, the historian, or the just plain curious. Back on the road with nothing in sight but the desert and the distant mountains, it's easy to imagine how the pony express riders and the pioneers who trudged across this area so long ago must have felt. Far from civilization with nothing but a fierce determination to get to their destination, they were probably too busy to think about being lonely.

Thanks to the *LIFE* article, those who enjoy a challenge eagerly filled up their gas tanks and water jugs and headed out for the Loneliest Road in America. As word spread, Highway 50 became so popular that, turning lemons into lemonade, the Nevada Commission on Tourism now offers would-be motorists an "I Survived Highway 50" kit.

We wonder what all those pioneers and pony express riders would make of that.

Ghosts Across Highway 50

When you're traveling along Highway 50 near Lane City at the stroke of midnight, you may see several glowing lanterns off in the distance.

This, locals say, is a ghostly procession of long-dead Chinese miners making their way toward their homes. These spectral Chinese men are reminders of an event that occurred over a hundred years ago at the nearby Chainman Mine in Robinson Canyon. This tragic event, some say, was the inspiration for Stephen King's haunting novel *Desperation*.

Mining has always been the lifeblood of these small northeastern towns. But mining is not without its dangers, as one unfortunate group found in 1876. According to that story, a group of Chinese miners were deep in the Chainman Mine when a cave-in occurred, leaving the men trapped.

In 1987, a mining company excavating in Robinson Canyon cut into the chamber where the miners perished and discovered the miners' remains, which were removed and buried. But that's not the end of the tale. After that, the ghosts of the abandoned miners started walking across Highway 50 at midnight, trying to return at last to their homes and families. Or so the story goes.

Geiger Grade

In the rush to profit from the riches of Virginia City's gold and silver lodes, the town grew from a small mining camp of makeshift tents to a budding cosmopolitan city of nearly twenty thousand. As millions of dollars worth of ore was taken from the mines, the need for homes, hotels, saloons, schools, and every other comfort and necessity of civilization increased. One of those necessities was for a more direct road from the Truckee Meadows (Reno) to Virginia City.

To fill that need, D. M. Geiger and J. H. Tilton developed a toll road known as Geiger Grade, which opened in 1863. It was a treacherous passage that forced stagecoach drivers and wagon teamsters to slow their vehicles to a crawl as their horses maneuvered its hairpin turns. More than one team made a misstep, sending horses, coaches, and passengers crashing down into the canyons below. And, under cover of thick desert brush, robbers often waited to rob innocent passengers of their valuables.

In 1936, the old Geiger Grade toll road was replaced by a wider paved road, known as State Route 341, or the Virginia City Highway, a two-lane road that winds its way up around the mountainside to Virginia City. One of those mountain passages that demands a driver's undivided attention, Geiger Grade is especially dangerous during heavy snowstorms. Some travelers say that the lonely ghosts of men who lost their lives in the canyons below still walk this road late at night. Others tell harrowing tales of a ghostly stagecoach that careens around the mountain and tumbles down into the canyon, only to disappear at the moment of impact.

We're not sure about the ghosts. But at the lookout, you'll see breathtaking views of the surrounding mountains. Down in the canyon is the original Geiger Grade road from the nineteenth century. Farther up from the canyon are Dead Man's Point and Robbers' Roost, two places where many men met untimely deaths and numerous stagecoaches were stopped and robbed.

At the Virginia City Highlands, nearer to Virginia City, the road straightens for a few miles. Sightings of the wild horses that roam freely here are common. There are no street lights on Geiger Grade; when the sun goes down, it is pitch-black. Nighttime drivers should use extreme caution, as horses sometimes wander onto the highway.

Donner Party Camped Here

The Millcreek Townhomes are located in the Donner Springs neighborhood in southeast Reno. The ill-starred Donner Party, whose members were forced to resort to cannibalism in the snow-covered Sierra, camped in this area in the early fall of 1846 before their fateful journey into California.

In remembrance of their having stopped here and the tragedy they later endured, a memorial, state historical marker 253, was erected on a strip of land between townhomes on Chirnmore Drive. It is not easy to locate. There are no signs directing drivers to the monument. In fact, many Renoites aren't even aware of its existence. Those who are say there is something eerie about the monument. Several people have reported seeing a ghostly little girl walking near it. At least one person who stopped at the monument had an experience she still cannot explain. She recounted this chilling tale to us:

"It was around ten o'clock. My husband and I were on a tour with about ten other people. As soon as the bus pulled up across the street from the little monument, my head started pounding. My legs felt wobbly, and I didn't know if I should get off the bus or not. My husband laughed at me for letting my imagination run away with me. He helped me off and walked over to read the plaque. I wandered over near the grove of tree stumps. 'Do you see that?' A woman asked. I looked toward the direction she was pointing and saw this glowing mistlike thing was slowly floating toward us. Everyone else was at the monument. She and I were the only ones who noticed it.

Maybe it's a ghost. I laughed.

She nodded. 'Yeah right. Maybe it's one of the Donner Party,' she said. 'Did any of them die here?'

Before I could answer, the guide explained that what we saw was nothing but fog. Low ground fog was especially prevalent in this area at this time of year, he explained. 'It's what causes pogonip.' Someone else agreed—those eerie ice crystals that sometimes form in the air.

I couldn't wait to tell my brother, a history buff, about the memorial. We decided to go see it the very next night, right after we got off work. I got out of the car and shined the flashlight on the plaque. While he was reading, we heard what sounded like someone crying. 'Is that a baby or a coyote?' my brother asked. Whatever it was, it didn't sound like any baby or coyote that I've ever heard.

All of a sudden there was this low moan like someone was in pain. My brother shined his light toward the grove of cottonwood tree stumps. While we watched, this raggedy old man just sort of appeared up from stumps and started toward us. We backed away to the monument. But he kept coming toward us and howling.

'Who is that?' my brother asked. I couldn't answer him; I was so scared my knees were knocking. Then the man zoomed right up to us and hung there in front of us, staring. I have never seen anything like that. We could see an old man's face, but we could see through it too.

'It's a ghost!' I said, still scared out of my wits. Let's get out of here. Suddenly there was a loud rush of cold air that almost felt like we were being pushed toward the car. Come on, I said. It wants us to go.

We ran for the car and locked the doors. Soon as I turned the key, the ghostlike thing floated back to the grove and dissolved into the ground. I'm not coming back here.

Ignoring me, my brother said, 'It seemed to be angry or very sad.'

Since a man named William Pike was the only member of the Donner Party who died while the party was encamped here, I wonder if we saw his ghost that night. His death remains a mystery; some believe he shot himself accidentally, and others think he was murdered. I'm not really sure what we saw that night. Maybe it was William Pike's ghost trying to tell us what really happened to him."

Desert Ghosts

Take a vibrant, tacky, all-consuming twenty-four-hour casino city like Las Vegas and compare it with Nevada's dry, dusty, quiet ghost towns. It seems they are worlds apart, but are they really? As Vegas is today, those ghost towns once were full of people following shining dreams of unlimited money and all it can buy. Regardless of whether those dreams were played out in the spin of a roulette wheel or in picking at a wall of rock hundreds of feet below the ground, the reward, or lack of one, can do funny things to people. In a moment, the wealthy can lose everything and the destitute can become fabulously rich. Old friends become bitter enemies. This highly charged emotional atmosphere has made Nevada the perfect breeding ground for spirits, old and new, playful and malicious. So join the *Weird Las Vegas* team as we see why, in Nevada, the haunted house always wins.

Elvis Has NOT Left the Building

The King of Rock was a flop when he first performed in Las Vegas, at the New Frontier Casino in 1956. The city was not ready for Elvis in those days. His fans were teenagers, much younger than the Vegas crowd, so he wisely moved on to bigger and better things.

By 1969, things had changed. His fans had grown up, and Elvis was booked into a brand-new casino called the International, which would eventually change its name to the Hilton. He sold out every show there. Vegas loved Elvis, and vice versa.

The King had a private suite on the thirtieth floor of the Hilton. After the shows, he would take the freight elevator from the nightclub to the upper floors, avoiding fans who were all too ready to rip the rhinestones off his white jumpsuit. It is in the backstage area and the freight elevator that the ghost of Elvis has appeared again and again. The apparition is an image of Elvis that first shows itself as a solid person, but then slowly fades away. Many employees of the casino reported seeing the spirit, but it might have remained just a rumor—until Wayne Newton went public with his own sighting.

In his autobiography, *Once Before I Go*, Newton states that while performing at the Hilton on the same stage on which Elvis had performed, singing a song that Elvis had sung, his attention was caught by a glimmer of light from one of the balconies. He looked up and saw what he recognized as the ghostly figure of Elvis Presley. Strangely, he writes, the ghost was wearing the

exact same outfit as the statue of Elvis that is in the Hilton lobby. Newton knew Elvis very well in life, so he knew what he was seeing. It was the King. He has no doubt.

Elvis is also said to haunt a residence called the Hartland Mansion, located at Sixth and Charleston. It's a place he stayed in from time to time when he wanted to escape the crowds of the Hilton, and apparently, he grew attached to it, even from beyond the grave.

One final bit of Elvis weirdness: The Haunted Vegas

Tours group performed a séance to contact Elvis on August 16, 2004, the twenty-seventh anniversary of his death. The séance was performed at the Greek Isles Casino, down the street from the Hilton. Just as the proceedings began, at 2:01 p.m., storm clouds rolled in, thunder clapped, and a huge downpour pelted the roof. As the séance continued, water leaked into the casino and onto the stage where the tour group was gathered. As soon as the séance ended, the clouds cleared up and the storm ended. The significance of this was realized only later. It seems that the day Elvis died, Las Vegas was hit by a freak rainfall that lasted for three hours and, according to the *Review-Journal*, caused the roofs of "countless businesses and homes [to] collapse under the weight of constant rainfall."

Death, Taxes, and the Ghost of Redd Foxx

Born into poverty in 1917 Chicago, Jon Elroy Sanford was nicknamed 58th Street Red during his teens and later changed his name to Redd Foxx.

Growing up poor, Redd Foxx was no stranger to street crimes and running cons—anything to avoid a real job. He even went so far as to eat soap to avoid the draft, claiming he was a victim of constant abdominal pain. Not surprisingly, the reprehensible behavior of his youth led not only to jail time but, as is often the case, to a career in show business. Redd Foxx developed into a superstar in the '70s in the hit sitcom *Sanford and Son,* Norman Lear's African American answer to his other creation, Archie Bunker.

Foxx loved Vegas. He lived there and delighted in spending his money there. But despite earning millions of dollars, by the 1980s Foxx had squandered almost all his wealth. Gambling, women, and drugs were a few of his vices. Alimony put another huge dent in his wallet, and to make matters worse, he failed to pay his taxes.

In 1989, in front of news cameras, the IRS busted into his home on 5460 South Eastern Avenue and seized all his possessions—while Redd stood in the street wearing little more than a pair of briefs and a disgusted look on his face. Two years later Foxx died, bankrupt and bitter.

Dan Parker, a neighbor of Foxx's, said that Redd had told him that when he died, he would return to Vegas. Foxx's mortal remains did indeed return for his funeral and burial. His immortal remains went back to his old house.

An Elvis Presley impersonator called Jessie Garron purchased Foxx's house and began to notice strange goings-on: doors slamming, voices in empty rooms. A psychic confirmed that it was the ghost of Redd Foxx and that he was upset about the IRS taking his house, the place where he was said to have been at his happiest.

Other former tenants say they often heard unexplained noises, saw doors open and close themselves, and window blinds rustle without the benefit of wind.

> **Foxx loved Vegas. He lived there and delighted in spending his money there. But despite earning tens of millions of dollars, by the 1980s Foxx had squandered almost all his wealth.**

Many paranormal experts conclude that Redd's tough upbringing won't allow him to "let go" and travel away from this mortal plane. Some suggest that having his belongings ripped from him during his final years made the old con man decide to stick it to the afterlife's version of "the man" and stay where he was most contented.

The building is now owned by Shannon Day Realty, Inc., but Redd Foxx, cosmic prankster, refuses to be evicted. Karen Henderson, a real estate agent at the company, has heard someone walk through the lobby, only to van-ish when she goes to welcome the visitors. Henderson says,"Just about any time I wear sandals or open-toed shoes, I get the sensation that the tops of my feet are being tickled. I just chalk that up as Redd being in a playful mood."

To honor the spirit of Redd Foxx, Shannon Day has painted little red foxes all around the agency. "I have seen some things I can't explain," says the current owner of Redd's former property. "I don't necessarily believe, but if he is here, I want him to feel welcome."

Bugsy's Back

Benjamin "Bugsy" Siegel is credited by many as the person who envisioned modern-day Las Vegas. A gangster from New York and a member of Murder Incorporated, Bugsy was sent to Los Angeles to oversee a horse wire service (which reported race results to the East Coast) and take over an actors' union. At the time, Billy Wilkerson, owner of the *Hollywood Reporter*, was building a casino/resort on the then desolate Highway 91. He made the mistake of inviting Bugsy and some of his mobster friends to invest in the venture. Predictably, the mobsters took over, and the casino became the Flamingo, Bugsy's pet name for his mistress, Virginia Hill. Unfortunately, Bugsy lost too much of his gangster pals' money in the venture, and his life came to an abrupt end at Virginia Hill's Hollywood mansion, courtesy of a rifle bullet in the back of his skull.

Shortly after his death, his ghost was sighted in his former Vegas digs: private rooms at the Flamingo that became known as the Presidential Suite. Frequent reports told of the appearance of a full image of Siegel, whom guests recognized from the gangster's many published photos. And it wasn't just his own suite that the ghost of Bugsy visited. A man staying in the room below the suite recounted his experience on the Web site www.theshadowlands.net. Seems the man awoke in the middle of the night to see a white-coated figure

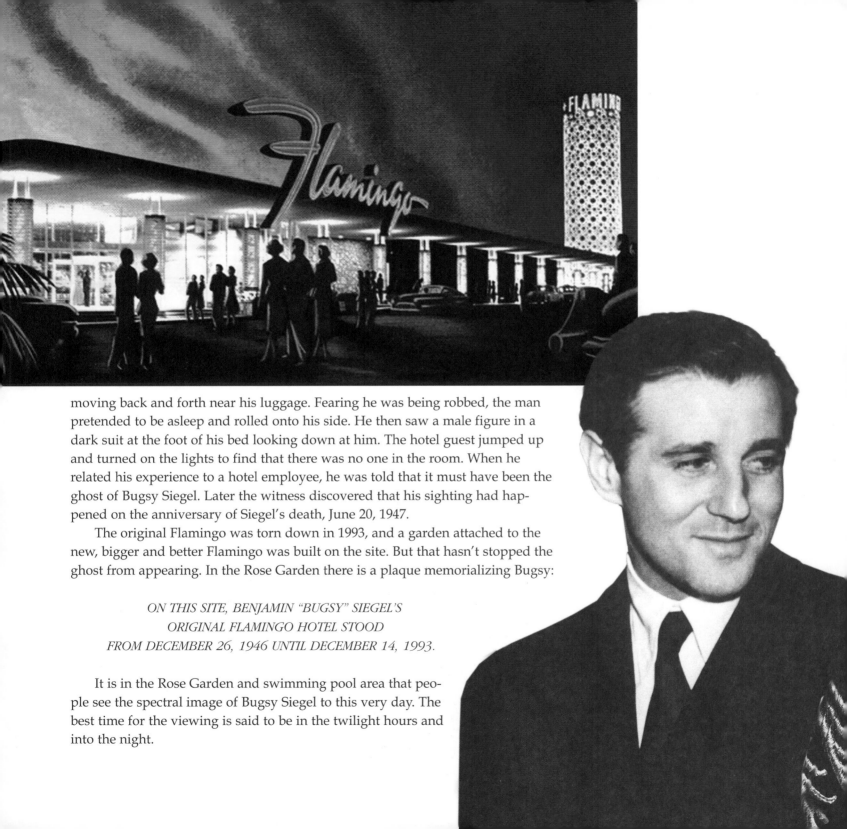

moving back and forth near his luggage. Fearing he was being robbed, the man pretended to be asleep and rolled onto his side. He then saw a male figure in a dark suit at the foot of his bed looking down at him. The hotel guest jumped up and turned on the lights to find that there was no one in the room. When he related his experience to a hotel employee, he was told that it must have been the ghost of Bugsy Siegel. Later the witness discovered that his sighting had happened on the anniversary of Siegel's death, June 20, 1947.

The original Flamingo was torn down in 1993, and a garden attached to the new, bigger and better Flamingo was built on the site. But that hasn't stopped the ghost from appearing. In the Rose Garden there is a plaque memorializing Bugsy:

ON THIS SITE, BENJAMIN "BUGSY" SIEGEL'S
ORIGINAL FLAMINGO HOTEL STOOD
FROM DECEMBER 26, 1946 UNTIL DECEMBER 14, 1993.

It is in the Rose Garden and swimming pool area that people see the spectral image of Bugsy Siegel to this very day. The best time for the viewing is said to be in the twilight hours and into the night.

THE "BUGSY BUILDING"

ON THIS SITE, BENJAMIN "BUGSY" SIEGEL'S ORIGINAL FLAMINGO HOTEL STOOD FROM DECEMBER 26, 1946 UNTIL DECEMBER 14, 1993.

THE HOTEL, WHICH HOUSED 77 ROOMS, INCLUDING THE NOTORIOUS MR. SIEGEL'S "BUGSY SUITE," OR "PRESIDENTIAL SUITE," AS IT WAS SOMETIMES REFERRED TO, WAS UNIQUE IN MORE WAYS THAN ONE. THE WINDOWPANES, FOR INSTANCE, WERE BULLET PROOF, AND, ALTHOUGH THERE WAS ONLY ONE ENTRANCE TO THE TOP-FLOOR SUITE, THERE WERE FIVE POSSIBLE EXITS. THIS INCLUDED A HIDDEN LADDER LEADING FROM THE HALLWAY CLOSET TO A BASEMENT TUNNEL, WHICH LED TO AN UNDERGROUND GARAGE, WHERE BUGSY ALLEGEDLY HAD A CHAUFFEURED GETAWAY CAR AWAITING AT ALL TIMES.

BUT MR. SIEGEL'S PREOCCUPATION WITH SAFETY AND ESCAPE ROUTES PROVED TO BE GEOGRAPHICALLY MISPLACED. ON JUNE 20, 1947, 300 MILES FROM LAS VEGAS, AT THE BEVERLY HILLS MANSION OF HIS GIRLFRIEND, VIRGINIA HILL, BUGSY WAS KILLED IN A HAIL OF GUNFIRE BY UNKNOWN ASSAILANTS.

SINCE THAT DAY, THE FLAMINGO HAS CHANGED OWNERSHIP 3 TIMES, INCLUDING ITS FINAL SALE FROM KIRK KERKORIAN TO THE HILTON HOTELS CORPORATION IN 1970.

BENJAMIN "BUGSY" SIEGEL

CARLUCCIO'S TIVOLI GARDENS

Liberace Lingers at Carluccio's Tivoli Gardens

Kelly Stanley has been a bartender at Carluccio's Tivoli Gardens since 1987. She's a seasoned veteran of the barroom and knows how to calm down belligerent booze hounds and reason with drunken dipsomaniacs. There is, however, one patron of Carluccio's that even Kelly Stanley has no power over: the ghost of Liberace, the former owner of the Italian-style eatery.

The first time Ms. Stanley encountered the flamboyant phantom was shortly after she started working at Carluccio's. "I got a call saying, 'Don't bother showing up.' All the freezers had gone out, and the food went bad. It seemed bizarre because there are a few different freezers and refrigerators and they all went out at the same time, but the electricity didn't go out. Later on we realized it was Liberace's birthday, and no one had made a big deal of it."

Since then, Ms. Stanley has always gone out of her way to honor the late entertainer- restaurateur on the anniversary of his birth. Sometimes she'll get out an old set of dishes that was used by the restaurant back when Liberace was alive and set a place for him at the bar. It seems to work, as long as no one makes jokes at the former owner's expense.

"One Halloween we're all at the bar and I start telling some off-color Liberace jokes and

anley recalls. "we weren't being mean. It's a bar, and
e tell jokes, but it happened to me three times that
ght. I got hit in the head three times by wine bottles
at were in a rack three feet away." When the Liberace
kes stopped flying from the bartender's lips, the bot-
es stopped flying into her skull.

Ms. Stanley isn't the only one to encounter the
ano-playing poltergeist; there are plenty of accounts
om co-workers and patrons alike. Frightened women
ve burst out of the ladies' room screaming that they
d been locked inside, perfectly balanced trays of food
ve been knocked over, water faucets
rn on and off by themselves, and
ere are hysterical poundings on
e door, but no one is ever on the
her side.

Oscar Ortiz has worked as a waiter
Carluccio's for almost a decade,
d he claims to have actually seen a
quined cape–wearing Liberace
miling back at him as he polished
ne of the many mirrors. Ortiz was

maintains Liberace is a good ghost who wants to make
sure his place is kept clean.

Carluccio's Tivoli Gardens is located directly next
door to the Liberace Museum in the Liberace Plaza.
Kelly Stanley recommends the Seafood Diablo. She also
recommends you not tell any Liberace jokes if you don't
want to be bonked on the noggin by a bottle of Merlot.

A Vegas paranormal investigation group claims that Fox Ridge Park in Henderson has a swing set that is haunted by a boy who was killed by a drunk driver. To make things creepier, as you approach him, the boy's face contorts into the face of a demon, just before he disappears.

It sounds like urban legend, but something truly weird does seem to be happening at the park. It was on the route of Haunted Vegas Tours, and many people who took photos there got very bizarre images. The local loiterers who frequent the park have taken back the night and run the tourists off . . . at least for now.

Swing Shift at Fox Ridge Park

Fox Ridge Park is a pretty weird sight at 1:00 in the morning. My friends and I heard about this place and we decided to check it out. So one night, we all drove up there to see if we could see anything. We get there—it's cold, it's really dark except for those little lampposts along the sidewalk. I swear, there was not a sound or anybody there. We're chilling for about five minutes and an eerie silence took over us all. We're standing there by "the swing" and we all just stop talking. From the direction of the swing we didn't see anything, but we heard something. Someone said "goodbye" in a little childlike voice. We all froze up and we just stared at each other. We weren't sure what it was, so we decided it was time to leave. It was a little weird that we all heard that and it scared me. I was bummed that I didn't see anything, but maybe we'll go back to see if we can catch anything.
—*Monty Gruber*

Ghost of the Union Plaza Hotel

Las Vegas claims to be the home of many a rhinestone-studded celebrity from the great beyond, but one of this city's more active phantoms is a blue-collar specter who now resides at Jackie Gaughan's Plaza Hotel, formerly the Union Plaza Hotel.

Dancers, comedians, magicians, and stagehands at this Fremont Street landmark have all supposedly encountered the ghost of a lighting man who hanged himself onstage after hours and has regretted that final, fatal decision ever since.

Employees often report seeing a "cloudlike figure" in their dressing room, feel as though they've stepped into a "cold spot," or sense they have been grabbed or shoved, only to realize there is no one else in the vicinity. Lights will flicker off and on during performances, and people have felt gusts of air blow on them without benefit of drafts or electrical fans. The departed worker is apparently more of a fun-loving trickster than a screaming banshee. He's been known to knock heavy objects to the floor and move or hide show props.

Dancer Sara Costa, a.k.a. Sarafina, claims this deceased lighting technician has a randy side to him as well. According to the leggy beauty, he has appeared in her mirror while she puts on her makeup, and she has even glimpsed him watching in the dark narrow hallways as she's changing in and out of her suggestive outfits.

Sarafina's co-worker, magician Jenny Alexander, claims to have seen the spirit on one occasion. It was late at night, and she believed she was the only person left in the theater until she saw a male figure passing in front of the light booth. She cautiously strode down the constricted one-way passage to the tiny electronic workplace, only to discover an empty space.

It would seem that even in death, this proletarian poltergeist does not seek the spotlight, preferring to remain undetected behind the scenes.

Pioneer Saloon, Goodsprings

There are some places that are said to be haunted, but they just don't give off that identifiably phantasmal feeling. Then there are other places, places that just ooze a sincerely eerie vibe and leave even skeptical sorts almost believing in things that go boo in the night. The Pioneer Saloon is exactly that kind of place.

Located a little over thirty miles south of the Las Vegas Strip, the Pioneer is one of the oldest bars in the state of Nevada. Constructed of stamped-metal tin in 1913, when the young mining town was home to about eight hundred souls, the Pioneer was a hotbed of action in its day. And some say the old clientele like the place too much to ever leave.

Bartender Karen DeWitt swears she's being watched over by the spirit of a friendly old prospector. "I've seen him around a few times. Sometimes you can catch him out of the corner of your eye, and sometimes he's just sitting there on a barstool. He never bothers anyone. . . . Looks just like you'd expect him to. He's in his seventies or eighties, white hair, beard. . . . He's just making sure I'm doing all right."

Cindy Niles, another employee of the saloon, also knows of the phantom patrons. "I've heard some pretty wild stories. One day a woman was looking at that picture over the door and asked me what that man's name was. I asked her why she wanted to know, and she said she had just spoken to him a couple hours ago but didn't see him leave. I had to tell her he was a regular here for years, but he had just died last week. She was pretty shaken up, but that stuff happens here."

Not all the apparitions are affable. This watering hole's most infamous otherworldly visitor is a spirit once named Paul Coski. Coski, in this life, was a no-account, cheatin' drunk of a varmint who, according to the coroner who presided after his death, "could whip any two men in or around Good Springs [*sic*], and made a practice of doing the same once in a while when he would get to drinking."

The framed coroner's report hangs on a wall of the saloon, serving the dual purpose of informing customers of part of the building's history while covering up some stray bullet holes. These are left over from the night in July 1915 when Coski was shot dead after being caught cheating at cards. A couple of slugs in his side killed him instantly, but according to some, that doesn't stop him

from still showing up and causing trouble.

A burly man in his early fifties who frequents the Pioneer claimed to have seen Coski one night. According to the patron (who prefers anonymity), "I walked out of the bathroom, and I saw this mean-looking guy staring at me. He was bleeding and wearing clothes out of a cowboy movie. . . . Next thing I know, he's gone."

The Pioneer is also well known as the place where Hollywood leading man Clark Gable drank himself into a stupor as he waited to hear the fate of his wife, Carole Lombard. Her plane had gone down in a fiery plane crash at nearby Mount Potosi, and it took search teams days to reach the site. The cigarette holes that Gable created as he passed out from drink and exhaustion are on display in the cherrywood bar top. Some say the ghost of the long-deceased actress still comes in, looking to console her man.

The Pioneer Saloon is located at 310 West Spring Street. Swing by and say hi to some of its current and former regulars.

Ghost of Whiskey Pete

Located some forty miles southwest of the Las Vegas Strip, smack dab on the gambling side of the California/Nevada state line border, in the town of Primm, is Whiskey Pete's western-themed resort and casino.

Whiskey Pete's is a favorite destination of Californians who can't wait to get to Vegas to gamble, as well as those who haven't lost enough during their visit and want one more shot at the big jackpot before they finally admit defeat and return to their mundane worka-day lives.

The family-friendly, happy-smiling cartoon mascot that now symbolizes Whiskey Pete is apparently not an accurate depiction of the man who once operated a gas station/moonshine parlor on this land. Pete McIntyre has

been described as a cantankerous old man when sober, with a personality that turned much darker when fueled by his bootleg booze.

Before Whiskey Pete died of miner's lung in 1933, he had asked some of his boozing buddies to bury him vertically so he could watch over his beloved land. Legend has it that his friends were drunk and so exhausted from digging a grave that would contain an upright coffin that they gave up at a certain point and slid the peddler of the prohibited palliative sideways into his would-be eternal resting spot.

The term would-be is apropos because Pete was accidentally exhumed late in the last century while workers were building a connecting bridge from Whiskey Pete's to Buffalo Bills Hotel and Casino (on the other side of I-15). There was little doubt it was Pete McIntyre, based on

the bottle of whiskey clutched in his skeletal hand, the shock of red hair still peeking out of his cowboy hat, and the fact that his casket was found at a sixty-degree angle. The body was moved and is now said to be buried in one of the caves where Pete cooked up his moonshine.

The ghost of Whiskey Pete has been spotted at the resort by visitors and employees alike. Often he has been reported playing with light switches, knocking over glasses in the kitchen, rustling drapes and bed covers. There have even been accounts of patrons arriving at the hotel with their cars dangerously low on gas, only to find their fuel needles pushed to full when they return to their vehicles in the morning.

Whiskey Pete, a nasty old bootlegging codger in this life, seems to have turned into a fun-loving, gas tank–filling ghost in the afterlife.

Haunted Hoover Dam

Nestled below the Grand Canyon and straddling two time zones, Boulder Dam, also known as Hoover Dam, was billed as the eighth wonder of the world when completed in 1935. Hydrating and electrifying California, Arizona, and Nevada, the engineering marvel beckoned thousands of unemployed men and their families to southern Nevada in the wake of the stock market crash. According to author Marc Reisner, it "rose in the depths of the Depression and carried America's spirits with it." But Hoover Dam has spirits of its own.

Rumors of men drowned and preserved in the dam's 3.25 million cubic yards of concrete are untrue. One man was swept to his death when one hundred tons of wet concrete slid like lava down the dam's central slot, but his body—and those of the other ninety-five workers who died on the project—were recovered. Or so they say.

Workers today sometimes see a phantom in a hard hat riding the elevator, and a young man in blue coveralls wanders the central part of the powerhouse. Loosened bolts are blamed on a ghost who floats among the generators. And there may be more to come. Though currently patrolled by armed guards day and night, the dam's 726 feet of sloping concrete was a popular spot for suicides in the past.

Key Pittman and the Mizpah Bathtub

If you peek into the foyer of the Mizpah Hotel in Tonopah, you will find a pair of skeletons peering back at you. They're toasting and playing cards, as if remembering glories past. Those were the days when Tonopah was one of Nevada's most famous cities, thanks to Jim Butler's jackass.

The Tonopah tale goes something like this. While Jim Butler was prospecting for silver one day in 1900, his mule moseyed off. When Butler located the errant animal, he noticed a chunk of ore at the mule's foot. Stooping to examine it, he realized he'd struck it rich. Butler staked his claim, and news spread. Tonopah became Queen of the Silver Camps, a place where fortunes could be made overnight.

When lawyer Key Pittman heard about the money to be had in Tonopah, he and his wife left their home in Alaska and moved to the boomtown. A man who liked a good drink and a good business deal in about equal measure, Pittman quickly jumped into the business of mining. Eventually, he too made a fortune in the mines and later was drawn into the political arena. Dubbed the Senator from Tonopah, Pittman won one election after another.

But times change. The mines played out, and people moved on. Today Tonopah is just another small town on Highway 95 halfway between Reno and Las Vegas. The Mizpah Hotel is closed, though still remembered as the place where Jack Dempsey worked as a bouncer and Wyatt Earp dealt poker and drank shots. Howard Hughes gave the hotel a Hollywood connection when he spent his 1957 honeymoon with actress Jean Peters in a fifth-floor suite.

Like most old hotels, the Mizpah has its restless spirits. The ghost of a prospector, who is said to have died in a mine cave-in beneath the hotel, can be heard moaning on certain nights. And a beautiful young prostitute who was strangled by her jealous boyfriend in a room on the fifth floor still wanders the hotel, particularly the hallways of the fifth floor. She is known as the Lady in Red ghost and is said to tease unsuspecting hotel guests. People are even warned not to ask her to appear unless they really want her to.

One of the oddest stories connected with the Mizpah Hotel concerns the death of Senator Key Pittman. In 1940, the Democratic Senator was up for reelection. In failing health, Pittman was urged by his friends and family to slow down, lead a quieter life, and not seek a sixth term. The sixty-eight-year-old Pittman paid them no heed. He liked his good times too much to give them up.

On the night before the election, Key Pittman was drinking and partying elsewhere when he was struck dead of a massive heart attack. It was his habit to cast his vote in Tonopah, so his body was spirited away to the hotel. The corpse was kept on ice in the bathtub until it "won" the election, thereby ensuring another Democrat would take his place. The dead man won by six thousand votes.

But the really strange part of the story is that there are no ghost tales told of Pittman. From all appearances, he went serenely to the other side, apparently content to have died as he lived, in the middle of a good party.

> Like most old hotels, the Mizpah has its restless spirits. The ghost of a prospector, who is said to have died in a mine cave-in beneath the hotel, can be heard moaning on certain nights.

Gold Hill Hotel

Driving from Carson City through winding desolation, it's hard to believe Gold Hill was once home to thousands of men trying to earn a living by scratching the earth's surface. In a pucker in the canyon leading to Virginia City, where a few houses dot the surrounding hills, you'll find the Gold Hill Hotel, "the first edifice known to Nevada to be worthy of the name of hotel," according to the historical marker. Built as Vesey's Hotel in 1859, "it sits on the site of the first recorded claim on what became the Comstock Lode." Additions were made in the 1980s, but the original stone and brick edifice must be what keeps the ghosts around.

Gold Hill's miners were the highest paid in the world, so when fire belched from the mine's interior on April 7, 1869, it made world headlines. Thirty-six men were trapped and never

recovered—their corpses remain in the works to this day. Dozens more were dragged the 30 yards from the mine to the Gold Hill Hotel, and most died there, crushed by the collapsing mine.

The Gold Hill has some bona fide spooks. Rosie, a former housekeeper, keeps the scent of roses nearby as you approach Room 4 at the end of the hallway. William, a former owner, haunts Room 5. William died in a fire at the hotel and enjoys spooking guests. He scared one amateur ghost hunter by shaking the bed so violently he had to lodge elsewhere.

I had no such problem during our visit. The dying miners were dragged downstairs, and Rosie seemed to be absent. And I was tired. So the door latch moved on its own, twice. So?

About 2:30, while drifting off, it feels as though a cat is walking across my face, forehead to chin, like two little pads moving softly. Three hours later, the bed, the entire frame, moves in jolts. I think about a newspaper article I read about earthquakes in Nevada. Then the bed shakes up and down, briefly, and stops. Later I realize William is just trying to entertain guests. Perhaps he has no message.

I didn't sleep a wink. As I was checking out in the morning, Melodie the manager laughed and says, "William, he likes to kiss the girls."

Paranormal investigators are convinced the hotel is home to more than two spooks. Guests in rooms 10 and 11 have had their covers tugged off in the night; one woman lost her lighter, only to find it standing upright under the center of her bed in the morning. A trio of phantom children used to appear in the Great Room downstairs, play on the staircase, and hide in room 11. Despite the horrifying circumstances of the deaths in the hotel, the activity is prankish.

—Skylaire Alfengren

O l' Blue Eyes Is Back, and So Is Marilyn, at Cal-Neva Lodge

Nestled among tall pine trees and enormous granite boulders, the Cal-Neva at Crystal Bay is famous for its swimming pool, which is divided by a line representing the California/Nevada border, its breathtaking views of the pristine waters of Lake Tahoe, and a history that is peppered with underworld activity and movie star legends.

Frank Sinatra brought worldwide fame and notoriety to the Cal-Neva when he bought it in the early 1960s. Sinatra envisioned turning the lodge into one of the most spectacular spots on the north shore. But he also wanted a place where he and his friends, the famous Rat Pack, could come and get away from it all.

Sinatra built a nightclub that rivaled most of those in Las Vegas and Reno. He proudly appeared on stage at his new place and offered top entertainers like Ella Fitzgerald and Tony Bennett as well. Friends like Sammy Davis Jr. and Peter Lawford, brother-in-law of President John F. Kennedy, were frequent visitors. Marilyn Monroe came to the lodge with her husband, Arthur Miller, while filming *The Misfits* in Reno, and they were entertained lavishly.

Marilyn Monroe has another, less enjoyable connection to Cal-Neva. She would eventually die in Los

Angeles, apparently from an overdose of sleeping pills. A week before her death Marilyn sought solace at the Cal-Neva. Her life was falling apart. There were rumors of an affair with both President Kennedy and his brother, United States Attorney General Bobby Kennedy. But the beautiful blonde had suddenly become persona non grata with both the President and his brother. She placed numerous phone calls to both men, but none were answered. Those who saw her at that time claim she spent her last days in a drug-induced stupor, alone in the cabin Sinatra had assigned her.

Marilyn's cabin still stands at the Cal-Neva. Even with its million-dollar view of the lake, it seems somehow too small and rustic for such a glamorous star. Some people regularly come and stay there, hoping to communicate with her. And some say they have. They claim that when she speaks from the afterlife, Marilyn says she is quite happy and content to stay on at the Cal-Neva indefinitely. This might seem strange in view of the desperation of her last days at Lake Tahoe, but some of her happiest times were spent here as well.

One of Monroe's favorite haunts is the swimming pool. According to those who have seen the apparition, she swims from one side of the pool to the other, steps up to the rail, and vanishes.

> **A week before her death Marilyn sought solace at the Cal-Neva.**

One man who stayed at the Cal-Neva must have thought he'd died and gone to heaven. He was swimming alone in the pool one night when he happened to look across the water and saw Marilyn Monroe swimming toward him. As she swam closer, she smiled. And then, just like that, she was gone.

Frank Sinatra lost his gaming license when he gave Mafia don Sam Giancana access to the Cal-Neva, allowing him to stay in one of the chalets. Giancana was one of the undesirables named in the Nevada Gaming Commission's *Black Book*, a list of people who were never to be permitted entrance to any of the state's gam-

ing establishments. For his blatant disregard of the commission's regulations, Sinatra was forced to give up ownership of the Cal-Neva as well as his shares in the Sands in Las Vegas. It must have been a crushing blow for Ol' Blue Eyes, who had worked so hard to make the lodge his showplace.

It has been more than forty years since Frank Sinatra owned the Cal-Neva, but he is not forgotten here. The nightclub still bears his name, the Frank Sinatra Celebrity Showroom. Photos of him and his pals line the walls outside the room, and his piano is center stage. It's not surprising that this showroom and the backstage area are most often associated with Sinatra hauntings.

Several Cal-Neva employees tell of ghostly encounters with the singer they reverently refer to as Frank. One said he saw a figure he thinks was Frank walk across the stage. "It was like he was singing or entertaining an audience." Sometimes the sound of laughter will drift across the empty room and equipment will suddenly break down for no apparent reason. This usually happens when someone questions the Cal-Neva ghost stories.

Never doubt the powerful presence of Frank. During one afternoon rehearsal in the showroom, a member of a group scheduled to appear there made a joke about the ghosts of Frank and Marilyn. As soon as he said that ghost-sighting stories were nonsense, all of the group's equipment stopped working. The entertainers and their technicians tried for over an hour to see what was wrong. Finally they gave up. There was nothing more for them to do but leave the stage. It was the last time they joked about the ghosts at the Cal-Neva.

Word is out that the Cal-Neva plans to convert its high-rise hotel to condos. No doubt there will be plenty of takers. However, the organizers had better set aside a few of the rooms to accommodate the former owner and some of his spirited celebrity guests who never really checked out of the place.

Virginia City: Alcohol, Money, and GHOSTS

It's the largest living ghost town in the country. Here, tomorrow is yesterday and yesterday is always.

A smattering of mansions and warped wooden sidewalks on C Street recall a time when Virginia City—home of the Comstock Lode, the world's largest silver strike—was known as the richest place on earth. At today's rates, more than five billion dollars worth of silver (and a smattering of gold) was extracted from its mines. The strike helped President Lincoln win the Civil War and was responsible for making Nevada a state. Silver was so abundant that ore less than fifty percent pure was used to pave A, B, and C streets. They still sparkle in the sun.

Virginia City was no place for the timid or the teetotaler. Hundreds of men died in the mines and in drunken street brawls. As one local puts it, "We had fifty-two saloons and no town drunk. . . .They took turns. We still do that."

On October 26, 1875, an overturned kerosene lamp and the winds of the notorious Washoe Zephyr reduced the heart of the town to ashes. John Mackay, an Irish immigrant who became the richest man of his day, thanks to Virginia City silver, stepped in. Mackay personally dynamited the fire away from mines and homes. In the grand spirit of the West, the town was rebuilt, bigger and better.

By the end of the century, though, the mines had played out and the boom times were over. Most people drifted away, but some stayed and the town survived. The people who live in Virginia City today are proud and protective of their historic past, their Victorian homes—and their ghosts.

C Street

Virginia City's C Street boasts the most spooks per square inch in the United States. After dark, shadowy specters hang out amid the tourists on the city's board-walk. Mark Twain has been observed pacing as a "shadowy figure in a white suit" in the window of the *Territorial Enterprise,* where he got his start as a journalist.

Delta Saloon

The "suicide table" is a big draw at the Delta Saloon. As you drive into town, billboards invite you to "See the famous Suicide Table." The table is a morbid attraction with a bloody history.

Black Jake owned the place, but that didn't stop him from shooting himself in the head when he lost a huge amount of money playing faro, the game of choice of the nineteenth-century gambling halls. He was "bucking the tiger" a bit too roughly when he lost it all and blood cascaded onto the green felt. Two other owners killed themselves at the same table, the last when a miner walked away from the game with $80,000, a team of horses, and an interest in a gold mine.

If the suicides weren't enough to dissuade superstitious gamblers from playing at the table, the ghost of Black Jake started to show up and sit in on games. When unseen hands kept interfering with gaming, the table was finally retired to the back room. Years later, it was dusted off and put on display.

There are other ghosts lurking at the Delta, including a woman in a long white dress who haunts the staircase. Known as Delta Dawn, she has kept certain bartenders from organizing weddings upstairs.

Washoe Club

One of the most haunted saloons in the state, the Washoe Club sits below the long-deserted Millionaire's Club, a western palace where silver kings stayed up all night, drinking and playing poker.

Of singular interest is a spiral staircase in the center of the Washoe Club. One of several ways to enter the Millionaire's Club, it had no center supports and was built without the use of nails. The stairs are now unsafe for use by mortals, but they still get some use.

The most infamous haunting at the club is the spirit of a woman called Lena, who appears by the staircase and other places around the bar.

The most persistent story about Lena is that she once worked at the Millionaire's Club as a prostitute. One day the manager got into a fight with her and pushed her down the spiral staircase, breaking her neck and killing her. Poor Lena still wafts around the place where she met her sudden death, perhaps trying to come to terms with it, perhaps looking for revenge.

Another ghost who haunts the bar, flaunting the liquor laws, is a little girl who was killed outside the club. It is historical fact that a girl was run over by a carriage on the street outside; legend has it that she was pulled inside and breathed her last breath in the bar. She is sometimes seen inside, and people find little footprints in the dust of the unused portions of the building. Perhaps tiring of the barflies, she has also been reported in other parts of town. She wanders the city in a deep blue dress with ivory lace and a matching bow in her blond hair, and has been spotted playing with toy trains in the tourist shops. She's also shown up in photos taken during the annual ghost walk.

There are other hauntings at the Washoe Club. In the back of the building, a cold storage room known as the Vault is meant for beer, oysters, and other perishables.

However, the story goes that during the winter, when the ground was too frozen to dig graves, the room was used for the temporary storage of human corpses. The bodies were unceremoniously stacked ten high. The chilled-out ghosts seem to have grown attached to this stopover on their way to the other side. A TV crew filmed a failed exorcism that was attempted at the Vault. When a cameraman looked into a glass box the word "stop" appeared in the dust.

If you appear near nine p.m. and sit at the end of the bar, you might find a miner, reeking of ether. Drinking ether was a favorite stupor-inducing practice of the times. This gentleman may tap you on the shoulder or jab you in the ribs. You could be sitting on his favorite stool. So slide over—he's been coming to this bar longer than you have.

Nevada Death Trip

Death: *It is the greatest mystery of all,* and because of that it fascinates us. Whether we like to admit it or not, most of us harbor a deep-rooted curiosity about that fnal journey we will all make one day. Maybe it's just morbid interest, or maybe it's because pondering the passing of others gives us a chance to reflect on the temporary nature of existence and the inevitable approach of our own demise.

Fortunately, we can satisfy some of that curiosity in the cemeteries and lone burial sites located all around the state. These places of the dead offer us—the living—history, mystery, strange tales, and sometimes even humor. There are also infamous death spots where those who flirted with death life finally consummated their relationship with the grim reaper.

This chapter is dedicated to the dearly departed of Nevada. We can't say for sure if there is an afterlife for their souls, but we do know that when people die, their story isn't necessarily over. To the contrary, sometimes it's really just beginning.

Resting in Peace in Sin City

Las Vegas has eclipsed Hollywood as the entertainment capital of the world. Stars love it here, so much in fact that many have chosen to spend eternity in the city that never sleeps. Among the celebs buried here is onetime Heavyweight Champion of the World Sonny Liston, who rests in Paradise Memorial Gardens. His headstone reads simply CHARLES "SONNY" LISTON, 1932–1970 "A MAN."

Baseball great, pitcher Bo Belinsky, is buried nearby. In addition to his name and dates of birth and death, the words NO HITTER 5/5/62 are inscribed on his headstone, thus commemorating the no-hitter he pitched for the Los Angeles Angels against the Baltimore Orioles. And Sin City talk is that Wayne Newton, affectionately known as Mr. Las Vegas, has already reserved his final resting spot here in this tranquil cemetery.

Onetime bootlegger and reputed mobster Moe Dalitz reposes in the Garden of Eternal Peace section of Palm Memorial East. Many Las Vegans believe he picked up Bugsy Siegel's dream and ran with it, helping to make the city the glamorous gambling mecca that it is today. Dalitz came to Las Vegas in the late 1940s and opened the Desert Inn with his business partners. A generous man, this friend of the late mobster Meyer Lansky donated to several local charities throughout his life. In 1976, he was named Humanitarian of the Year by the American Cancer Research Center and Hospital.

A favorite Las Vegas story involves Dalitz's testimony during the 1950 Senate Special Committee to Investigate Crime in Interstate Commerce headed by Tennessee senator Estes Kefauver. When asked by Kefauver if his Las Vegas investments were financed by money he had made as a bootlegger, Dalitz replied, "Well, I didn't inherit any money, Senator. If you people wouldn't have drunk it, I wouldn't have bootlegged it."

> **Sin City talk is that Wayne Newton, affectionately known as Mr. Las Vegas, has already reserved his final resting spot here in this tranquil cemetery.**

Unmarked Graves of the Unknown Eighty-sixed

The phrase "You're eighty-sixed" is best known today as saloon slang. Many a bartender has ordered that unruly patrons be eighty-sixed from the bar, meaning they were no longer welcome. But did you know the term has its roots in old Las Vegas?

The story goes that when the mob ran the hotels and casinos there would be the occasional disagreement, but rather than politely asking the offending party to leave and not come back, the old-time gangsters did what old-time gangsters have done for years. They whacked 'em.

Now even in Bugsy Siegel's day you couldn't leave a body riddled with bullet holes right in the middle of a busy casino floor, so the corpse would be thrown into the trunk of a car and driven approximately eighty miles away from the city into the unpopulated nearby desert. A six-foot hole was then dug, and the carcass of the formerly ill-mannered victim was dropped in and buried.

Eighty miles out and six feet under, or eighty-sixed.

And that concludes today's lesson on terms that used to mean hiding a dead body so the cops couldn't pin a murder wrap on you, but now refers to boozehounds who have been banished from their favorite watering holes for being annoying jerks. Needless to say, we don't know exactly where in the desert these old-time victims lie. But they're out there.

The Dog Whose Name Must Not Be Spoken

The growth of Las Vegas owes a lot to the Boulder Dam. The dam was completed in 1936, five years after its beginning. By harnessing the Colorado River, the states of Colorado, New Mexico, Utah, Arizona, Nevada, Wyoming, and California prevented further flooding of farmlands and ensured electrical power and water for the western part of the country.

The work on the dam was grueling and dangerous. Anything that would make the day a little easier to bear was welcome. When a little black shepherd dog was born at the Boulder Dam work site, the men adopted him as their mascot. The dog played no favorites; he loved them all. It was even said that he could warn of impending danger and would summon help when a person found himself in a life-threatening situation.

One spring morning the little dog fell asleep behind a dump truck. Unaware that the dog was there, the truck's driver jumped into the cab and backed up over the napping canine. The men buried their beloved pooch and in time a plaque over the dog's grave site. It stood there for many years with his name and story carved into it. He lies there still, on the Nevada side of the observation deck.

The dog's name was removed from the plaque in the late '70s. Why? Because the workers of long ago had named the dog Niggy, now deemed highly offensive. And so, while his story remains, his name does not. Today the little dog is known simply as the Dog of the Dam. And his name is never spoken.

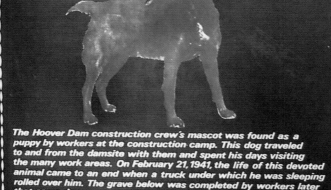

The Hoover Dam construction crew's mascot was found as a puppy by workers at the construction camp. This dog traveled to and from the damsite with them and spent his days visiting the many work areas. On February 21, 1941, the life of this devoted animal came to an end when a truck under which he was sleeping rolled over him. The grave below was completed by workers later that same day.

Quehoe's Quorpse

The "Mad Indian" Quehoe was southern Nevada's own boogie man, a mad killer to most, an anti–folk hero to some, fighting back against the white man's oppression.

Whichever he was, Quehoe's killings terrorized inhabitants in the early days of the last century.

Quehoe, it was said, would kill for next to nothing. He killed his half-brother, another outlaw, at a white man's behest. He killed some prospectors for their shoes and others for their food. Things finally got to the point where every time a dead body was found in the region, Quehoe got the blame. In one instance, a man he was said to have murdered turned up very much alive, surprised to hear about his gruesome demise. Posse after posse set out to track the killer down, but he easily eluded them all.

In February 1940, three prospectors found a mummified body in a cave on a mountain overlooking the Colorado River. The desiccated corpse inside was none other than Quehoe. A burlap bandage wrapped around one of his legs led some to believe he had suffered a snakebite that may have killed him. Among the items in the cave was the badge of a man he had killed, a watchman at the Gold Bug Mine.

Quehoe's postmortem adventure would become almost as infamous as his life. The corpse was hauled down the mountain and taken to Boulder City, where a fight broke out over who owned the outlaw's remains. The prospectors who found it, the sheriff, the chief of police, and even the Elks Lodge all wanted it. To further complicate matters, two people claiming to be Quehoe heirs claimed dibs on the body.

Sheriff Gene Ward put the corpse on display in a glass case at the courthouse, claiming that this was for identification purposes. After everyone had gotten a good look, the body was taken to the Park's Palm Funeral Home in Las Vegas. There it caused another sensation as curiosity seekers stormed in to look at the outlaw in his glass-topped coffin. The troublesome Quehoe also rang up a high bill for storage at the funeral home.

Curiously, no one stepped up to pay it, so Quehoe stayed at the funeral home for three years until Frank Wait, the police chief who had hunted him for years, finally paid the bill.

Wait gave the body to the Elks Lodge, who were in charge of Helldorado Days, early Las Vegas's annual rodeo–street fair–carnival. The Elks created an exhibit at Helldorado Village, complete with Quehoe's mummified remains and a papier-mâché replica of his cave, with actual artifacts that had been found there. Quehoe's Cave was the highlight of the Helldorado Carnival until the mid-'50s when someone stole Quehoe's body and all the artifacts.

After the theft, Quehoe's bones were dumped into the Bonanza Wash and, when first found, were thought to be evidence of a recent murder. When the bones were determined to be older, however, it was clear they were the remains of our friend Quehoe. The city quickly sold them to the first bidder, and after that they passed through various hands until they came into the possession of an ex-lawyer named Roland Wiley.

Wiley was the type of eccentric that early Las Vegas attracted. He had been Clark County district attorney from 1939 through 1942 and had participated in the legal haggling over Quehoe's remains. He was also a profoundly spiritual person and had constructed a religious theme park, which he called Cathedral Canyon, near his ranch outside Pahrump. He completed his project by the mid-'70s. A replica of the Christ of the Andes statue stood in the middle of the small canyon. There were pathways, changing light patterns, and electrical-powered waterfalls. A suspension bridge took visitors across the canyon, where they could visit small niches carved into the sides and holding more saintly statues. There was no admission charge; Wiley paid for everything himself.

This would become Quehoe's final resting place. Wiley bought what was left of the Indian, now literally just a bag of bones, for one hundred dollars. He buried those remains at the edge of Cathedral Canyon in 1978.

Wiley died on August 15, 1994. Since his death, Cathedral Canyon has fallen into disrepair and has been trashed by vandals. The Christ statue, the gates, and bathrooms that were carved into the canyon walls are about the only things left. But Quehoe's grave is intact at

the side of the parking area overlooking the canyon. The slab of concrete that covers it reads QUEHOE 1889–1919 NEVADA'S LAST RENEGADE INDIAN, HE SURVIVED ALONE.

Why Wiley chose to bury him on the edge of Cathedral Canyon has never been stated. One can speculate that a man as spiritual as Wiley could find forgiveness for Quehoe, who may have been as much of a scapegoat as a killer. Perhaps Wiley just wanted to give the red man's soul and his weary bones some rest.

Overview: Cathedral Park; insert opposite page: Quehoe's grave; Below: The suspension bridge; Bottom: the bathrooms.

The Tragic Death of Carol Lombard

The romance between Carole Lombard and Clark Gable fascinated Americans during the golden age of movies. It started in January 1936, even though Gable was married at the time. His wife granted him a divorce, and within two weeks of its being official (in March 1939), Gable and Lombard eloped in Kingman, Arizona. Married in the southwestern desert, the couple had no way of knowing that a few years later their union would tragically end there too.

It was January 16, 1942, and Lombard had just completed a successful national tour selling war bonds. The tour ended in her home state of Indiana, and she planned to fly back home to Los Angeles. She boarded, along with several other passengers, TWA flight 3, which left at four a.m. It touched down in Albuquerque, New Mexico, where fifteen returning servicemen boarded. Four passengers gave up their seats to the servicemen, not knowing how fortuitous their decision was. The plane touched down again, for refueling, in Las Vegas. It left Vegas at 7:07 p.m. for what was to be the final leg of the journey.

Twenty-three minutes later, the plane slammed into a cliff on the side of Mt. Potosi, thirty-two miles southwest of Las Vegas. Miners saw a flash of fire as the plane hit. The crash was confirmed when the pilot of TWA flight 10, heading to Salt Lake City, sighted the burning wreckage.

The cause of the accident is unknown, although folklore says that the pilot left the plane in charge of an inexperienced copilot while he chatted with his celebrity passenger. For whatever reason, the plane was 6.7 miles off course, but would have missed the

MT. POTOSI, NEVADA
IN MEMORY

Of the 22 individuals who perished on this mountain on January 16, 1942, in the crash of Transcontinental and Western Airlines (TWA) flight 3, including Carole Lombard, 15 Army Air Corp pilots, a crew of 3, and 3 passengers.

peak if it had been flying a few hundred yards to the left.

As a search party made its way up the snow-covered mountain, a devastated Clark Gable flew in from Los Angeles. He wanted to join the searchers but was dissuaded. It took the party fourteen hours to reach the crash site, where the rescuers quickly realized there were no survivors. Ms. Lombard's charred body was identified by its blond hair.

Clark Gable was inconsolable. He and Carole Lombard had been the perfect love match. He would go on to marry others, but some of his closest friends believed he never recovered from the loss of Carole.

Lombard was listed as the first woman killed in the line of duty during World War II and was given a posthumous Presidential Medal of Freedom. A plaque honoring her, the other passengers, the three-man crew, and the fifteen servicemen marks the crash site. Parts of the wreckage are still scattered around the area, although most of the smaller bits have been scavenged.

If you want to see the crash site, be prepared to spend the day doing so. It involves driving a high-clearance vehicle an hour up an unpaved road that some describe as butt-bruising, and then hiking for two to three hours on foot to reach the site.

Less adventurous travelers can stop by the Pioneer Tavern in Goodsprings, just a short drive off I-15. It was here that Gable paced the floor while awaiting word from the rescue party. The tavern, which has quite a history and a couple of resident ghosts, has a room dedicated to Lombard and Gable, and a fragment from the wrecked plane sits atop the Franklin stove in the middle of the bar.

Some day, they'll go down together
They'll bury them side by side
To a few, it'll be grief
To the law, a relief
But it's death for Bonnie and Clyde.
—Bonnie Parker

The Bonnie and Clyde Death Car, Primm

Bonnie Parker and Clyde Barrow had been celebrated in story and song even before they met their grisly end in a police ambush on a lonely road near Gibsland, Louisiana, on May 23, 1934. History suggests that the public enjoyed reading about criminal exploits like theirs during the nation's Great Depression. John Dillinger and Pretty Boy Floyd were but a couple of the infamous fugitives who enjoyed a certain admired notoriety at the time. But when it came to romance and bullets, no story was as riveting as that of Bonnie and Clyde.

Bonnie Parker and Clyde Barrow never made it to Nevada. Long before Las Vegas was anything more than a tiny outpost in the southern Nevada desert, the cold-blooded duo died, as violently as they had lived, in a merciless hail of bullets. After posing for their post-mortem mug shots, Bonnie and Clyde were buried in Texas by their families.

Yes, they went down together, as Bonnie predicted in her poem "*The Ballad of Bonnie and Clyde.*" The 1934 Ford sedan in which the celebrated bank robbers took their final ride, however, continued its strange journey long after the death of the two outlaws. For years, the bullet-riddled car traveled all over the United States, but it seems to have found its home at the Nevada state line.

The car began its voyage to notoriety on April 29, 1934, when it was stolen from the driveway of Jesse and Ruth Warren, of Topeka, Kansas. On May 22, six lawmen ambushed the car from the side of a county road near Gibsland. They pumped 167 rounds of hot ammunition into the sedan, killing both occupants; fifty bullets hit Bonnie

and twenty-seven hit Clyde, making a bloody mess. The coroner's report mentions that Bonnie had all the fingers of her right hand shot clean off. Inside the stolen auto was a mini mobile ammo dump, including three automatic Browning rifles, a 10-gauge Winchester lever action, one sawed-off shotgun, seven Colt automatic pistols, three thousand rounds of ammunition, and one saxophone. (Clyde was said to blow a mean sax.)

The car, already the target of souvenir hunters, was towed to Acadia, the parish seat, and locked up in a secret location. But its show business career was just about to begin. A man named Duke Mills approached the Warrens with a plan to exhibit the car at the upcoming World's Fair in Chicago. Ruth Warren attempted to retrieve her car, but Sheriff Henderson Jordan demanded that she pay $15,000 for its return (the Warrens had bought it for a little under $800). Ruth hired a lawyer and successfully sued for the automobile's return. She ended up driving the bloodied and bullet-riddled sedan from Acadia to Shreveport, LA, where it was loaded onto a truck and delivered back to the driveway from where it had been stolen.

Ruth then began renting the car to carnival exhibits. Eventually, a showman named Charles Stanley bought the death car outright from Ruth for $3,500. He exhibited it at fairs and other venues until 1952, when he sold it to a man named Ted Toddy for $14,500. Toddy was a movie producer who used the car to promote his 1967 movie *Bonnie and Clyde*, with its infamous death scene.

In 1975, the car was sold at auction for $175,000. The buyer was Peter Simon II, from Jean, Nevada. Some Nevadans still remember when Simon exhibited the car at his Pop's Oasis Casino in Jean, a literal pit stop on the way to Vegas.

DIVISION OF INVESTIGATION

U. S. DEPARTMENT OF JUSTICE

WASHINGTON, D. C.

May 28, 1934.

APPREHENSION ORDER
No. 1227-307.

Dear Sir:

In Re: MRS. ROY THORNTON, aliases BONNIE BARROW, MRS. CLYDE BARROW, BONNIE PARKER; CLYDE CHAMPION BARROW, aliases CLYDE BARROW, ROY BAILEY, JACK HALE, ELDIN WILLIAMS, ELVIN WILLIAMS.

Identification Order 1227 on the above named subjects is hereby cancelled, inasmuch as they were killed near Arcadia, Louisiana on May 23, 1934.

Very truly yours,

J. E. Hoover,

Director.

The only time the death car left Nevada after that was in 1987, when the next owner, Clyde Wade, got it up and running and entered it in a famous coast-to-coast race as a publicity stunt. Wade was then the curator of the Harrah Casino's Automotive Museum in Reno. He had covered the bullet-shattered windows with Plexiglas, both to preserve the original glass and to keep the wind out. He had no intention of winning the race, but hoped the publicity would help him sell it.

Apparently, the stunt worked, because Gary Primm, a casino owner and car aficionado, bought the car for $250,000 in 1988. He used it to promote his casinos in what used to be called Stateline and is now officially Primm, Nevada. The MGM Corporation owns the Primm casinos today and exhibits the car, along with other Bonnie and Clyde memorabilia, at the Primadonna Resort Casino.

Bonnie realized that the public would be curious about her and Clyde long after the law caught up with them. But she could not have guessed the extent of that curiosity or how long it might endure. Every day at Primadonna, crowds still press their faces to the glass and stare in fascination at Clyde's bloodstained shirt and the bullet-riddled vehicle that took the outlaws to their fate.

Over the years, some have called the authenticity of the death car into question, but the one in Primm is the only one sanctioned by a court of law. In 1969, Toddy won a suit of injunction and became the only person who could legally use the Bonnie and Clyde name. Now and then other death cars pop up, but the one at the Primadonna is the only one authenticated.

The death car exhibit is open twenty-four hours a day and has no admission charge. If you are driving between Los Angeles and Vegas, you are well advised to stop at the state line to see this genuinely weird historical artifact.

The Jones Boys of Gold Hill Cemetery

Fourteen-year-old Henry Jones and his nine-year-old brother, John, died on Christmas Eve 1871. The youngsters were buried in the Gold Hill Cemetery; their headstone read:

THEY ARE NOT DEAD, BUT GONE BEFORE,
OUR PRECIOUS, DARLING BOYS
DEATH WRAPPED THEM IN A SNOWY SHROUD
TO WAKE MID HEAVENLY JOYS
THEIR HORSE STOOD OVER THEM WITH CARE
BY THE HAND OF GOD WAS HOLDEN THERE,
THREE DAYS AND NIGHTS ON THE
MOUNTAIN THEY LAY
GUARDED BY ANGELS TILL BOURNED AWAY

Loving as the headstone may seem, the Jones boys' short lives were spent under the rule of an abusive father. On the night of their deaths, the boys were sent to find a stray cow. It didn't matter to their father that it was Christmas Eve or that wind-driven snow was quickly piling up on the Comstock in deep drifts. "Don't come back without that cow," he warned them.

Knowing their father's mean temper, the boys trudged out on horseback into the blinding snow. As the hours passed, the children became hopelessly lost. Yet they knew they must not return without the cow. They were found frozen to death in their tracks a few days later.

News of the children's death spread across the Comstock. All of Gold Hill and Virginia City were outraged. How could Mr. Jones so coldheartedly send his sons out on such a mission, everyone wondered. After the boys were buried in the Gold Hill Cemetery, the sentimental headstone was erected over their graves.

During a séance months later, Alf Doten, a well-known Comstock journalist, claimed to have made contact with the boys. At last freed from their father's cruelty, the little boys were reportedly happy in the hereafter. Their ghosts were even spotted in the cemetery from time to time.

As if the Jones boys hadn't suffered enough in life, vandals made off with their monument in the mid-1970s. Three decades later, using an old photograph, the Comstock Cemetery Foundation arranged to have a new gravestone constructed. On May 26, 2001, one hundred and thirty years after their deaths, the Jones boys were remembered with the dedication of their new headstone.

Their ghosts are still occasionally seen in the Gold Hill Cemetery.

Where Tupac Shakur Got Gunned Down

Gangsters have been getting rubbed out in Sin City since before the introduction of neon. But gangstas getting whacked in this burg is a relatively new phenomenon. For example, gangsta rapper Tupac Shakur was fatally shot at the intersection of Flamingo Road and Koval Lane in an as yet unsolved drive-by shooting.

Dictionary.com defines gangsta rap as "A style of rap music associated with urban street gangs and characterized by violent, tough-talking, often misogynistic lyrics." One of the most prolific and celebrated pioneers of that musical genre was Tupac Shakur.

Shakur was no stranger to the thug life; in fact, he often embraced the lifestyle in reality as well as in song. The son of two members of the Black Panther Party (a controversial African American civil rights and self-defense organization active during the 1960s and 1970s), Shakur displayed enough artistic ability to be accepted by the prestigious Baltimore School of the Arts. However, he was forced to drop out before graduation when his mother moved the family to Oakland, California. It was there that, according to Shakur, he began hustling and living on the street.

In 1992, he released his debut album, 2Pacalypse Now. Album sales were brisk, probably helped along when then Vice President Dan Quayle publicly condemned the explicit lyrics during his reelection campaign. Following on the heels of his musical success, Shakur garnered critical acclaim for his portrayal of Ernest Dickerson in the film *Juice,* a story of four young men coming of age on the streets of Harlem.

But fame and success would be followed by violence and troubles with the law. Shakur was charged with shooting a couple of off-duty policemen in Atlanta in 1993 and was sentenced to fifteen days in jail for assaulting Menace II Society director Allen Hughes in 1994.

Later that year he was shot by a pair of muggers in a New York City recording station and was also found guilty of sexual assault of a female fan.

Sentenced to prison for four and a half years, Shakur accused New York rap star Notorious B.I.G. (a.k.a. Biggie Smalls) and producer Sean Puffy Combs of masterminding the shooting in New York. At the same time, his third album, "Me Against the World," landed on the charts at number one.

Suge Knight, co-founder of Death Row Records, decided Shakur was a musical talent worthy of investment. The burly entrepreneur, who also enjoys a reputation for living dangerously, posted close to a million and  a half–dollar bond eight months into Shakur's prison stretch and signed the rap artist to his own lucrative label. Shakur was soon on the outside again and making records for Knight.

Fast-forward now to eight forty-five p.m. on the night of September 7, 1996. A young man is captured on MGM Grand video surveillance getting into a physical altercation with Shakur, Knight, and members of their party. The man is questioned but released without giving police his name.

Roughly ten minutes later Shakur, Knight, and the rest of the entourage make a stop at the Luxor, then start out for Knight's Las Vegas home, southeast of downtown.

It is reported that at eleven fifteen, Shakur and Knight were chatting with some ladies at a red light at the intersection of Koval and Flamingo when a white Cadillac pulled up on the passenger side of the automobile, where the rapper was seated. According to witnesses, two men jumped out of the Caddy and emptied thirteen rounds into Knight's shiny black Beemer, hopped back into their vehicle, and sped off. Shakur absorbed four bullets during the brutal confrontation, while shrapnel from another bullet lodged itself in Knight's head.

A wounded Knight pulled a U-turn and raced back down East Flamingo. In attempts to circumvent traffic, he ran red lights and hopped road medians, which ultimately flattened all four of the vehicle's tires. Police quickly caught up to the BMW, loaded Shakur into an ambulance, and took the hip-hop legend to University Medical Center.

According to Knight during an interview with MTV, Shakur was calm and even joking during the frantic ride to the emergency room: "My whole thing was Pac—he was shot. I'm like, 'You're shot! Let me get you to the hospital.' I'm driving, telling him I'm gonna get him to the hospital, kicked back. Pac looked at me and said, 'You know what? You need a doctor more than me. You the one shot in your head.' And we laughed the whole time finding our way to the hospital."

Six days later, after doctors had removed one of the rap star's lungs and given him a fifty percent chance of survival, Tupac Shakur died at the hospital from respiratory failure and cardiopulmonary arrest due to the bullet wounds.

Six months later Notorious B.I.G. was gunned down in a similar drive-by fashion on Wilshire Boulevard in Los Angeles. Many people believe Smalls had a connection to the Shakur hit, and that he was killed in an act of street vengeance. So far that correlation has not been proved. Such is the life (and death) of an outlaw.

Silver Terrace's Mysterious Glowing Headstone

A walk among the headstones at Silver Terrace Cemetery tells the story of Virginia City's frontier days. Few of the dearly departed who rest here died of old age; most left this life rather suddenly and at an early age. Accidents, suicide, murder, and disease hastened the inevitable. Among the cemetery's residents are miners, saloon keepers, and gunslingers. But don't look for

Julia Bulette and other ladies of the evening here. Judged not pure enough to spend eternity reposing alongside the Comstock's upstanding citizenry, these soiled doves were buried on Flowery Hill or other locations far from the general population.

Tread reverently. Burials still take place in Silver Terrace, which is made up of thirteen cemeteries, some in better shape than others. Several headstones date from the Comstock era, but vandals have defaced, destroyed, and stolen many of them over the years. Much of the intricate filigree iron fencing has long been

carted away as well. Luckily, the mysterious glowing headstone still stands. On nights when the moon shines brightest, it can be seen from different locations throughout the Comstock.

Only a few people know which headstone it is. Those who do aren't talking. The locals accept the eerie glow that emanates from Silver Terrace as just another fact of life and death "here on the hill." Several attempts have been launched to locate the strange light, but all have met with failure.

The glowing headstone is often the topic of discussion at the local saloons. One story concerns a spiritualist named Lavinia, who resided in Virginia City at the height of the silver rush. It is her headstone that shines against the darkness, this story goes. It's Lavinia's way of proving she is still with us in spirit. Some residents believe that the phenomenon is not a headstone at all, but a ghostly glowing young girl who comes to life and dances across the cemetery on certain nights. This, they say, is why no one can find the mysterious headstone.

One person in Virginia City who claims to have his boots firmly planted on terra firma insists that there is nothing paranormal about the glowing headstone. He explains that the material the stone is made of is similar to that of a child's glow-in-the-dark toy; it absorbs light during the day and glows in the darkness.

Yessir, it all sounds quite logical. Right up to the time someone else saunters into the saloon and asks why no other headstone, of the hundreds out there, is made of the same glow-in-the-dark material. Gotcha! Gimme a brewski, and let's see if we can figure this thing out.

Some residents believe that the glowing headstone phenomenon is not a headstone at all, but a ghostly glowing young girl who comes to life and dances across the cemetery on certain nights.

Pets and Their Masters Lie Side by Side

In the Old West, when someone died, you just chose a suitable place to bury them, set up a homemade tombstone, and that was that. On a desolate road outside Searchlight, the old ways still reign.

Near the Colorado River, adjacent to some high-power lines beside an unpaved road, is what the locals call Veterans Cemetery or Memorial Cemetery. It is a strange combination, an improvised cemetery with both humans and animals.

There is more than one version of how this all came to be, but if you believe the July 16, 1978, issue of the *Nevadan,* it happened this way. A prospector named Tobey Barnes had a beloved dog that died. When Tobey himself went to his reward, he asked to be buried next to his dog. Later other people requested to be buried at the same plot of land. The paper quotes Tobey's friend John Kay, who said, "We've buried sixteen people out there, last count. Cost you fifty dollars to get a hole dug, and there's no up-keep." The article states that Barnes's grave was unmarked and that his dog "lies in a better tended grave than his former master."

It seems that people from Searchlight and the surrounding area have been burying their pets and relatives here since the early 1960s. Records show that the first graves for humans are from 1962. All these early interments were veterans from the First or Second World War.

Burials of people and animals still take place at this remote locale, which is officially called Six-Mile Cove Cemetery. The graves range from elab-orate stonework to homemade wooden markers decorated with lawn ornaments. The graveyard exhibits a warmth of feeling that is all but lost in most of the modern-style burial grounds of today.

Six-Mile Cove Cemetery is located seven miles east of Searchlight on Highway 164, then right on the unpaved power-line road.

Puss 'n' Boots Hill

The Boulder City Pet Cemetery kinda is and kinda ain't an official pet cemetery. You won't find it listed in the phonebook. Good luck finding it on a map. Even if you do know where it is, you may still have trouble finding it.

The cemetery started in 1953, when Boulder City resident Marwood Doud, a self-taught veterinarian, was looking for a suitable place to bury pets. The city council didn't want a pet cemetery next to the city's regular cemetery, so they gave the thumbs-up to its current location. Trouble is, until the 1990s this pet cemetery was officially on federal land. Over the years, hundreds of pets were buried there.

The cemetery faced a crisis in 1976 when the state of Nevada asked the Bureau of Land Management to clear the land. They actually wanted people to come and dig up their dead doggies and kitties and move them somewhere else. The government killjoys used nasty phrases like "begun illegally" and "without official permission" to describe the cemetery. A group of pet owners formed the Incorporated Desert Pet Cemetery Association and worked out a deal with the state that stopped the proposed desecration of the burial ground. When Boulder City bought El Dorado Valley in 1995, the cemetery finally became city property.

This final resting place of many a pet lies south of the intersection of highways 93 and 95. There is a gap in a white fence by the side of the northbound lanes of Highway 95. Beyond that is the oldest part of the cemetery, with graves from the 1950s. Looking like a Wild West boneyard, the wooden markers and tombstones here are weathered and falling down. Desert brush grows freely. Presumably, the beloved pets' owners have all gone to their own reward and can no longer care for the graves. A Las Vegas newspaper once called this section "Puss 'n' Boots Hill."

As you walk away from the highway, the dates become more recent and the markers look newer. There are no signs of planning or boundaries; the graves are laid out haphazardly. Some are ornate; most are simple. There is a grave with a doghouse and another with a water bowl. Many look neglected, although there are some that show recent visitation, with elaborate decorations.

And there is some folklore here as well. One visitor reported that a white cat followed her around as she wandered among the grave markers. At first she thought it was just a normal cat, but soon realized that this was the spirit form of one of the graveyard's residents. An Internet posting gave this report stamina, causing some to make a midnight visit to this humble graveyard, where the ghost cat may follow you around — "if it likes you."

Stoney the Elephant, R.I.P.

Craig Road Pet Cemetery in Las Vegas has one thing no other cemetery has: Stoney the elephant. Stoney was a star of the Luxor Casino's dinner-theater show "Winds of the Gods." His death came about, according to all accounts, as the result of an accident. What's not clear is whether or not Stoney got the care he should have.

It seems that Stoney suffered a leg injury in September 1994. His leg was not healing, and animal

rights activists were protesting his treatment. In August 1995, Stoney was due to be moved to an elephant-breeding farm in Arkansas, but he injured another leg as he was being moved, in full view of animal rights protestors. He was euthanized later that day.

All the information about Stoney's death comes from biased sources: the animal rights activists and the casino, which would like to play down any negative aspects of this incident.

It is hoped Stoney has found peace at the Craig Road Pet Cemetery. His burial place is evident by its pronounced lump, rising higher than any of the other graves.

Abandoned in the Silver State

All *around Las Vegas* there are reminders of the past: once thriving places now abandoned and left for dead. Forlorn vestiges of our beloved roadside culture—gas stations and truck stops, drive-in theaters and trailer parks— are found along just about any lonely desert highway. There are obsolete military facilities and deteriorating remnants of our industrial heritage, rusting mills and tapped-out mines. Perhaps strangest of all, though, are the numerous ghost towns to be found scattered about the state. Left to the ravages of time, they languish year after year, as if waiting for someone to rediscover them and the human dramas that once played out within them.

Stepping into an abandoned place is like walking into an unknown world that others once inhabited and then deserted. Who might these people have been? What were their daily lives like? Why did they leave, and where did they go? These are the questions we ask ourselves while exploring Nevada's forsaken monuments. Ride along with us on this journey into the past.

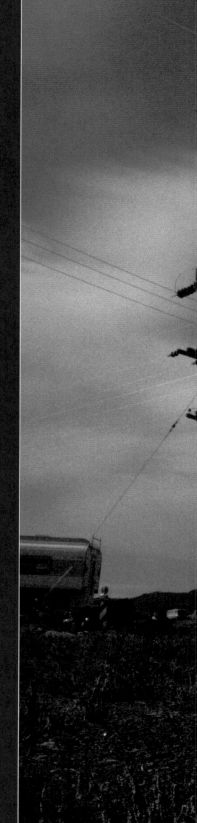

Rhyolite

In its boom years of 1905–1908, Rhyolite had a population of 8,000 hopeful souls. Today it is Nevada's most popular and most photographed ghost town. There are a few factors that make this so. For one, it's close to Las Vegas; for another, it's just down the road from Beatty, which itself would be a ghost town if it were not on Highway 95. Beatty calls itself the "gateway to Death Valley."

You will see the Rhyolite turnoff about four miles west of Beatty on Highway 374. Drive up the road, past the Goldwell Open Air Museum, and you're there. The site is now owned by the Bureau of Land Management, which maintains it.

Rhyolite came into being in August 1904 when two prospectors, "Shorty" Harris and Ed Cross, stumbled across a piece of gold ore. It is said that the ore's greenish

color and lumpy shape gave the mining district its name, the Bullfrog. And then there is the story that it was named after Ed Cross's favorite song, "The Bullfrog on the Jump." In a classic Nevada prospector move, Harris made his way up to Goldfield to record his claim, but stopped at some of the local drinking establishments to celebrate and brag about his find. Folklore has it that Harris got so drunk that he did not file a claim until the next day. When he returned to Bullfrog, people who had overheard Harris's drunken bragging the night before were already there staking their own claims. Another version of the story says that the next day he gambled away his half interest in the mine. Whatever the case, Harris made only $500 and a mule from his end of the deal. The Bullfrog Mine would list at $200,000 on the San Francisco Exchange a short time later.

Several camps sprouted up around the Bullfrog, but Rhyolite was the only one that turned into something like a real city. By June 1905, there was piped water in town. The sudden influx of people necessitated building a two-story schoolhouse. The problem was, by December 1908, when the building was completed, the population was already shrinking as the mines played out and there were not enough students to fill its rooms. A similar fate would befall the much photographed Cook Bank building, which was built in 1908 at a cost of $90,000. In 1910, the owners sold the doors of the bank's massive vault in an effort to recoup some of their losses as the town dried up. When the *Rhyolite Herald* announced the closure of the Montgomery-Shoshone mine on its front page in March 1911, it might as well have been an obituary for the city.

The Rhyolite train depot is one of the few buildings in town that is still intact. This is partly because it was constructed with railroad-rail instead of rebar. It was completed in August 1908 and serviced the Las Vegas–Tonopah rail line, Rhyolite's first train service, as well as two other rival lines. The depot closed in 1918. The 1920 census showed that Rhyolite had only twenty residents.

In 1924, the rail depot was purchased by N. C. "Wes" Westmoreland, who had owed the Old Arizona Bar in Vegas. He transformed it into a roadhouse, the Rhyolite Ghost Casino, and ran the whole operation for twenty-three years. When he died, the property was sold in probate. For a while, it was run as a museum and souvenir shop, but today it's empty and fenced off. The only building now occupied is the frequently photographed Bottle House, and it is not really occupied. The caretakers live in a motor home behind the house.

The Bottle House was built between September 1905 and April 1906 by Tom Kelly, an Australian miner who began the project when he was seventy-six years old. He constructed a wooden frame, then filled in the walls with discarded beer bottles from the local bars, mortaring them together with mud. Kelly never lived in the house, but raffled it off in June 1906 and walked away with a $2,000 profit. From 1953 until 1989, the Thompson family occupied the house. Caretakers now live nearby and will be happy to give you a tour.

Rhyolite is incredibly photogenic. The crumbling shell of the Cook Bank building is one of the most photographed ruins in Nevada. A couple of 1920s western movies used the town as a backdrop, and a portion of the 2006 movie *The Island* was shot along the main street. Even the school got another bit of use when in the 1980s a record company used the building for a party for its distributors; they poured a new concrete floor for the one-time event.

A Lingering Deeth

Pull off at exit 333 of Interstate 80 and it is as if you have stepped into the Twilight Zone. Deeth should be a ghost town; in fact, it is listed in several guides to ghost towns. But someone seems to be living here. There are houses that are falling in on themselves, with shells of cars rusting in the overgrown yards. But then there are houses that look new and inhabited, with satellite dishes on the outside. Looks can be deceiving, however. Go to the front door and it is wide open. The only inhabitants are a family of birds, living in a nest formed around a light bulb on the ceiling. As the town died, the folks who lived here just left—in some cases, without packing up.

Deeth may have gotten its name from a man named Deeth, or it is an obvious corruption of the word "death," the fate that would await an unprepared traveler crossing the desert. It became a town in 1869, springing up when the Central Pacific Railroad passed through this part of the world. The Deeth post office opened in

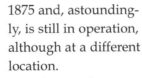

1875 and, astoundingly, is still in operation, although at a different location.

The town's population peaked at 250 in 1912. The 2000 census reported the population as 201, but this includes the surrounding area. The actual population of the town itself is consistently given as being around 20. Most of the people who live in the area surrounding Deeth are ranchers or work at a nearby mine. Some of the area residents commute to Elko, only thirty miles away on the freeway. So Deeth ain't dead yet. But take a tour through the abandoned railroad tie house and you will know why it keeps getting listed in those ghost town guidebooks.

Cursed Belmont

Historian Shawn Hall says that Belmont is the "queen of Nye County ghost towns—in fact, one of the top ghost towns in the state." In 1867, Belmont was the new Nye county seat; thousands populated what had started as a small camp, mining silver and lead ore, less than two years earlier.

In 1905, the state legislature moved the county seat to Tonopah. By then, Belmont's population was less than fifty as residents fled the failing mines, and now there was one more reason to leave town. In 1911, the post office shut down. There were a few more spurts of mining that kept a few residents in town, but by 1922 it was deserted. Well . . . almost.

Rose Walter

There was a time when Belmont's population was one, that being Rose Walter. Rose had been married to a miner who died of silicosis; for whatever reason, she decided to stay in the town, and when the rest of the people wandered away, she became Belmont's guardian, chasing away potential vandals with a pistol. The June 1974 issue of *National Geographic* quotes Rose as saying, "I aim for the head and never miss!" In this instance, she was talking about rattlesnakes, not people, but folklore has it that she once had an encounter with Charles Manson.

"I knew Rose Walters, and Rose said they [the Manson "Family"] did stay there," says Dick Ashton, former owner of Dirty Dick's Belmont Saloon. "There was five of 'em; they were there for about a week and later left, and they went from Belmont to Death Valley and they got captured coming out of Death Valley."

Rose did not make the connection between these hippies and the Manson Family killings, says Ashton, because she had no TV and limited radio. But in Belmont's deserted courthouse there is graffiti carved in the wall saying, "Charles Manson Family 1969," giving credence to this bit of folklore.

Rose Walter, Belmont's last remaining full-time resident from its mining days, died at the age of ninety-three in January 1987. Nowadays Belmont's population hovers at around ten, although few of them stay for the wintertime. The population centers around two businesses, the Belmont Monitor Inn and Dirty Dick's Belmont Saloon.

The saloon is open only on summer weekends and gets about thirty to forty customers per week, except on the Fourth of July weekend when a biker run brings up to three hundred people through the watering hole.

The inn, in the former building of the Combination Mining Company office, is now a bed-and-breakfast. Owners Henry and Bertie Berg say that it is the perfect retreat for people who want to get away from the complications of urban life.

Ghosts in the Ghost Town

It seems even death won't make some of Belmont's residents leave. Dick Ashton, the aforementioned former owner of Dirty Dick's, had a strange encounter in the Belmont Inn in the late 1970s, when he was asked to house-sit the building, which was undergoing restoration, while its owners, John and Kathy Richardson, were visiting relatives.

"And at two o'clock in the morning, I woke up. . . . I could feel a thumb and forefingers gently pressing on my throat. And both of those Australian shepherd dogs were sitting outside in the snow barking, and I kept thinking, Dick, you're dreaming, wake up, and I thought, What is this hand doing around my throat? and, Who is this? and I kept swinging in the air with my other arm. Finally I rolled out of bed, and when I looked out the window and watched the Australian shepherds, they went back under

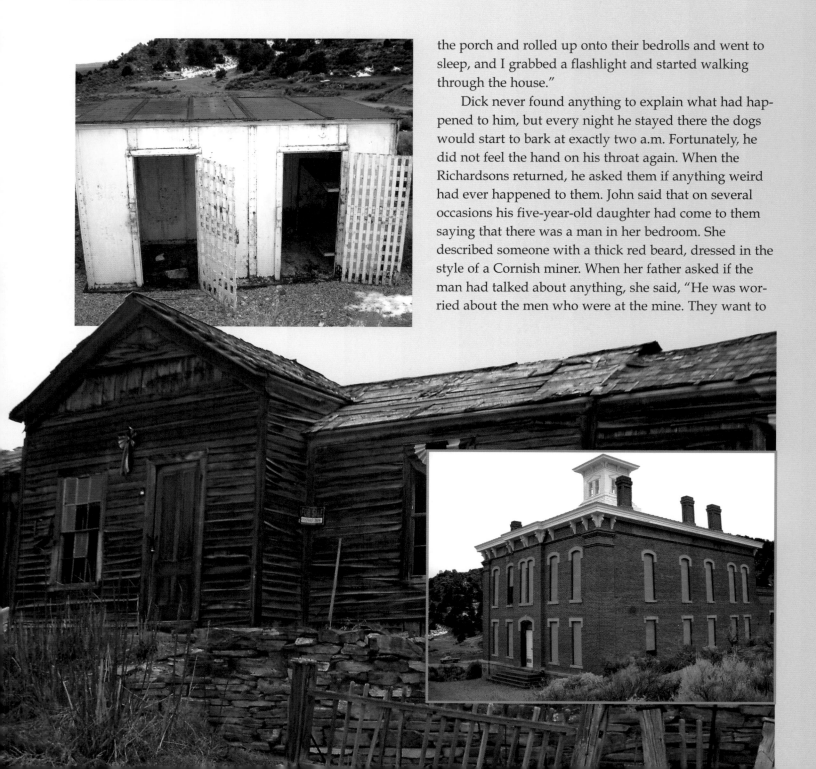

the porch and rolled up onto their bedrolls and went to sleep, and I grabbed a flashlight and started walking through the house."

Dick never found anything to explain what had happened to him, but every night he stayed there the dogs would start to bark at exactly two a.m. Fortunately, he did not feel the hand on his throat again. When the Richardsons returned, he asked them if anything weird had ever happened to them. John said that on several occasions his five-year-old daughter had come to them saying that there was a man in her bedroom. She described someone with a thick red beard, dressed in the style of a Cornish miner. When her father asked if the man had talked about anything, she said, "He was worried about the men who were at the mine. They want to join a union, and he is not sure that he wants to join a union, and he's the   foreman and he's having trouble with the conveyer systems. They don't line up, and they are spilling the ore off of the side. The crusher won't crush the ore down forty-eight mesh like it ought to do."

"This five-year-old was using terms from mining that just astounded John," says Ashton, "and me too."

Lynching Curse

Like any western boomtown, Belmont had its share of riots, murders, and violence, but the blackest mark on *Belmont's* history is the double lynching of Charlie McIntyre and Jack Walker in 1874. Who these men were and the specifics of their deaths are a jumble of history and folklore. Usually said to be miners, they were rumored to be members of the Molly McGuires, union organizers.

Officially, Jack Walker was jailed because of a fight that occurred at the Tiger Saloon. The resulting gunplay left one man dead and another wounded. McIntyre was already in jail for pulling a gun "not in self-defense," although he had not hurt anyone.

The two escaped from jail by tunneling their way out; they were soon found hiding in an mine shaft. They were taken back to jail, but on June 4 a lynch mob made sure that they would never complete their sentences.

Their death was cruel, even for a lynching. After the jail guards were tied and bound, Walker and McIntyre were taken to the basement of the old courthouse, although some say it was a saloon. Holes were drilled through the ceiling and ropes dropped down from above. As the lynching began, it became obvious that the short drop had not broken the men's necks, and they writhed in the agony of slow strangulation. To finish the job, one of the mob fired a few slugs into their squirming bodies.

Legend has it that one of the dying men placed a curse upon the town during the lynching. An article in the March 24, 1946, *Nevada State Journal,* entitled, "ONCE THRIVING TOWN KILLED BY CURSE," states that before the last man died, seeing the blood on the ceiling left by his slain comrade, he choked out, "You're killing two innocent men. As long as that blood stays up there, this town'll never amount to a tinker's dam."

An article in the March 1951 issue of *FATE* magazine repeats the same story, but like a game of telephone, the last clause has changed slightly: "as long as that blood stays on the ceiling, this town will die." Dick Ashton says that he was told the clause was "sagebrush will grow on your streets."

The *State Journal* article says that residents tried to clean the bloodstains off the ceiling any way they could, but that the stains would always return. And of course the town did go from county seat to ghost town within a few years. Dick Ashton says that the story of the curse may have been contrived, or at least embellished, by onetime Belmont resident Lee Brotherton: "I think Lee . . . went down there and threw some of that red paint up there for the tourists." Cursed or not, Belmont became a ghost town, a fate shared by other mining towns that did not have curses placed upon them.

Belmont's most famous building, the county court-house, was deeded by Nye County to the state of Nevada in 1974. It is now a historic state monument, run by the division of state parks. Dick Ashton says that it is the "smallest state park in the state of Nevada." The courthouse is open for guided tours only a few days out of the year, in the summer months. For more informa-tion, contact the Nevada Division of State Parks in Carson City.

Pioche: The Wildest of Wild West Towns

One of the most notorious mining camps ever to exist was Pioche (named after Francois L. A. Pioche, a San Francisco financier who owned the mining claim to the area). It is said that, in the 1860s and '70s, it was wilder than other infamously lawless western towns such as Tombstone and Dodge City—and that's really saying something! In its heyday, Pioche was the archetypical Wild West town, where the only law was that of the gun. The mining camp grew rapidly after the first discovery of gold and silver in 1863. By the early 1870s, it had become one of the most active mining towns in all of Nevada, with a population of nearly 8,000. Dozens of saloons and brothels sprang up practically overnight, adding to the already chaotic atmosphere of the place.

For evidence of the legendarily lawlessness of Pioche, one need look no further than the town's own Web site, www.pioche-nevada.com, which offers this description:

Pioche in the 1870's was considered one of the wildest mining camps in the west. According to a number of sources, "hired gunmen were imported at the rate of about twenty a day during boom times to fight mining claim encroachments." Evidence of the "toughest town" image was the reference that early day residents would make when they would point with pride to "Boot Row" where seventy-five men were buried before anyone in the roaring mining town died of a natural death.

Despite Pioche's rowdy reputation, the mines there would eventually produce some $40 million worth of gold and silver during their years of operation. Alas, though, once the ore deposits dried up, Pioche's days were numbered. Today it is considered a "living ghost town" with a population about one tenth of what it was in its prime. Many of the original buildings are still intact; one is the Lincoln County Courthouse, which was condemned in 1933, years before its construction costs were paid off.

One of the most interesting attractions for visitors now is the town's cemetery, famed for its Boot Row, also known as Murderer's Row. Here, in mostly unmarked graves, lie the remains of as many as one hundred murderers, Overhead, huge black steel ore conveyor buckets still dangle in midair, suspended from the high-tension pulley cables of the tramline as if frozen in time.

Pioche is located in Lincoln County a few miles from the town of Panaca, just off U.S. Highway 93 North.

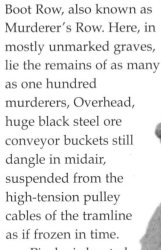

Francois L. A. Pioche

Submerged Nevada

We associate Nevada with heat and dryness, but it has at least two abandoned places that are completely underwater. So get out your scuba gear if you want to take a look at these sites!

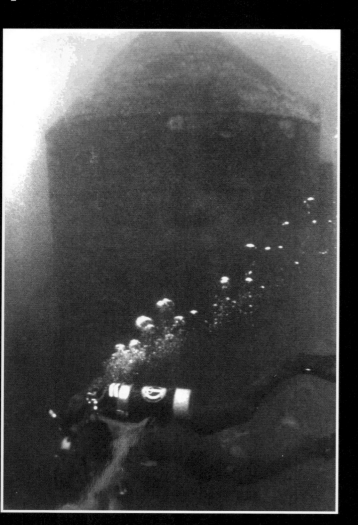

Factory Under Soda Lake

In northern Nevada is a lake with no inlets or outlets. Soda Lake was created by a collapsed volcanic cone; water from underground sources filled up the resulting depression and the lake was born. In the 1840s, pioneers encountered the welcome body of water after crossing the parched forty-mile desert. Settler Asa L. Kenyon claimed it around 1855. A survey made that same year noted that the lake was filled with brine shrimp—what you and I call sea monkeys.

In 1886, a factory was built on the shore of the lake to extract the naturaly occurring soda in the water. These days we think of soda as something in baking soda and laundry powder, but back then it was used in the manufacture of glass, soap, and most importantly, in certain mining processes. The commodity was in high demand at nearby Virginia City.

In 1907, for then unknown reasons, the water of the lake began to rise. The soda factory became completely submerged by the next year. This led to a series of lawsuits against the government, as a newly built irrigation system and series of dams known as the Newlands Water Project was the most likely explanation for the rising waters. Although none of the canals went directly to the lake, subterranean seepage made its way in. The lawsuits ended on November 21, 1921, with a landmark decision by the U.S. Supreme Court that the U.S. government cannot be sued for "unintentional" actions.

By the 1970s, the sunken factory had gone from lawsuits to local folklore, in the form of rumors of a "city" beneath the water. In 1978 a group of divers explored the lake looking for remnants of the factory. It was still there,

preserved by the silty quality of the lake. In 1982, a group called RAID (Reno Area Interested Divers) attempted to map the bottom of the lake and get it listed on the National Register of Historic Places. The Churchill County Museum promoted both dives.

In addition to the factory, divers found what they called a "ghost forest," the remains of a grove of cottonwood trees at the southeastern end of the lake. Located just a few miles west of Fallon, off Highway 50, Soda Lake and its submerged factory are a popular spot for divers adventurous enough to endure the murky waters and the sea monkeys.

Left and right: In 1978 a group of divers explored the lake looking for remnants of the factory. It was still there, preserved by the silty water. Soda Lake and its submerged factory are now a popular spot for divers adventurous enough to endure the murky waters.

Submerged St. Thomas Arises

It emerges from the murky depths of Lake Mead every decade or so—the legendary sunken city of St. Thomas.

St. Thomas began at the behest of Brigham Young as an attempt to expand the Mormon empire. It was settled in 1865 as a farming community, its citizens at first thinking that they were in Pah-Ute County [a former county in the Arizona Territory]. It was the Nevada taxman who let them know their true location —and that they owed back taxes. St. Thomas was a barter-based economy; the community's inhabitants had no money of any kind, and there was no way that they could pay the bill.

In 1871, Brigham Young visited the town and told the populace that they could leave if they wanted to. Most did, some burning their houses as they left, not wanting their hard work to fall into the hands of squatters. By 1880, some people had moved back, and St. Thomas prospered not only as a farming community but also as a roadside stop, being one of the few settlements between Salt Lake City and Los Angeles, before the rise of Las Vegas. St. Thomas got another boost in the 1920s, with the rise of archaeological tourism, as it was close to the newly built Lost City Museum. But even then, time was running out for the little town.

In 1932, the federal government claimed the land, planning to submerge it as part of the Boulder Dam

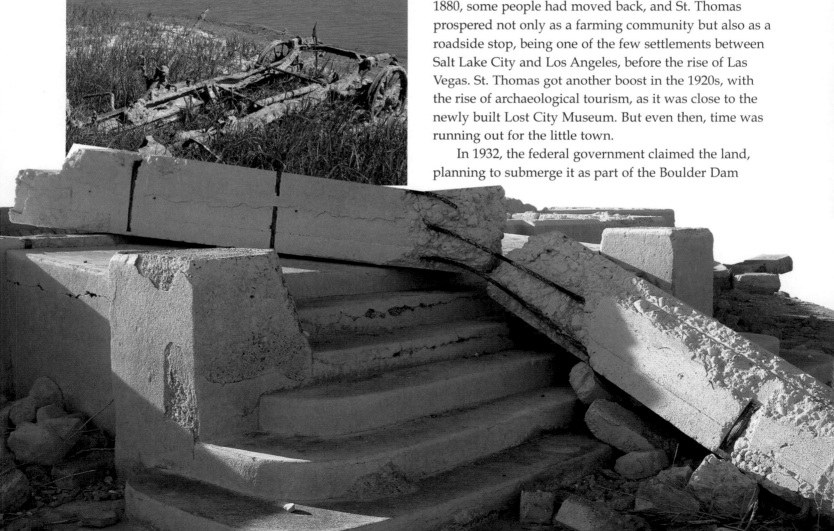

project. In 1934, the graveyard was moved to a new location. In 1938, the rising waters of the newly forming Lake Mead began to engulf St. Thomas, now deserted except for one man named Hugh Lord, who refused to believe the water would cover the town. As the water lapped at his front porch, a rowboat arrived to rescue the stubborn last inhabitant. He lit his house on fire before they rowed him away.

Since then St. Thomas has been a curiosity for divers who explore its remnants beneath the recreational waters of Lake Mead. At one time there was an underwater forest, but the park service cut down the trees, seeing them as a hazard to water-skiers.

Since its submergence, St. Thomas has arisen from the depths seventeen times. A historic low-water point was 1965, when water was being diverted to fill Lake Powell. Presently, almost all of St. Thomas is on dry land, as drought has brought Lake Mead to a new low. To find St. Thomas, go to the Lost City Museum in Overton and ask for a map. A Boy Scout troop has marked out trails through the reeds that grow tall in the summertime. All that is left of the city is its concrete foundations. Its streets are long gone, but toward the water's edge we found the rusting remnants of a 1930s-era car, which likely had not seen dry air for a long time.

The Sunken Steamship S.S. *Tahoe*

On August 29, 1940, small crowds gathered at Glenbrook and Deadman's Point to say good-bye to the S.S. *Tahoe.* Although many of them had tried to save the old steamship from its fate, now there was nothing more to do but watch as the Queen of the Lake was towed out and sunk in the waters she had once ruled.

The 169-foot boat had been launched amid much fanfare in 1896, with Captain Ernest John Pomin at the helm. For the next thirty years, she would carry mail and tourists around Tahoe. With room for two-hundred passengers, she was elegance itself; rich touches of mahogany paneling and lush Brussels carpeting were part of the decor throughout. But soon automobiles became the preferred mode of transportation around the lake, and the usefulness of the *Tahoe* came to an end.

The summer sun slipped behind the Sierra, turning the sky orange. The signal was given, and the grand old dame was slowly towed out and sunk off Deadman's Point. Some of those who were there that evening claimed they heard the distinct sounds of moaning and weeping emanating from the old boat as it dropped beneath the water and into history.

Today the National Park Service recognizes the S.S. *Tahoe* as a national underwater historic site. It is the only such site in the country. The vessel rests on the lake bottom at about four-hundred feet. This depth, combined with Lake Tahoe's altitude, make a dive to the old ship very dangerous.

Tonopah's Jinxed Air Field

Stargazers take note. According to *USA Today*, Tonopah is the best place in the United States to see the stars. Unlike Las Vegas, there's no light pollution in this tiny town, which sits on Highway 95, halfway between Reno and Las Vegas. There's not even a stoplight.

Nowadays there's not much goin' on around here, but things were different in 1940. With war raging in Europe and threatening to involve the United States, our military decided the country needed a well-trained fighting force. Toward that end, construction began on the Tonopah Army Air Field (TAAF), seven miles east of Tonopah. Two years later the base was ready for occupancy, and not a moment too soon.

Personnel began arriving, along with the aircraft on which they would train—the Bell P-39 Airacobra—the same fighter plane that was being used by the air force in its operations in the Pacific. The Airacobra was involved in the majority of the 132 deaths that would occur at the airfield over the next three years.

People living in the Tonopah/Goldfield area soon grew accustomed to witnessing or reading about one fiery crash after another in the skies over the desert. The large number of mishaps led airmen who trained here to claim the base was jinxed. Everyone dreaded an assignment to Tonopah. With the conclusion of World War II, the government decided that this was not the best site to train fighter pilots. Some claimed it was the base's high altitude; others said it was the surrounding mountain ranges. Whichever it was, there was no doubt that the Tonopah base was an unlucky place to be.

Allen Metscher, local historian and president of the Central Nevada Historical Society in Tonopah, remembers, as a child in the 1950s, visiting the vacated base with his father. Metscher was fascinated with the empty barracks and hangars, noting that "to a little boy from Tonopah, it seemed like an abandoned city."

Metscher's interest was sparked; he was intrigued with the stories of the dead airmen, the number of crashes, and eyewitness accounts of them. Years passed, but he never forgot his visit to the base or the stories. Through his research, he gathered the names of all those who perished at the jinxed airfield and a monument was erected at the Central Nevada Museum in Tonopah. Today all that remains at the air base site are memories of those who perished here long before their time, bits of scattered rubble, and an abandoned hangar that serves as the Tonopah airport.

Double Negative: Abandoned Art

When Michael Heizer's *Double Negative* was bequeathed to the Los Angeles Museum of Contemporary Art in 1985, it caused a conundrum. The work of art could not be displayed at the museum, as *Double Negative* is empty space carved into Mormon Mesa, eighty miles northeast of Las Vegas.

Two long trenches, fifty-feet deep and thirty-feet wide, are carved into opposite sides of the mesa, directly across from each other. Their juxtaposition suggests that a huge straight object once filled the space. The vast majority of the missing object floats in the void between the two trenches thus, negative space is surrounded by negative space: double negative.

Michael Heizer was a pioneer of the art movement of earthworks, where art merges with the environment, which was popular in the late 1960s and early 1970s. Earthworks were influenced by ancient art such as earth mounds and the lines on the plains of Nazca, Peru.

The Nevada location was selected mostly because the land was available. Virginia Dwan, a gallery owner from New York City, funded the project. Heizer and a work crew spent two months, starting in December 1969, blasting and bulldozing 240,000 tons of sandstone to create the sculpture. Heizer displayed photos of the completed work at Dwan's gallery.

It was Dwan who donated the sixty-six-acre site to MOCA in Los Angeles, making it the first museum to have an earthwork in its collection. Since its creation in 1970, only a few thousand people have visited the site. MOCA solved its dilemma of how to exhibit the earthwork by scheduling trips to the site, as well as publishing a book about it, and *Double Negative* became the standard to which all other earthworks were compared.

If you would like to see *Double Negative*, you can get directions from the Lost City Museum, which is a few miles beyond the Overton Airport. The unpaved road to the site is rough, and four-wheel drive is recommended, although we had no problem getting there in an economy rental car. You can walk inside the trenches, which have had a few landslides over the years but still give a good sense of the negative space. And you get an incredible view of the Virgin River, which is a positive.

Currently, Michael Heizer lives near Hiko, Nevada, where he has been building his ultimate Earthwork City since the '70s. The work isn't finished, so people aren't allowed to see it just yet; it is fenced in and on private land.

INDEX
Page numbers in **bold** refer to photos and illustrations.

DEDICATIONS AND ACKNOWLEDGMENTS

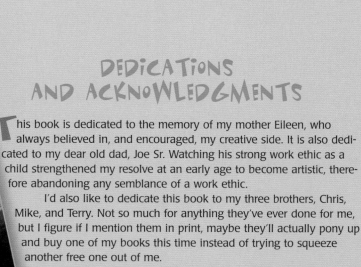

This book is dedicated to the memory of my mother Eileen, who always believed in, and encouraged, my creative side. It is also dedicated to my dear old dad, Joe Sr. Watching his strong work ethic as a child strengthened my resolve at an early age to become artistic, therefore abandoning any semblance of a work ethic.

I'd also like to dedicate this book to my three brothers, Chris, Mike, and Terry. Not so much for anything they've ever done for me, but I figure if I mention them in print, maybe they'll actually pony up and buy one of my books this time instead of trying to squeeze another free one out of me.

Last but not least, I'd like to thank my beautiful girlfriend, Jennifer. Partly because of all the faith she has in me, and the inspiration I derive from her, but mostly because I didn't mention her in the last book, and I have yet to stop hearing about that.—*Joe Oesterle*

Many people helped make this book possible, people who gave me their time for interviews, people who indulged me and helped me find obscure and forgotten photographs. Many are mentioned in the text but I would particularly like to give special mention to Philip Earl, former curator of the Nevada State Historical Society in Reno, and Dennis McBride, of the Boulder City Museum. Both are dedicated researchers with a passion for Nevada history that goes beyond the academic. And both realize that legends and folklore are an important part of history. The staffs of many museums and libraries across the state have been very helpful, but in particular I spent many long hours at the library at UNLV digging through reels of microfilms of old newspapers, as well as electronic archives of more recent news.

Ray Nelke, of Collectors of Unusual Data-International, has been supportive of me over the years, even when my communication has been irregular. He sent me many bits of data that helped my research. Bruce Walton is a researcher of subterranean mysteries who found incredible information and assembled it into photocopied booklets in the 1980s. His dedication inspired me to delve deeper. I am happy to say that Walton's work has now found a wider audience, thanks to the Internet. Richard Toronto and his Web site, Shavertron.com, has been helpful in the same way. San Francisco–based artist Sharon Leong did something that few people would—look up articles on microfilm at the San Francisco Public Library, including some that were of unspecified dates. Without her help the Ancient Mysteries chapter would be lacking some critical information.

Photographer Richard Faverty, of Beckett Studios in Las Vegas, was kind enough to let me spend many hours at his studio working on photos for this book. Thanks to authors John Keel and Brad Steiger, whose writings have fascinated and inspired me over the years. And special thanks to Skylaire Alfegren, who brought me on board this project in the first place.—*Tim Cridland*

CONTRIBUTING AUTHORS

Skylaire Alfvegren has worked on cars for the Mexican mafia and roped cattle on the border of Area 51. Having witnessed her first UFO episode alongside Air Force personnel as a child, she began her writing career at seventeen with "File o' the Damned," a column of Fortean investigation for *Fizz* magazine.

Not yet of legal drinking age, she was hired as a consultant for *Strange Universe*, the Fox Network's nationally syndicated "paranormal news program," wrote regularly for *L.A. Weekly*, and built a laboratory to grow *Amanita muscaria*.

Translated into four languages and plastered helter skelter online, her gonzo reportage has appeared in countless magazines, books, and journals. Descended from the dark elves of old Scandinavia, she is currently applying her vast knowledge of California—the esoteric, the dark, and the weird—to the small screen, and recently founded the League of Western Fortean Intermediasts as a network for explorations into the mysteries and peculiarities of the Southwest. To eyeball further dementia, visit www.skylaire.com.

Janice Oberding has been investigating the paranormal for more than thirty years. She is the author of *Las Vegas Haunted*, five other books, and hundreds of articles on the paranormal. Coproducer of the popular Las Vegas Paranormal Conference, Janice lectures widely and has appeared and consulted on numerous television shows on the paranormal, including the History Channel, Living TV, the Travel Channel, and Fox Television. Her Web site is www.HauntedNevada.com.

Troy Paiva captures the disappearing man-made world with his evocative and exotic night-photography technique. Troy uses old and obsolete, low-tech equipment to create brilliantly lit tableaus of the abandoned debris of a modern, disposable culture—taking pictures of junk *with* junk.

In 2003, Troy's first book, *Lost America* (Motorbooks International), was published, to critical acclaim. He has previously contributed writing and photography to the *Weird U.S.*, *Weird Texas*, and *Weird California* books. Make sure to visit Troy's Web site: www.lostamerica.com/lostframe.html.

Jarret Keene is author of the poetry collection *Monster Fashion*, the rock-band bio *The Killers: Destiny Is Calling Me*, and editor of *The Underground Guide to Las Vegas.* He lives in Las Vegas.

PICTURE CREDITS

SHOW US YOUR WEIRD!

Do you know of a weird site found somewhere in the United States, or can you tell us about a strange experience you had? If so, we'd like to hear about it! We believe that every town has at least one great tale to tell, and we're listening. It could be a cursed road, haunted abandoned site, odd local character, or bizarre historic event. In most cases these tales are told only in the towns in which in they originated. But why keep them to yourself when you could share them with all of America? So come on and fill us in on all the weirdness that's lurking in your backyard!

You can email us at: Editor@WeirdUS.com,
or write us at:
Weird U.S., P.O. Box 1346, Bloomfield, NJ 07003.

www.weirdus.com